LOVE AFFAIRS

LOVE AFFAIRS

Marriage & Infidelity

RICHARD TAYLOR

 **Prometheus Books**

59 John Glenn Drive
Amherst, New York 14228-2197

Grateful acknowledgment is given to the publishers of the following works for permission to quote from them: The epigram on page 5 from Bertrand Russell's *Marriage and Morals* (The Liveright Publishing Corp.); the lines on page 39 from Phyllis McGinley's "The Honor of Being a Woman," in *The Province of the Heart* (Viking Penguin Inc.); the lines on page 51 from Cyril Connolly's *The Unquiet Grave* (Persea Books, Inc.); the epigram on page 91 from Dorothy Parker's "General Review of the Sex Situation," in *The Portable Dorothy Parker* (Viking Penguin, Inc.); the lines on page 177 from Anne Morrow Lindbergh's "Even . . . ," from the *Unicorn and Other Poems*; and the lines on page 187 from La Rochefoucauld's *Maxims*, translated by Louis Kronenberger (Random House, Inc.).

Published 1997 by Prometheus Books

Inquiries should be addressed to
Prometheus Books
59 John Glenn Drive
Amherst, New York 14228–2197.
VOICE: 716–691–0133, ext. 207; FAX: 716–564–2711
WWW.PROMETHEUSBOOKS.COM

07 06 05 04 03   8 7 6 5 4

Library of Congress Cataloging-in-Publication Data

Taylor, Richard, 1919–
    Love affairs : marriage and infidelity / Richard Taylor, — Rev. ed.
        p.   cm.
    Rev. ed. of: Having love affairs, 1990.
    ISBN 1–57392–128–9 (pbk. : alk. paper)
    1. Adultery. I. Taylor, Richard, 1919–   Having love affairs.
II. Title.
HQ806.T39   1997
306.73'6—dc21   96–50919
                                                                      CIP

Printed in the United States of America on acid-free paper

To fear love is to fear life, and those
who fear life are already three parts dead.

—Bertrand Russell

Contents

Preface, 1990

When this book first appeared there were many persons who thought they had no need to read beyond the title in order to know its contents; they were sure it was a wicked book, subversive of morality. They were rather like the self-styled Christians who picketed *The Last Temptation of Christ,* seeking thereby to prevent its showing, or at least to discourage people from viewing the film. Asked whether they had ever seen it, these critics replied that they would not dream of doing so! Such is the power of self-authenticating opinion. Its possessors, so certain of everything, imagine that they have the power to know without seeing.

Many assumed that *Having Love Affairs* defended or even advocated infidelity and was thus subversive of marriage. It was viewed as an embarrassment by my university, and colleagues who happened to see the book discretely avoided mentioning it. All of this was in spite of the book's opening sentence, which I here repeat: "This book is meant to be a contribution to human happiness and . . . to a strengthening of the institution of marriage."

For a long time after the book was published I received requests for interviews on radio talk shows, sometimes distant ones. These were easily managed simply by my being at my telephone at an agreed upon time. It was rare to find that the hosts of these programs had actually read the book except, sometimes, superficially. The very subject was considered to be such a departure that merely to bring it up was thought to be worth airing. It was generally assumed that only one view really needed to be conveyed on this subject: "Thou shalt not."

Problems are seldom solved by avoidance, and controversial issues are not resolved by declining to think and talk about them. Even a sympathetic effort to understand why people become involved in love affairs is somehow regarded as an attempt at compromising morality. But it is of no use to men or women who are deeply and helplessly caught up in love affairs just to be told "thou shalt not"; nor can such a negative approach be regarded as expressing any decent moral standard.

9

What I have tried to do in this book, then, is first, to understand how and why love affairs get started, often ending with explosively destructive consequences, and second, to try to point out ways of mitigating their destructive power. These two goals still seem to me to be good ones. While I think I succeeded fairly well with respect to the first, I am less sure of any great success with respect to the second.

So far as understanding is concerned, I am sure that I learned more during the book's development than from any other research and writing that I have ever undertaken, and what I learned is of great importance. Talking with many people, candidly and at length, about something of momentous importance in their lives is extremely instructive. And since the publication of *Having Love Affairs,* I have continued to learn so much so that I almost wish I had not yet written it, feeling that I could now write an even better book.

My views on the subject of love affairs have not changed significantly, except with respect to emphasis. Although at first I did not doubt the destructive power of sexual infidelity, for example, I now believe that I underestimated it. The wounds it inflicts are far more difficult to heal than I had supposed. I am still convinced, however, that they can be healed, and more or less in the ways I suggested; I remain convinced that such wounds are not healed by simple condemnation.

I also believe now that becoming involved in a love affair is symptomatic of an already failed marriage. This would seem obvious to some, but for different reasons. The success of a marriage should not be measured by its duration or by the fidelity of its partners, for there are many lasting marriages, never marked by infidelity, whose partners nevertheless have no overwhelming love for each other. Indeed, this seems almost to be the norm, and it is, in the truest sense, the meaning of a failed marriage. When I state, then, that an affair is symptomatic of a failed marriage, I mean that it is indicative of love that has been lost. But the erosion of love, and its gradual replacement by other forces holding a marriage together, is common even in the absence of any sexual infidelity. This is perhaps the most baneful thing I have learned from my interest in these matters, and it is worth stressing in spite of the general resistance to such an idea. A genuinely happy and fulfilling marriage, resting on indestructible love and requiring nothing more, is rare. But it is also the foundation of a unique happiness and, possibly, of the only perfect fulfillment of which we are capable.

One theme of this book, concerning which my conviction of its truth has not been lessened at all, is that marital infidelity encompasses much more than sexual transgression. *Any* betrayal is an infidelity, even the slightest and most commonplace deception. Someone who withholds from a spouse knowledge of personal finances, of associates, of how time away from home is spent, or anything whatever that would be of interest to the other, is being faithless. Equally to the point, such infidelity can be far worse than sexual inconstancy. Thus, for example, the maintenance of a secret bank account is an infidelity indicative of greed along with deception and, in the face of a lying declaration of love, nothing could be more indicative of love lost.

The original edition of this book carried no dedication. Perhaps it should have. I therefore dedicate it to all the romantic souls who believe, as I do, that there is no happiness in the world comparable to loving another person, totally and unqualifiedly, and finding that love returned.

25 January 1990

Preface, 1997

This book is meant to be a contribution to human happiness and, whatever may be the appearance to the contrary, to a strengthening of the institution of marriage.

I have sought to do this by trying to *understand* why people become involved in sexual infidelity, and by trying to find ways to reduce the overwhelming damage of such behavior to precious relationships and, especially, to marriage.

This is a departure from the manner in which the subject is usually treated; namely, moral condemnation. That way of dealing with love affairs accomplishes nothing. For in the first place, no one has ever given any very clear meaning to the idea of something being "morally wrong," other than being an expression of this or that person's strong feelings about it, and, in the second place, merely moralizing about someone's behavior seldom has much effect in changing it. What is needed instead is clear-cut rules or guidelines.

In spite of my stated purpose—to strengthen the institution of marriage—the original edition of this book was, as I had anticipated, received with considerable hostility from many quarters. People simply assumed that, since I did not condemn sexual infidelity on the part of married people as morally wrong, then it must be that I thought it was all right.

Of course I do not think that infidelity is "all right." But I also do not think it is immoral. I think it is frightfully destructive of certain things that are very precious and essential to happiness. And for this reason I think it should be understood, not just dismissed as immoral, and we should try to learn something from the experiences of others.

Wars have never been prevented by intoning the commandment, "Thou shalt not kill." They are prevented, if at all, by understanding their causes and trying to do something about them. Similarly, love affairs have never been prevented by intoning, "Thou shalt not commit adultery." And to make that simple point is *not* the same as saying that there is nothing wrong with having love affairs.

When my book was first published, I anticipated hostile reception from two very different quarters; namely, persons oriented towards traditional religious ideas, and feminists. And I was right about this. Religious people sometimes seem to think it sufficient simply to proclaim, "Thou shalt not...," and feminists sometimes react negatively to my claim that there are very basic differences between men and women in their expressions of, and responses to, love and sexual intimacy. Men and women are very complex, not easily cast into formulas born of "political correctness," and they are also very different.

My book resulted in many radio interviews and a few television appearances. Some of the hosts of these were, I think, somewhat disappointed that I did not come on as singing the praises of having love affairs. And one female interviewer, doing the program by telephone, simply cut me off upon hearing me say that men and women are very different.

I am much indebted to all the people who have, over the past several years, talked to me about their personal lives. I learned a great deal from them and, more important, I came to understand a lot that I already knew. I am also much indebted to Professor David Riesman of Harvard University for his helpful comments on the parts of the book he read, and his encouragement in finishing the work. Most of chapter 4, "Within the Halls of Ivy," appeared in *Change* (May–June 1981) and is reprinted with permission.

R. T.

1

Introduction

It is just this not seeking of one's own things which is everywhere the stamp of greatness, that gives passionate love also a touch of sublimity.

Arthur Schopenhauer

The joy of a love affair is that someone seems to love you who does not have to, or who, in fact, positively should not. Married people have many reasons—one almost wants to say ulterior motives—for caring about each other, and one can always wonder whether these might not really be the basis for affection. They are likely to have a house and other possessions, children, common endeavors which neither could pursue alone, and, above all, some sort of position in the community which is enhanced by their being married and would suffer by their separation. In other words, there are many things holding married people together besides love, and these are sometimes sufficient even when there is little or no love in the marriage. This is well and good, of course. No one can doubt that, from the standpoint of children, for example, a family is usually much better when intact than broken, even though some of the things holding it together are mundane. Nevertheless, these considerations rob marriage of the romance that everyone craves.

Partners in a love affair, on the other hand, have none of these things to hold them together, but have, on the contrary, the same kinds of forces working to drive them apart—for example, the need for secrecy and deception, which is always degrading; the existence, in the background, of a husband or wife or both; and, in such cases, the loss of reputation if they are discovered. All these lovers have, it seems to them, is passionate love—which is, of course, a lot, but it is still only one thing. This certainly attests to the power of passionate love, and it is doubtful whether there is anything in human experience as totally fulfilling as

15

being loved in this way—intensely, intimately, and gratuitously. It is, perhaps, the ultimate joy that everyone wants more than anything else. The most vehement condemnations of it seem often to come from those who have abandoned hope of experiencing it, and who therefore represent it to themselves as something base in order to assuage their own sense of deprivation. Someone involved in such a love affair—overwhelming, forbidden, explosively dangerous—can think to himself, with some truth at least, that here is one person who cares for him from no ulterior motive, who has nothing to gain by it and very much to lose, but who does, nevertheless, love.

This does not mean that love affairs are better than marriage, for they seldom are. Love between married persons can be so vastly more fulfilling that none but the hopelessly romantic could suggest otherwise. The passionate love that so explosively blooms in an affair is not, moreover, as gratuitous as it may seem. While the usual ulterior reasons for it may be lacking, others are certainly present, and in particular, the ordinary and not very romantic needs of its partners.

It is nevertheless true that, notwithstanding their destructive consequences, the joys of illicit and passionate love are overwhelmingly exciting and good. Those who never experience a love affair, and who perhaps even boast of their faultless monogamy, year in and year out, have really missed something. Virtuous they may be—and even this can be questioned—but truly blessed they are not, except in the case of a truly fulfilling marriage which precludes temptation. What we need to do, then, is not simply dismiss sexual infidelity, but understand it.

2

Background

Morality consists of suspecting other people of not being legally married.

—George Bernard Shaw

Off and on over the course of three years (1979–1981) I repeatedly inserted this or a similar advertisement in the classified section of five newspapers in three cities:

Professor researching causes and consequences of extramarital love affairs wishes to contact persons willing to answer questionnaire or be interviewed. Confidentiality assured. Write: Prof. R. Taylor, Dept. Philosophy, University of Rochester, NY 14627.

Many years later (1996) I inserted a similar ad in several other newspapers. My book had gone through several printings, and I wanted to develop a new edition. The orientation of the book needed changing, I thought, and the original title had also proved misleading.

The newspapers chosen were all in upstate New York, where I lived and worked. They were mostly near universities and colleges, whose faculties and students tend toward a higher than average level of sophistication, and they were seen in two large metropolitan areas, where there was a wide readership.

There were eventually perhaps sixty or seventy responses to the first ad, rather fewer to the later one, although I kept no count. To each respondent I sent a brief questionnaire and a self-addressed envelope. Some were never returned, but most came back. The purpose of the questionnaire was not to elicit data. I merely wanted, instead, to see whether the involvements of the respondents constituted genuine love affairs, as I understood them, and especially, whether either or both partners were married persons. It was not necessary, so far as the problems that interest me are concerned, that either of them be married in any strict legal sense, but I was especially interested in relationships involving third persons. Therefore, I have treated men and women who cohabit and more or less make some kind of a home together—a practice that is very common among college students, for example, as well as others—as being essentially "married," and having a relationship of "husband" and "wife," even though the relationship is not formalized by law and may, as in the case of many students, be kept secret from parents. And since it is love affairs that interest me in this study, and not the wide variety of problems concerning marital relationships as such, I have concentrated on the problems arising from involvements with third persons. It is these triangular relationships that give rise to the questions dealt with here.

I also sought in my questionnaire to learn whether the affairs had ended, and if so, whether badly or well, whether they had been destructive of other relationships, and so on. The responses enabled me to decide whether an interview might be interesting or instructive, which was in fact my purpose in sending the questionnaire.

Thus my questionnaire was in no sense a research tool, and I did not pretend otherwise. It was simply an avenue to a highly informal face-to-face discussion, and a means of sorting out which of these possible discussions might be worth pursuing. Actually, in many cases no questionnaire was used at all. I made known to my students on two campuses, for example, that I was engaged in this project, and invited them to come forth with experiences of their own that might be interesting or enlightening. Many did.

After considering the responses to my ad and the initial conversations with prospective interviewees it became clear that, in many cases, further discussion would have served no worthwhile purpose. There is, for example, nothing inherently interesting in the fact that this or that person has had numerous bed partners. Some respondents, moreover—most but not all of whom were men—seemed motivated only by a desire to boast, and were not entirely believable. No effort was made to learn more about these individuals and their relationships. Some of the responses, on the other hand, whether they were written replies to my questionnaire or elicited from more casual inquiries, seemed promising, and usually I was successful when I tried to pursue them further. The interviews were conducted over lunch or tea. Sometimes I met with respondents in the student rathskeller, but always in a public place. At times I recorded our conversations, but usually I merely made notes during the meetings or immediately thereafter.

I do not, therefore, pretend that there is anything scientific in my approach to these matters, beyond the fact that my descriptions are free from invention, distortion, and embellishment, although I have been careful to conceal the identities of the persons interviewed when asked to. I made no analyses of my responses, no data were tabulated, and the responses were not categorized. All I have tried to do is gain wisdom and insight into an important aspect of human experience, one that is filled with implications for ethics. This has seemed to me preferable to simply plucking ethical norms from religion or from inherited cultural values, which is the approach of most persons not trained in philosophy. I believe I have succeeded in this, for even though I am neither young nor naive with respect to relationships of this kind, it is hardly possible to come to know the inner and private lives of many people without becoming wiser, the more so in the cases of people who are complex, talented, and interesting.

It should also be clear that soliciting personal information through classified newspaper ads cannot possibly be scientific. Questionnaires distributed in such a way are not nets cast, but bait offered, which can accordingly be declined. Thus, for example, before even answering the ad, my respondents had to have some reason of their own to respond, and most of those who saw it had, of course, no such reason at all.

Some persons would prefer to make people all alike, at least with respect to strict monogamy, but that is neither possible nor desirable. Whatever outward conformity may be forced upon people, it will always conceal an immense diversity of inner feeling which will, from time to time, express itself, secretly if not otherwise.

I am going to examine love affairs, not with the thought of condemning or approving, but with the thought of understanding them, and then formulating guidelines for making them less destructive.

None of the accounts of people's affairs that I have recorded here and there are "composites," that is, drawn from different accounts and then put together as one. Each story authentically records what just one person told me. The only changes I have made, beyond putting them into readable prose, are in names and, sometimes, incidental details that would otherwise destroy anonymity.

3

The Meaning of Marriage

No happiness is like unto it, no love so great as that of man and wife.

—Robert Burton

This book is written in the conviction that there is no happiness that matches the happiness or fulfillment that can be found in marriage, and its aim is to strengthen that overwhelmingly important institution. Thus, marriage is important not only for the stability of society, for the protection and education of children, for the orderly ownership and transfer of property and so on, even though these are of overwhelming importance, especially as they affect children. Marriage is, beyond all this, important as a basis for human happiness and, it is my belief, it is for most people the firmest basis for genuine and lasting happiness.

Our culture nourishes the idea that the pursuit of happiness is the pursuit of wealth, or, at least, success in work or career, this usually being measured in terms of the goods that they yield. Virtually everyone does pursue such success, to be sure, but how can this possibly compare with the happiness that is found in a marriage that rests upon total and lasting love? People who are truly married, that is, whose marriage is built on the kind of love that will be described here, are blessed beyond any treasures that can be measured by money. They have, we can suppose, a roof over their heads, the wherewithal to meet life's daily needs, and security in their declining years; they look with shared joy upon their children, and together rejoice in their achievements. In the warmth of their family circle, and having, with no great command of wealth, the means to keep the evils of the world at bay, these married people have every ingredient of happiness that is possible to human nature. For them to seek happiness anyplace else, whether in fame, power, wealth, or whatever, would be sheer distraction.

21

What has just been said must not be misunderstood. I have not said that marriage is a sure or reliable route to happiness. It most certainly is not. Nor have I meant to suggest that married people are happy people. Most of them, in varying degrees, are quite unhappy in their marriages. What I suggest is that no happiness exceeds or even matches that which is *sometimes* found in marriage. That it is seldom, perhaps even rarely, found there does not detract from the truth of this.

About half of all marriages end in total collapse. The rate is higher among those whose education and level of sophistication is higher. Nor should one by any means assume that those marriages that do not end in divorce are, perforce, happy marriages. Rather few of them really are. People who are less than totally happy in marriage, and even some who are totally miserable, often remain married for reasons having nothing to do with happiness—for the sake of their children, for example. Sometimes the numberless practical difficulties of divorce keep people together in loveless marriages—difficulties with respect to property, social standing, religious prohibition, and so on. Among the roughly half of those who remain married, often after one or more failed marriages, those who have found the kind of total and ultimate happiness I have alluded to are quite rare.

This is not always apparent. People who are not very happy in their marriages seldom display this; on the contrary, they tend to conceal it. It is only when you are somehow able to see beneath the surface of things that you see the sad reality. This is why, so often, we are surprised to learn that friends, whom we thought we knew so well, are considering divorce. They seemed to be getting along perfectly well. Of course! Domestic discord is seldom exposed to the public.

Consider a bar, white at one end and black at the other, with every shade of grey in between:

This bar stands for a representative sampling of marriages, the degree of whiteness at any point being the degree of happiness found in a marriage, and black, of course, the degree of unhappiness. Now all those marriages that fall below the approximate midpoint of this bar contain such deep unhappiness, to the point of total misery, that they end in divorce. This is simple fact. But how absurd it would be to suppose that those marriages that fall *above* that point are all happy ones! This would require that our bar be all white from that point upward, when what we are trying to represent is obviously a continuum. Some marriages, namely those that fall within the small white area at the upper end, are indeed happy, a few of them totally so. But from that point on they are a mixture of happiness and discord, descending to mild frustration, annoyance, boredom, bitterness, resentment, conflict, and pain. Some, indeed, that come close to ending in divorce, along with the approximately half that actually do, contain more unhappiness and downright misery than those further along on the scale, because of the many forces that sometimes keep an otherwise dreadful marriage together. People do sometimes stay in a failed marriage. Indeed, this is fairly common.

From this we can see, too, the folly of making divorce more difficult by erecting legal obstacles. This is the course advocated by many religious leaders and other defenders of "family values." Indeed, the Roman Catholic church would make divorce legally impossible, even for non-Catholics. The effect, however, of making divorce *harder*, in this sense, is only to move the line on our graph further to the right and increase the amount of black in it; that is, divorce does indeed become less frequent, but the unhappiness in those marriages thus "preserved" is greatly intensified. A marriage that has failed, in the sense that both partners are made unhappy in it and want finally to go their separate ways, is hardly made better by their being compelled to stay together. On the contrary, their bitterness and misery are greatly intensified, so that the right half of our graph becomes blacker than ever.

Certainly it is worth trying to discover, then, the explanation of a truly happy marriage. We need to know not merely how marriages are kept intact, but how ultimate and lasting happiness is found in some of them. Indeed, it would be hard to think of any of life's questions more important than this one.

For this we shall need to have a clear idea of the nature of the love that is sometimes found in marriage; the kind of love that sometimes, albeit rarely, blesses married lovers with total and lasting happiness; and also, what can destroy it. With respect to the latter, we shall limit ourselves to the single thing that is probably most explosively devastating of such happiness, namely, marital infidelity. And we need to ask: Why does it occur? How is it prevented? And, when it does occur, how can its destructive power be mitigated?

*   *   *

But what are we talking about? What, in other words, does it mean to be married?

The distinction between being married and being unmarried seems about as clear and absolute as any we know. It is like the distinctions between night and day, male and female, or north and south. A given person is either married or single; one cannot be neither, nor can anyone be both, nor can anyone be half married and half not. Or at least, so it seems.

This distinction is, moreover, of overwhelming social importance. Immoral conduct and civil wrongs are sometimes defined in terms of it. What is permitted of the unmarried is forbidden to the married. The legitimacy of children turns on it, as do tax liabilities, inheritance rights, sometimes occupational roles, and so on. With respect to the themes of this book, adultery is defined in terms of this distinction. So it follows that if the distinction itself, between being married and being unmarried, is not perfectly clear and unambiguous, then the same lack of clarity infects the idea of adultery and, perhaps, all marital infidelity, of whatever kind.

People assume that a person, hitherto single, becomes a married person at a single stroke, at a certain moment of time, easily identified. Typically two persons, one male and one female, set that time and, until that moment arrives, are considered "engaged" to be married. Then, typically, there is a wedding, presided over by a clergyperson or, less often, by someone holding a civil office, such as a town justice. In the course of this ceremony, this person intones the words, "I now pronounce you man and wife" and, everyone supposes, from that very moment, they have become what they were not before—a married couple. Certain things, hitherto permitted, are now prohibited, and vice versa. Certain expressions of affection from other persons are now forbidden. Each of these two persons, from this moment, possesses exclusive rights with respect to the other. New forms of ownership of property are suddenly created, as well as new privileges, and liabilities, with respect to taxes. A commitment, presumed to be lifelong, comes suddenly into being. The knot is tied.

But now let us consider certain "what ifs."

What if, for example, this wedding is presided over by a self-styled cleric whose right to fill such a role is recognized by almost no one but himself? Someone who, for example, has no authority from the state to perform such an act? Or by a justice of the peace whose commission has expired? Or what if certain documents, essential to the legality of any marriage, somehow fail to get filed? Or what if they are never executed or signed in the first place?

Most jurisdictions, for example, require the issuance of a marriage license before a marriage takes place. Some lay down additional requirements, such as medical tests, or a waiting period, the reason for this being to ensure sobriety. After the wedding the clergyperson, or judicial officer, is supposed to validate the marriage license and forward it, perhaps with other documents, to a hall of records.

What if some or even all of these are omitted, and a formal wedding takes place in their absence? Thus, the nuptials have their wedding, in a church, with witnesses, wedding gifts, reception, and all, and go off on their honeymoon. But, by prearrangement with the pastor, no marriage license is submitted, and hence no record is made of the event, either in the records of the church or those of any hall of records.

Are these two married, or not? Everyone considers them so, for no one, except they and the clergyperson, suspects that any step has been omitted. Yet in many jurisdictions such a couple could not claim to be legally married at all.

Does this ever happen? Yes, and with considerable frequency. There are even well-established clergy, impeccable in their orthodoxy and devotion to their faith, who for reasons of their own insist upon proceeding in no other way. That is, they are happy to preside at a *wedding,* which they may prefer to call a "service of commitment," but refuse to solemnize a legal *marriage,* insisting that, after the wedding, the couple go elsewhere—to a town justice, for example—if they wish to take that step. And that is a step which they are free to omit.

Would a love affair with some third person by either of these two constitute adultery? What if they file joint income tax returns? What if they purchase real property in joint names, or make investments in their joint names with rights of survivorship? Would it occur to anyone to question the legitimacy of these things? Or the legitimacy of their children?

Most jurisdictions do not consider marriage to be legally possible between persons of the same sex. As homosexuality has become increasingly accepted, however, at least to the point that little stigma attaches to openly homosexual couples, many such couples have insisted upon becoming married. And liberal clergy have accommodated them in this wish, with a formal wedding. Some companies, moreover, extend the medical and retirement benefits of married people to such couples, thus treating them as married, and in most jurisdictions, they can adopt children, as joint parents. But are they really married? No, because the record of such a marriage would have no legal validity. And yet they have done everything that the heterosexual couple has done—the wedding ceremony, the certificate of marriage, signed and witnessed, and so on. The only difference is that here the basis for challenging the legal status of the marriage is perfectly obvious, whereas in the case of the heterosexual couple, no such basis is even suspected. If a man and a woman *say* they are married, or indeed, merely act as if they are married and treat each other as such, then everyone assumes that they are married, whereas no one simply assumes this is the case of two persons of the same sex. With them, it is instantly recognized as a pretense.

*   *   *

Having noted this one circumstance, which is perfectly clear, but almost never considered—namely, the failure to certify a "marriage" in the office of records—let us now consider others which render the concept of marriage even less clear.

The Roman Catholic church does not recognize the possibility of divorce, and yet annulment is very common. When an annulment is granted, then it is considered that the couple were never married at all, and the grounds for annulment are numerous. Many such considerations can be raised, even in the minds of persons outside the church, to challenge the validity of a marriage, even one that fulfills every requirement of the law.

Suppose, for example, that a couple never consummates their marriage. Are they really married? Or suppose one of them enters into the marriage simply and solely to gain possession of the other's wealth, fulfilling no other expectation of marriage at all. Or suppose one is a foreigner, and marries a citizen only to gain instant citizenship, the two henceforth going their separate ways as virtual strangers. We can suppose that, in all such cases, every requirement of the law is met—a large wedding; reception; gifts; all certificates properly signed, witnessed, and filed, and so on. And yet, in all such cases, the question can be asked, are they *really* married? And just as an affirmative answer can be rationally defended, so can a negative one and, increasingly, the church renders a negative one.

The upshot of all this is that the status of being married is far less clear-cut, far more ambiguous, than people imagine.

*   *   *

What, then, is marriage? What is it that truly unites certain people in marriage, if it is not (as is so commonly thought) a solemn ceremony, and not (as is less often appreciated) the filing of legal documents, and not even both together?

What is essential to marriage, we now suggest, is not anything easily seen, such as a ceremony, nor is it a legal formality, nor is it these two together. It is, rather, the strong bond of love between its partners that makes possible their lasting commitment to each other. It is this that matters, and this *alone* that gives rise to every moral consideration concerning the behavior of married people. Succinctly put, we are saying that it is lasting love that makes two people really married. Everything else is secondary, important to the administration of civil law, but of little relevance to marriage itself.

Thus, the woman who marries an American citizen just in order to gain automatic citizenship for herself, and then never sees him again, is not really married to him at all, even if every formal requirement of marriage has been met. Similarly, the man who marries a woman to gain her fortune, and thenceforth dismisses her completely from his affection and concern, is not really married to her. He has only created a semblance of marriage and used this to gain an advantage. And the couple who spend the final decades of their lives under the same roof, known to all as "Mr. and Mrs.," but who, during that whole time, hardly speak to each other and share as little as possible, are not really married. They have only the external shell of a marriage, the very minimum needed to meet certain requirements for social security benefits, inheritance of property, and so on.

One should not say, merely, that such "marriages" as these are not "good marriages." Instead one should say that they are not really marriages at all. They merely meet the minimal legal criteria. These can be important sometimes—as when questions of eligibility for certain benefits are raised, the inheritance of pensions, custody of children, the avoidance of gift taxes, and the like. But they have almost no importance at all with respect to genuine marriage.

To see this even more clearly, consider the woman whose only reason to marry was to gain automatic citizenship, who then never sees her "husband" again. And suppose that this man then eventually comes to love, lastingly and intimately, another woman. Is he an adulterer? Or what of the man whose only motive for marrying is to gain control of a fortune. Suppose that, upon discovering this, his "wife" secretly bestows all her property on some charity devoted to helping the poor, thus removing it forever from his grasp. Has she betrayed him? Or consider our third example, of the lasting but loveless "marriage." Does that "marriage" end only when the two are parted by death? Or did it not, instead, end long before?

These points are not just philosopher's quibbles, for all the ethical (as distinct from the civil and legal) questions surrounding marriage entirely depend on them. And if anyone were to insist upon thinking of being "really married" exclusively, or even primarily, in legal terms, then this would automatically reduce all questions of ethics to mere questions of legality. The scope of what is ethically acceptable is much wider than what is legally permitted and, conversely, vast moral wrongs can sometimes be committed even within the law. Betrayals, lies, and cruelties are not, in every case, breaches of legality.

A marriage is dead when the love that sustained it dies. If such love was never there to begin with—as in the case of the woman who marries just to gain citizenship, or the man who marries just to get his hands on a fortune—then the marriage was dead from the start or, rather, it never came alive. And, in the light of what has just been said, a dead marriage is no real marriage at all.

This has a significant consequence with respect to marital infidelity. Sexual intimacy on the part of a married person, with someone other than wife or husband, is considered adultery, and therefore morally wrong. It is on the basis of this that even persons long separated from their spouses, and persons in the process of divorce, are by many persons—clergypersons and other moralists—deemed adulterous if they become involved in such intimacy. It is even sometimes maintained that persons separated, and in the process of divorce, should not even date other people. They are, after all, *still married*, it is said.

But are they? Not really. A dead marriage is not a marriage, notwithstanding whatever may appear in any documents. People are made married by lasting love and commitment. The legalities of marriage are important for some purposes, but they have no importance to the actual relationship of marriage when this is considered in its ethical dimension. Lasting love and commitment are what count here. When this love dies, and the commitment is no longer there, then every ethical factor involved in true marriage goes too. If your marriage is truly dead, you cannot, by falling in love with another person and acting in ways appropriate to that love, commit adultery, no matter what may be implied by the legalities involved. Your fidelity, from the standpoint of ethics, is not to an estranged spouse, but to the person with whom you share the bond of total love that can give rise to lasting commitment.

This is how we shall think of marriage in the pages that follow. Lasting love is obviously a nobler idea than mere legality. To think of the institution of marriage just in terms of the latter, or in other words, to try to maintain that people are really married if they meet these easily identifiable criteria, and not really married if they do not, is to trivialize the whole notion of marriage. And it is only in the light of this nobler conception of marriage that real meaning can be given to the idea of infidelity. Infidelity, or breach of faith, is, in its fullest sense, an ethical concept, and only secondarily a legal one. And in the light of this, we shall see something else that is seldom sufficiently appreciated; namely, that marital infidelity can take many forms, of which adultery is only one, and further, that adultery, in the legal sense of the term, does not always constitute marital infidelity.

A further important consequence of viewing marriage as primarily an ethical concept rather than merely a legal one is that it permits us to speak of both fidelity and infidelity in, for example, homosexual unions, even when there is no trace of legality. Consider, for example, two persons who are united by a lasting bond of love and commitment, who regard themselves as married and who are even so regarded by their church, but who are of the same sex. Would it not be a trivialization of the notion of fidelity to say that there is no way that either of these can break faith with the other? Are there not, on the contrary, numberless ways? Does infidelity take only one form, limited to persons of different sex who are married by the minimum requirements of the law?

*   *   *

It is not uncommon to hear marriage spoken of as a *commitment*, and sometimes it is even suggested that it is a form of *contract*. One is especially likely to hear this view from someone long married, and the more so if the marriage has been less than totally fulfilling.

Of course, there is nothing really wrong with this. People who have "stuck it out," as it is said, "through thick and thin," who have stayed together through the years, even after the love and passion that brought them together has faded, do have a justified basis for pride in what they have managed. They stayed together, made a life together through all the sometimes unrewarding years. And why should this not be praised? Surely, it seems, the world would be better if more married people did this, if they settled for what they had, instead of becoming discontented and abandoning their marriages in search of a greater happiness which, very often, they can hardly claim to deserve. It is no wonder that preachers and politicians urge that divorce be made more difficult, and that people, having taken on the responsibilities of marriage, should be expected to honor them. They swore to a lifetime commitment, so now let them do it.

Commitment, however, is basically a concept of business and commerce, the idea of *contract* even more obviously such. A purchaser commits himself with a down payment. A bank files a letter of commitment. A manufacturer commits itself to replacement by guaranteeing a product. And a contract is a means of formally sealing a deal; one party agrees to do what it would otherwise have no reason to do, in return for a valuable consideration offered by the other party.

What is apparent in the idea of commitment, then, is the idea of give and take. Each side seeks to further its own interests and is willing to give up something in order to accomplish this. The focus is thus, for each party, on what it is going to get from the deal. It is a concept that is very basic to civilized society, so much so, in fact, that philosophers sometimes say that society itself rests upon a tacit, unwritten contract between its members. There is thus certainly nothing wrong with the concepts of commitment and contract, or with the primacy of self-interest which these ideas rest upon. Without them it would be quite impossible to settle questions of who owes what to whom, other than by violence.

Some persons have carried this idea of marital commitment to its logical conclusion by the creation of what are called prenuptial agreements. Here the idea is that a man and a woman, contemplating marriage, set forth in writing and sometimes in considerable detail, what each expects to get from the arrangement, and what each is willing to give in return. Such an agreement can cover matters as diverse as who contributes what in the way of finances, allowances, child care, freedom of movement, housework, home maintenance, and even such details as responsibilities for doing laundry, washing dishes, lawn care—whatever the two might want to put into it. If either fails to live up to any of the commitments thus made, then he or she will be clearly in breach of a contract, solemnly drawn up and signed, and, in principle, the other could seek legal enforcement.

From the standpoint of reason, there is certainly nothing wrong with this idea. Once you take the position that marriage is a mutual commitment, then there can be nothing wrong with spelling out the details of just what it is that each is committing himself or herself to do. The basic marriage vows, solemnly recited and witnessed by each party at their wedding, commits them to a lifetime partnership together with certain vague attitudes, such as honor and love and so on. The prenuptial agreement simply fills in the specifics and details of this vague and general commitment.

What should be obvious, however, is that however practical and sensible this whole idea of commitment may be, it can hardly be put forth as the expression of a high ethical ideal. To strike a bargain or make a deal is one thing. To love and cherish is something quite different, and it is not hard to see which is nobler. The latter, in fact, includes the former, but not vice versa. A man cannot love and cherish his wife, and at the same time disregard her needs and interests, but you can certainly enter into a contract or commitment with someone for whom you have no affection whatsoever.

Persons long married who, with total justification, point to their lasting commitment to each other do, indeed, have something to be proud of, but they should not imagine that they have fulfilled the highest ideal of marriage. A genuine marriage is not measured by time served, but by deep and unfailing love. Sometimes that love is found only after the bitter pain of divorce. Thus divorced people, while they have failed with respect to commitment to their marital vows, may nevertheless sometimes achieve, in a new marriage, a higher ideal, and thus have a stronger basis for pride than the long married.

This little story, about an elderly New Hampshire couple, pretty well illustrates both what is, and what is not, admirable about lifetime commitment:

> My sister and I never thought that Mom and Dad had much of anything in common beyond the interest they took in us while we were growing up. They hardly ever did anything together, except sometimes go visit some relative. He had his friends, and she had hers, and their interests were about as far apart as any could be. They even lived, more or less, in different parts of the house. Dad had his shop, and his gardening, and a room that was more or less his, where he read his magazines, and Mom had her church work. We never saw them get angry

with each other, except for little annoyances, but then, they never expressed much feeling of any kind.

We realized one day that their Golden Wedding Anniversary was coming up. Neither of them had said a thing about it, but we decided to do something about it, as a surprise. We invited about thirty people to come over, swearing them to secrecy, and arranged for food and refreshments for a party on the lawn. We even paid a couple to come play the guitar and sing.

It was a huge success. The local newspaper even came and took pictures. Dad got all dressed up, and at the end, when everyone was leaving, there the two stood, on the porch, holding hands, and Dad was smiling—something he did not do very often. I'm sure they were happy, that day, and proud, too.

Yes, but proud of what? Doubtless they had reason to be proud of something, but not, certainly, of the wonderful married life they had together created. What they had done was fulfill their commitment to each other, a commitment they had made in their vows a half century ago. One cannot help viewing this with a certain admiration, but it is certainly not the fulfillment of any ideal of marriage.

4

Love and Marriage

Love consists in this; that two solitudes protect and touch and greet each other.

—Rainer Maria Rilke

During the first half of the twentieth century and, of course, before then, there was, in our culture, a generally accepted model of marriage much different from today's. Educated people now look back upon the typical marriage of that period with either a shudder or amusement, but it is worth noting that there were deep and positive values in it.

What chiefly distinguished traditional marriage was a clear delineation of roles. The husband was protector and breadwinner, the wife was mother and home-maker. For a wife, and especially a mother, to be gainfully employed cast a shadow over her husband's character. He was deemed unable to support his own family, a man who had to "put his wife out to work," and she was considered demeaned as well. Similarly, a man was not thought responsible for routine indoor housework, and if he ever engaged in it—by wiping dinner dishes, for example—this was seen as "helping." Child care fell to the mother. The father's role there was ultimate disciplinarian, and children accordingly looked up to him with awe. His stern and reproachful glare could wither them. Middle-class men did not, in those days, appear on the street except in suit and tie, and they visited the barber weekly, even those who were balding. If wives participated in the organized activities of their husbands, it was likely to be as members of ladies' "auxiliaries." The professions, other than that of teaching children, were, by custom, mostly barred to them. There were almost no female attorneys, physicians, or even clergy. A courthouse was not thought to be a fit place for a respectable woman to be, and women's role in hospitals was as nurses. Divorce then was far less common, and was attended with shame. A divorced woman was vaguely thought of as wanting, in some respect, a "relict," in the quaint terminology of an earlier time, and a divorced man was in some degree disgraced. Even at midcentury, it was still thought that a divorced man was disqualified from running for high political office, this having been considered a significant obstacle to the nomination of Governor Adlai Stevenson to the United States presidency. The children of divorce almost always stayed with their mother, her maternal role thus continuing as before, and the husband's support of her normally continued until death. Thus were the distinct roles preserved, as much as possible, even beyond the life of the marriage.

Women now look upon that picture with horror, seeing it as female subjugation. We need not enter into the question of whether that is a correct appraisal. What should be noted, however, is that this delineation of roles was fairly successful in providing a basis for stable *and, sometimes, happy marriage.* And the reason for this is clear. Marriage formed a fairly successful foundation for the mutual fulfillment of needs and, therefore, for married love.

Thus, a husband found fulfillment in his work and his position in the community. He was, if successful, looked up to there, and respected. And he was similarly honored and looked up to at home, by wife and children. It was not uncommon for the wife to tidy the house and change her clothes in anticipation of his return. A woman's standing in the community was often simply a function of her husband's position there. Things did not always work out that way, of course. Men sometimes failed, or otherwise suffered disgrace in a small or large degree, but sometimes all went as it should, and stability, and even happiness, often followed.

A married woman often found fulfillment in these conditions—fulfillment of a kind different from her husband's, certainly, but nonetheless real. Thus a wife was likely to think of the home as *hers*, and as a source of deep pride. When the children turned out to fulfill their parents' aspirations as adults, the credit for this went largely to their mother. Men of achievement were likely to venerate their mothers as the source of their strength, and the annual celebration of the maternal role, Mother's Day, gained recognition well before any similar recognition was given to fathers. Wives, free from the onerous responsibilities of having to earn money through work, were able to indulge their individual interests, like gardening, and to join into pleasant and worthwhile association with other women.

This traditional scheme of marriage enabled husbands and wives to get along very well sometimes, even in the face of deep differences of personality, education, and temperament. A man's rewards in his work were not directly dependent upon his wife's personality and a woman's rewards in her home were not directly dependent upon her husband. Thus needs were fulfilled. And, when both found a considerable degree of happiness in the meeting of those needs, they were sometimes able, in their home and family life, to fulfill each other's deeper needs for comfort, emotional security, and affection. Such people, in spite of their different roles, and in spite of even deep differences in temperament, often loved each other deeply and lastingly, and such marriages were thus sometimes happy ones, in the fullest sense.

All this is noted, not with the idea of urging a return to that kind of marriage and role distinction. That would be quite impossible, and for many reasons a step backwards anyway. But what is important here is to note that this kind of marriage, the product of a long cultural evolution, did often provide for the mutual fulfillment of the needs of its partners, and thus, in spite of the limitations it imposed on both husbands and wives, it often formed a secure basis for genuine married love, as it has been defined here.

*   *   *

Western culture, and especially American culture, fosters a notion of love between the sexes that is totally at odds with the love that is found in genuinely happy marriages. This does not mean that the two are totally incompatible, but only that they are totally different. In order to keep them distinct and be clear with respect to what we are talking about, we shall call the first conception *romantic love*, and the second, simply, *married love*.

Romantic love is what is glowingly portrayed in film, novels, plays, poetry, and song. It is totally familiar. The picture presented here is of two people, male and female, irresistibly drawn to each other, passionately embracing when they are together and, sometimes, almost upon first sight of each other. Their thoughts are totally occupied with each other when they are apart. Tender notes, and tender sounds, go back and forth. The pulse of each quickens at the mere thought of the other. They yearn to be in each other's arms, yearn for every thrilling intimacy, and, they yearn to be married, that the bliss they have found with each other may be unending.

This kind of love is represented in story and song as triumphing over seemingly impossible obstacles, and, in truth, it often does. Men and women of totally different cultures, sometimes of cultures possessing age-old hatred of each other, fall in love across this cultural barrier—and are cheered on by outsiders. Hearts are warmed by the sight of a couple eloping. Thrones are sometimes abandoned for the solicitation of a romantic love. Sometimes men of true greatness, holding the highest offices in government or in the corporate world, are brought to disgrace for responding to this lure. A man holding the highest judicial office quite suddenly finds himself in total disgrace and headed for prison because he fell in love with the wrong person and briefly lost his capacity for rational conduct. A powerful senator is driven from office for a similar reason. It is almost as though a man, hitherto noted for intelligence and decorum, suddenly begins to stagger about like a zombie, everything hitherto precious to him, the things upon which his life and career rested, being cast to the winds, his sole obsession now being to be in the arms of his beloved.

Popular songs extol this passion. They lead us to imagine that on some enchanted evening we will find our true love, suddenly and out of the blue, across a crowded room; that there is one person, somewhere, waiting to be discovered, with whom instant and lasting bliss will be found and without whom life will be irreparably bleak. The very irrationality of romantic love is held up as part of its wondrousness. We are expected to *fall* in love, the very word suggesting that we are helplessly out of control. Or someone is described as swept off her feet, again suggesting a kind of helplessness. Expressions like *head over heels* and *crazy over* come into play here, the whole point being that romantic love is beyond intelligence, reason, or control.

Probably no writer has expressed the power and irrationality of romantic love more vividly than Arthur Schopenhauer, in his remarkable essay "The Metaphysics of the Love of the Sexes." He wrote of the part it plays,

> not only on the stage and in novels, but also in the real world, where, next to the love of life, it shows itself the strongest and most powerful of motives, constantly lays claim to half the powers and thoughts of the younger portion of mankind, is the ultimate goal of almost all human effort, exerts an adverse influence on the most important events, interrupts the most serious occupations every hour, sometimes embarrasses for a while even the greatest minds, does not hesitate to intrude with its trash interfering with the negotiations of statesmen and the investigations of men of learning, knows how to slip its love letters and locks of hair even into ministerial portfolios and philosophical manuscripts, and no less devises daily the most entangled and the worst actions, destroys the most valuable relationships, breaks the firmest bonds, demands the sacrifice sometimes of life or health, sometimes of wealth, rank, and happiness, nay, robs those who are otherwise honest of all conscience, makes those who have hitherto been faithful, traitors; accordingly, on the whole, appears as a malevolent demon that strives to pervert, confuse, and overthrow everything;— then one will be forced to cry, Wherefore all this noise? Wherefore the straining and storming, the anxiety and want?

And Schopenhauer's answer to this long and convoluted question is very simple: It is the sexual impulse.

The symbol of romantic love is, of course, Cupid, the smiling, naked infant boy, armed with bow and arrow, who adorns valentines. It is an ancient symbol, found in the poetry of the Romans of antiquity, but of more ancient Alexandrian origin. We have, however, ceased to note what is most important in this symbol, and that is the weapon that is always present. The arrow is a poisoned one which, upon finding its target, destroys all reason and intelligence, leaving the victim to stumble helplessly about in response to a kind of intoxication, culminating in embrace.

It is, alas! precisely this passion of romantic love, fed mainly by blind sexual passion, that impels people into marriage. And, what is worse, this is thought in our culture to be exactly as it should be. Ecstatic expressions, sometimes tears of joy, surround the newlyweds, even in the face of what should be glaring portents of disaster to come. The whispered endearments between the lovers, the billing and cooing that are erroneously thought to cement their commitment to each other, the sometimes almost comic courting that has gone on for weeks or even months, all this begins to fade once the climactic moment has come and gone and these two find themselves now confronted with the job of making a life together. Before very long, as likely as not, those sweet whisperings, the words of endearment, the soft caressing—all these come to be replaced with bitter sarcasm, sometimes shouting, threats, and the crash of breaking dishes. It is inexpressibly sad, and the fact that it is common, almost normal, makes it no less so.

Clearly, the romantic love that leads partners to the altar of marriage is no stable basis for marriage at all. The bare statistics of divorce prove this, and the obvious coldness of many, and perhaps even most marriages that do not end in divorce, proves it too. Many of those couples who do not, for whatever reason, dissolve their marriage in divorce, nevertheless allow it to die. Once believing they would find fulfillment in each other, they eventually come to sleep in different rooms, share meals with little significant conversation, and even, sometimes, vacation separately. They have come to realize that such fulfillments as they can hope for will not come from each other. Sometimes they find them in their careers, totally outside the home. Sometimes they seek them in the achievements of their children, sometimes in artistic expression, or in whatever engrosses them. A husband retires, at every opportunity, to his shop, to rebuild antique cars, or to his office, when nothing summons him there. A woman spends her days and evenings painting, or working in her church, or . . . the list of substitutes for the happiness that was supposed to reward the married is, of course, endless. These substitutes often keep a dead marriage somehow "together," but the point is that they do not enliven it. They merely make it bearable. And in time this couple will celebrate their decades of marriage with anniversaries, proud of the fact that they *stuck it out*, raised their family, and even, perhaps, that they retained a degree of fondness for each other, under the same roof and at the same table, year after year.

*   *   *

It is time now to recall what was said earlier; namely, that no earthly happiness matches that which is sometimes found in marriage. And the question arises: How can this possibly be true, in the light of the dismal portrait of marriage just given?

There is such a thing as genuinely happy marriage, but what has to be emphasized, once more, is that it is rare, even among the barely half of those marriages that, at least to appearances, survive. And what makes them happy, as marriages, is the love that unites their partners—nothing else. Doubtless there are married people who are, to some extent, happy, even when such love exists only minimally, but their happiness is not found in their marriage. It is found in their careers, or their children, or whatever engrosses them. Their marriage survives on some such foundation as this, and they even account themselves happy, but they assuredly do not know the kind of happiness that is built upon genuine married love.

Married lovers appear to live for each other, and this appearance is not totally misleading. Given the choice between doing something for themselves, or doing something for the other, they choose the latter. Each knows the other's ongoing habits and needs, and anticipates them. About to make her accustomed pot of tea, a wife finds it already done. The husband discovers that the trash he was about to set out at the curb is already there. He brings flowers, always as a surprise, but one that never really surprises; yet the delight in them never wanes. He knows her vanities, and never fails to note, and comment on, her tasteful dress and her beauty. She, in turn, knows, even though she barely understands, the depth of his involvement in something seemingly frivolous—his boat, perhaps, or his coin collection. She buys him an antique coin to add to the collection, paying several times its worth, and he receives it joyously, saying nothing about the folly of her purchase. While he has no personal interest in gardening, he notes her achievements there. In the company of others, these two listen to each other, pay attention to each other more than to others, and, even after decades together, they can be seen walking hand in hand, as if involved in unending courtship. They do not want to spend a day apart if what they are doing can be done together, and the years do not change this. It would be unthinkable for either to direct even a hint of sarcasm or belittling remark at the other. Each finds it hard to imagine life without the other. They are in love, and their love knows no season or age; it is, in truth, until death parts them.

Such love is rare, even in marriage, but it probably does not exist outside marriage. Its marks are such as have just been described. *But what, exactly, is it?* If romantic love is a kind of overpowering attraction or, as it is sometimes described, a chemistry between people which defies intelligence and reason, then what is married love?

Married love is the mutual fulfillment of needs. It is as banal and, at the same time, as exalted as that. It would be tempting to say that married lovers are solicitous of each other's needs *because* they love each other, but this would be to put things backwards. It is important to see that the love follows and is built upon such mutual fulfillment.

This is not hard to test. Imagine, for example, two lovers whose romantic craze culminates in marriage, which is the normal course of things. Soon thereafter they begin to discover certain things about each other that were scarcely noted before or, perhaps, not even suspected. The husband picks his nose, for example, or laboriously picks his teeth at the table, even in restaurants. Or the wife is given to foolish and extravagant purchases—nothing that threatens them with poverty, but nonetheless, things that constantly irritate and cannot be justified by common sense. Or the husband is untidy, leaving dirty clothes strewn about, bathing too infrequently, letting food fall from the table onto his clothes or the carpet—that sort of thing. Again, these are hardly things that are likely to shatter a marriage, but they perpetually annoy and, as a consequence, certainly dampen feelings of married love. The marriage may remain, but deep love cannot. Expanding on this, think of a wife who giggles a lot, especially in company, and is given to uttering silly, witless opinions, without any effort of thought or reflection. If her husband is of the opposite temperament—rational, reflective, and judicious—then his repeated embarrassment at his wife's behavior hardly kindles the love he thought he had for her. Think, finally, of a wife of refined taste and personal beauty and grace who finds herself married to a man given to slouching before a television set, unshaven, in his undershirt, drinking beer . . . it would be easy to embellish the description.

Of course people, romantically in love and more or less aware of each others' unappealing habits or tastes, imagine that they can change these. A reflective and well-read man imagines that his romantic but shallow lover will adopt his approach to things once they embark upon married life; the neat and tidy woman similarly imagines that her romantic but sloppy husband will change for the better, with her example constantly before him. This seldom happens to any considerable extent. People remain, after marriage, pretty much what they were before, but with one very significant exception. The romantic love, whose main ingredient is sexual passion—the love that led them to this great step, and which they imagined would last and last—soon begins to wane in the presence of all these small but constant frustrations, and before long they are likely to find that each is, in Schopenhauer's graphic description, saddled with "a detested companion for life," except that in this modern age that detested companion, having become an implacable foe, can be shed in a divorce court. And we do need to remind ourselves that this dreadful course of things comes quite close to being normal.

The examples that have been given of unmet needs are common, everyday ones. They are not examples of people who come to blows, or even, necessarily, quarrel a great deal, for sometimes married people, confronted with the impossibility of changing each other's behavior, learn to somehow put up with it. Married love is most often killed, not by outright hostility, but by simple lack of considerateness. Each partner indulges his or her needs, more or less oblivious to the needs of the other. A wife's day-to-day achievements, small in themselves but significant to her, go unnoticed by her husband. She has a talent for poetry, which he scarcely notices. Or she is an uncommonly resourceful parent, which he takes for granted. Or, on the other side, a husband takes pride in his skill at gardening, which his wife hardly notices, or he has developed great ability in restoring antique cars, an ability which everyone seems to admire except her.

Needs are not met—simple, everyday, even seemingly trivial needs—and love slowly dies, even though the marriage may remain intact. Or conversely, needs *are* met, and love, married love, flourishes. A husband, without poetic gifts of his own, avidly reads his wife's poetic creations, and with admiration. A frugal husband finds that his wife practices the same frugality, rejoicing in a dollar saved here, or ten cents saved there. The fastidious wife takes comfort in her husband's similar habits, and could not imagine him untidy or slothful. Bereft of any mechanical ability herself, she follows with deep interest his restoration of old cars, daily noting his progress. And so on, to every small, seemingly insignificant, banal aspect of their married life. These people are in love, and the love endures, quite literally in sickness and in health, in riches or poverty, and through old age and until death. All these things, of course, they swore to in their marriage vows, but this kind of love cannot possibly be sustained by vows. All that people can *vow* to do is stick together. The promise to *love* someone forever is necessarily empty. Married love is neither created nor nourished by promises and vows. It is nourished by the mutual fulfillment of needs, even, and indeed especially, the most ordinary of needs.

Some human needs are quite universal, such as the need for recognition of one's personal worth. The insult, the slight, the put-down—these are everywhere resented, while praise, admiration, and applause, even for trivial or sometimes nonexistent achievements, are received with an inner glow, just because they nourish that sense of self-worth. People who understand this side of human nature never lack friends, and it is probably this, more than any other single factor, that carries such people through life with singular success.

People are very different, however, and some needs are idiosyncratic. One person loves quiet, while another must be constantly doing things or mingling with others. This simple fact is probably the commonest cause of marital incompatibility. It is an incompatibility of very ordinary needs. Such spouses seem forever to be out of step or trying to go in different directions.

Here, for example, is the story given to me by a highly intelligent and articulate attorney who happens to be possessed of an extraordinary love of life, a man who laughs easily and is always on the lookout for unexpected moments of joy:

> My marriage to Linda seemed, at least on the surface, to be just right. We had many common interests, shared the same religious background, and we each had two young children by previous marriages, more or less the same ages. My twelve-year-old son was the oldest. Both of us were profoundly devoted to all these children.
>
> The marriage seemed all right, probably as good as most, and neither of us, during most of our twelve years together, supposed that it was anything but permanent. There was, however, a basic difference between us. Linda liked order, wanted always to know just where we were headed, and detested the frivolous. Her idea of child rearing rested heavily on discipline and control. She thought we should always have a clear idea of what we wanted the children to be doing and keep them always oriented in the right direction.
>
> This need carried over to me as well. Soon after we were married, Linda told me that some of my friends of many years were unacceptable to her. She thought their dress was tasteless, their manners uncouth, and none of them belonged to suitable country clubs. As time passed, I found my social relationships becoming ever more constricted, until I finally had no regular friends except hers. Most of my friends of long standing I was able to get together with only away from home.
>
> When we moved to another city, and set about to make friendships there, I was continually pressured to ingratiate myself with those Linda thought would enhance her social standing, and before joining any church, she investigated several to see which had the most prestigious membership. Even her work for charitable organizations seemed based more upon her need to be recognized for what she was doing than on any genuine desire to help those in need.
>
> This was just not the way I was accustomed to going about life, but I pretty much went along with it. Linda was a woman of strong will, and it didn't seem worth creating frictions over things that were not going to change anyway.

We had a camper trailer that could sleep all of us, and we took long trips with it, into the West and up into Canada. This could have been fun, but for Linda's always wanting to decide what we were supposed to be getting out of it. My oldest son, for instance, loved to read. He always had his nose in a book, even on these long trips. But if there was some mountain or lake to look at, Linda would insist that he put down the book and appreciate the things he was supposed to enjoy. Any book that seemed to her frivolous, she simply vetoed. When we came to fun things like a Ripley's Believe-It-Or-Not Museum, or a wax works, Linda vetoed those too. We all had to learn that life was serious business.

It is easy now to see what happened to our marriage. After the first couple of years, it just ceased to be fun. I like the unexpected, the novel, even things that are silly. Living without laughs is not for me. I loved the children and wanted to enjoy them for what they were and let them work out their own interests. I like talking with strangers, people I meet on the street, especially young people, and I don't care whether they have anything to offer. The world is too full of fun things to be always passing them over to get to some goal. I love zoos, and museums, and operas, and bird songs, and novelty, and I think it's all right to be silly.

I can mark the end of that marriage with a single banal episode. I was sitting in my kitchen on a hot afternoon in my undershorts, having a dish of peaches and ice cream. Linda came in and burst into a screaming fit of reproof, that I should be thus sloppily garbed and so pointlessly occupied. That seems to me now to epitomize everything that was wrong with that marriage.

The affable gentleman who told me all this became involved in several love affairs before the marriage finally ended, all of which he described as meaningless. But then he eventually met a concert musician who shared his love of life, and these two have now, for several years, shared a totally fulfilling marriage. Both are deeply involved, and successful, in their professional lives, and the basic need, unmet in the first marriage, is now abundantly fulfilled. As he described it to me, "We laugh all the time, even in bed."

*   *   *

It is important to note that no mention has been made here of sex, even though this is the first thing one is likely to think of when contemplating need fulfillment in marriage and, especially, a young marriage, or one still in the giddy stage known as the honeymoon. In the not-too-distant past, marriage was even thought of largely as the gateway, and the only acceptable one, to sexual gratification. It was a need that must remain unmet prior to marriage, and then, immediately thereafter, could be indulged without restraint or hindrance. It is fortunate that this incredibly artificial notion of virginity and marriage is no longer taken seriously. Being quite at odds with human nature, it only bred unhappiness, and led many couples to the altar quite unprepared for the real, day-to-day requirements of successful marriage.

There is no doubt that romantic love, described earlier, rests mostly upon sexual attraction. Schopenhauer, quoted earlier, maintained unequivocally that it is entirely reducible to that. And there is no doubt that many persons, probably most, marrying for the first time, expect that the enchantment and bliss of romantic love will be carried on, unabated, through the many years of marriage. Tasting that bliss, they want it to last, and they think that marriage will guarantee this. Of course people with more knowledge of the world, and especially those who have experienced marital breakdown, know better. That is, partly, what makes romantic lovers so comical.

Sexual intimacy is, of course, a natural part of marriage and, usually, very important to it. It is even difficult to think of marriage apart from it. But this is worth very little if all the other numerous day-to-day needs are largely unfulfilled. Lovers can fall into each other's arms ecstatically, and there is surely no comparable ecstasy in the other joys that married people, if they are lucky, find; but the joys of sex are short-lived if these other fulfillments, however pale in comparison, are not found.

5

Understanding Love Affairs

Women are not men's equals in anything except responsibility. We are not their inferiors, either, or even their superiors. We are quite simply different races.

—Phyllis McGinley

A love affair is defined for our purposes as an intense, passionate, and intimate relationship between a man and a woman, at least one of whom is married to, or cohabits in a marriage relationship with, someone else. By defining a love affair in this somewhat restricted way I am, therefore, excluding from consideration so-called platonic relationships, which may be intense but not intimate, as well as homosexual relationships, which involve all sorts of questions that will not occupy us here.

My definition also excludes from the class of "love affairs" the mere cohabitation of unmarried people, where neither is married to, or has any marriage relationship with, someone else. Thus, even though male and female students who live together and more or less make a home together *are not* involved in a love affair, they *are* involved in a marriage relationship. All that is lacking is its formal legality, which is no longer thought to have great significance even in the minds of the general public, and which presents few ethical problems that do not arise from marriage itself. If, however, either partner in such a relationship becomes intensely and intimately involved with a third person, then a love affair exists. I am concerned about precisely those problems arising from this kind of relationship.

No one any longer gives much thought to unmarried persons becoming lovers, living together, and so on, with the occasional exception of parents, in the case of young people, and here the concern is more with daughters than with

41

sons, and is usually felt more by fathers than mothers. With this exception, cohabitation is seldom considered immoral.

*   *   *

Of course one need not embark upon a series of interviews to learn that there are not two kinds of people in the world, namely those who do, and those who do not, have love affairs. It is certainly true that some people fall in love only once, get married, and never become involved in an affair, but they are not different in kind from those who do. Either they are simply people whose needs are, in some way or another, and to a degree sufficient for themselves, fulfilled by that one person, or (which is more common) they are individuals who feel themselves restrained by the conventionality of their lives and values. Thus a person who takes pride in personal constancy, or rejoices in what is believed to be the constancy of wife or husband, has little real basis for pride and rejoicing. It is likely to be a matter of mere luck or, what is worse, timidity. The conception of an "unfaithful" wife as one who is loose, or an "unfaithful" husband as one who is weak, is as naive as any idea can be.

Similarly, anyone who has ever observed or thought about these matters knows better than to treat love affairs lightly. They are serious, often more serious in their depth of feeling and in their power over those involved than most marriages—which, in spite of the aura of sanctity surrounding this institution, are sometimes superficial, trivial, bland, and virtually meaningless. Hence there is no good reason for saying that the institution of marriage is, as such, important, while love affairs are, as such, devoid of positive significance. Both can be important, because people are important, and in both relationships we are dealing with feelings which are at the foundation of all human happiness and misery.

In my conversations with people not many of the things I learned were new or surprising to me, though some were, to some extent. I seldom found people who were merely seeking pleasure or a forbidden form of entertainment, although a few (usually men) could perhaps be so described. In fact, even those few love affairs in which sexual passion appeared to be the essential ingredient were nevertheless usually very meaningful in ways having little to do with sex.

Most (or well over half) of the people who answered my ads were women. Virtually all, whether male or female, were fairly well educated; many were professional or semiprofessional persons or their spouses. Many of those interviewed (though fewer than half) were from academic communities, though not all of these were reached through my ad, because they were already known to me as friends, students, or recent students. A number of the relationships concerned unmarried (though often previously married) women who were involved with older men—many of whom were still married. I had no opportunity to talk with any young, unmarried man who was involved with an older, married woman. This, of course, does not mean that such relationships do not exist, but rather that the men involved in them perhaps feel no particular need to talk about them.

*   *   *

The eagerness of some respondents (especially men) to boast of their prowess and wide range of their experiences surprised me a little, though it should not have. After all, these individuals had evidently responded with just that motive in mind. What surprised me more was the connection between a certain kind of childhood upbringing and sexual expression in adult life. There are, that is to say, sexual practices that are highly irregular. The clearest examples are: The simultaneous pursuit of both homosexual and heterosexual intimacy; three people (usually two women and a man) all making love with each other; two doing so while a third person observes; or, what is more common, the simultaneous involvement in two love affairs (more common with men than women). Virtually all the women whose sexual behavior was in some such sense irregular had received their earliest education from nuns, or had received the same kind of restrictive and morality-oriented instruction from parents whom they viewed as cold and aloof. The men whose childhood associations had been similar in content tended to have excessively strong feelings about sex, and, at the same time, they tended to be perfunctory and uncommunicative with their partners. This kind of abruptness on the part of their partners is a common complaint of women ("He just wants to screw me and then fall asleep"); frequently such men have been inculcated with the same type of early moralistic education mentioned above.

The effect of associating sex with sin, in the minds of children, is also evident in this account:

> My parents are both religious, especially my mother, and I was too when I came to college. I almost joined the Christian Varsity Fellowship here my first year, and felt very troubled inside when something kept telling me not to. But I didn't. I have never had sex with a boy, and it doesn't bother me at all; but once when I wrote to my mother and asked her how she would feel about that she became very alarmed and wrote back a six-page letter, mostly quoting the Bible, saying why I must not. She should not have gotten so upset, because I had no intention of actually doing it.
>
> I stayed here over the summer, and, to my own amazement, I got all involved with the worst kind of man imaginable. I had never been in love, and this was a purely physical attraction, and nothing else, because we didn't have a thing in common. He was overweight, drank a lot, was into all sorts of drugs, punk rock music, fast cars, all the things I knew I should have nothing to do with. But he was thoughtful, would take me any place I wanted to go in his car and wait for me for hours while I shopped, bring me flowers, anything I wanted. He always wanted to sleep with me, and I did sleep with him once, but we didn't actually have sex. I know I am not really in love with him, and couldn't be, but I can't help being physically attracted, probably because he is everything I was always taught was bad and, in some ways, he is actually very good.

What can be inferred from accounts like this, which are common, is something that is, I suppose, fairly obvious and should not really surprise anyone;

namely, that teachers and parents who try to ensure the sexual purity of their children by impressing upon them the forbidden (and hence highly alluring) character of sex defeat their own purpose. They in fact sow the seeds of corruption in the minds of their children, seeds that sometimes germinate with great force, creating a fascination with sex and its more or less bizarre expressions.

*   *   *

Another connection between childhood and sexual expression in the adult lives of women should be noted; namely, that women whose fathers were hostile, rejecting, or simply lacking in demonstrative affection often develop an excessive need for affection in their teenage years. Often they seek this affection from an older, married man. This need can be easily exploited, and later on, after repeated injury, some women turn cynical and cold toward men.

The relationships between parents and children are, of course, too complex for easy generalization, but it cannot be denied that this kind of connection exists. This deep-rooted need for the affection of an older man is sometimes found, for example, in the backgrounds of female college students who sometimes form an overwhelming attachment to kindly professors. To say that these women are "looking for a father" is to oversimplify, and yet it is not entirely false. Their need is very natural and keenly felt. Sometimes this is a result of divorce, when young girls, typically remaining with their mothers, are left feeling abandoned and uncared for by their fathers. Those feelings are lasting and the need that springs from them is not easily met, especially by young men who are often quite self-centered and incapable of real and unselfish tenderness.

Sometimes fathers are overtly hostile and rejecting of their daughters, with the same effect. Consider, for example, the likely effect of a background like this:

> I have four sisters and a brother, all older than I am (I'm twenty-nine), and none of them has ever been married. When I went to my tenth high school reunion there must have been two hundred people there, and I was the only one who had never been married. The reason is my father. All of us were afraid of him, and we all grew up to hate him. To everyone else he seemed to be a perfect husband and father. He was a wonderful provider, and everyone thought of us kids as models. But that was just because we were afraid. I can still see that upraised hand, and feel the chill when I did anything wrong and Mother would say, "I'll tell your father." Just his glowering look was enough to terrify me.
>
> I suffered the most. I was never supposed to be born. After four children, when my mother got pregnant with me, my father gave her five hundred dollars to go to New York and get an abortion. Abortions were illegal then. She went, but came back with the money, saying she just couldn't go through with it. My father never let me forget that I was not wanted from the start.
>
> I never called him "Daddy." I had an uncle I loved, and who used to pick me up and hug me, and until I was five I called him "Daddy," sometimes right in front of my father. Of course I knew he was only my uncle. When my father

came home from a trip, we were all supposed to run and greet him, and my brothers and sisters did this very well, but I always held back. I wasn't glad to see him at all. Needless to say, he never hugged me or held me in his arms, and in fact if he even so much as touched me it just made my flesh creep.

The sweet person who gave me the above account was, when she told it, totally involved in a love affair with a married man, her boss. Her description of him was of a man possessed of one quality above all others, and this one to an extraordinary degree: He was totally loving, gentle, affectionate, and tender.

Of course hers is an extreme case. What is far more common is a father who is ostensibly devoted to his children, who says and does more or less what is expected of any father, but who is nevertheless stiff, undemonstrative, cold, and emotionally removed from them. The effect of this upon girls is very often that, as adults, they seek warmth and affection from men much older than themselves, and sometimes men who in fact have very little else to offer.

Thus, the following contains elements that are common to the lives of many women:

Why would I fall in love with a plumber, twenty years older than myself, who has only an eighth-grade education? Well, I had three children, and had never felt loved in my life. My husband's idea of romance was to get drunk and make love. I merely endured it. I felt nothing. So of course he said I was "frigid."

Will, the man I fell in love with, is a huge, strong man, and I am quite small. He would pick me up and hold me like a child, or sometimes I would just curl up on his lap, and he would touch my feet, and my arms, and face, and stroke my back and my hair. He was very sensuous, and loved touching, even stroking my cat, or anything that felt nice to him. My father wasn't affectionate at all, and it was not until I was thirty and found Will that any man had actually held me on his lap. It was also the first time I actually enjoyed sex. With Will I had the sense of being taken care of, for even though he was very big, he was gentle and kind, just by nature. It wasn't anything he had learned. In fact he was very uneducated, and I never saw him reading anything except *Field and Stream.* He even believed that we had all descended from Adam and Eve, though he was not religious, and never went to church—he just supposed that that was what everyone believed. Still, he was intelligent; he could fix any machine, and was clever at his job.

I loved him for six months, but finally had to end the relationship for fear of losing my husband and children. There was nothing left in my marriage, but I didn't want to risk having my husband get custody of the children.

I believe anyone would be obtuse not to see a close connection between the feelings this intelligent, artistic, and educated woman had for a plumber, and the brief allusion to her childhood memory of her father.

Often women enter college after having spent their formative years with fathers who were emotionally remote from them, and with a similar result. Often such a father is outwardly concerned and even devoted, glad to pay the huge costs of education, and may even give his daughter a car when she leaves home for college; but they will still be strangers to each other. Such women cannot remember ever being held by their fathers or tucked into bed by them or having their backs rubbed at night or being cared for by their fathers when sick. Their fathers still, as always, greet them with a perfunctory kiss on the cheek when they go home, then launch into one-sided but outwardly amicable conversations in which it is quite apparent to the daughter that there is no real interest at all in things that concern her but, instead, a kind of father-daughter role playing. Such a lifelong barrier to genuine affection is impenetrable, destructive, and beyond compensation by paternal gifts, generosity, or even the genuine pride fathers take in their daughters. It causes in a young woman a constant resentment for her father that precludes real love, a resentment that is carefully concealed, of course, behind a facade of respect. She becomes exceedingly vulnerable to the affection of some other fatherlike man, whose motivations may be less noble than they appear to her.

It is a popular and romantic notion that true love is some kind of ultimate good—a saving virtue—and that parents who genuinely love their children, who demonstratively and unabashedly express that love to them, will have that love returned, and eventually their children will lavish others with love, many times over. I do believe, however, that this is true.

*   *   *

Finally, it is worth noting the considerable number of love affairs described to me in which the male partner was, at the beginning, sexually impotent, or nearly so, for a short or long period of time. This was often reported by the women involved, but only once by a man—in this case, a student. It seems, in fact, to be fairly common among students, where there is far more insecurity and loneliness than outsiders are likely to suspect. I believe that part of the explanation is the increased freedom and candor of college women, under the influence of feminism and the sexual revolution. Often they are not passive at all, but quite outspoken about their expectations; and when a man feels that much is expected of him, sexually, a very common reaction to this is fear and anxiety, and an inability to meet any expectation whatever. Hence, the following account:

> Dan and I became constant and exclusive friends our first semester, but we didn't sleep together for weeks, even though it would have been easy and I was quite willing. He sort of avoided the subject. Then when Thanksgiving break came he let it be known that he would be going to his girl back home, and made it clear that he would be sleeping with her a lot. I was completely crushed, because he had never mentioned her before, and it made me feel like I must not be very much if he wanted to sleep with her and had no interest in sleeping with me. But a couple of days later he called me from home and said there wasn't any other girl at all; and later he told me that he had just made it up because he was afraid,

and so I wouldn't think he couldn't make love, and that all he wanted was to be with me! We started living together as soon as he came back. My roommate just changed places with his, and it has worked out perfectly ever since.

Another kind of explanation (I do not know how common it is) for this type of temporary impotence in young men is a manner of upbringing in which one is taught to have an excessive regard for feminine qualities and female virginity. Thus, the next account, which is the only admission of impotence that I received from any man in all of my many discussions with them, although there were many women who offered comparable descriptions of their male partners:

> I had never been in bed with a girl until I met Julie just a week before leaving home to come to college. I spent one night with her, although we didn't do any-thing. When I went home, after being out all night, and told my parents where I had been, they spent the whole day wringing their hands and carrying on, ask-ing me and each other where they had failed as parents and asking me to think about how my behavior was going to affect my sisters and that sort of thing. After I got to college Julie often came to visit me on weekends, and always slept with me then, but for three months we still never had sex, even though I tried several times. I was just too scared to do anything. Sometimes I got so tense that I had to get up in the middle of the night and just run, for an hour or more, to get it out of my system. Eventually, we became lovers and, in fact, that finally got to be the only thing there was in the relationship. We weren't in love at all any more, at least I wasn't, but we both did want to make love every chance we could, and that finally got to be the only thing we ever did together.

A love affair in which the male partner is more or less incapable of making love violates, of course, the popular stereotype of love affairs as little more than sexual extravagances; nevertheless they are often intense, and not so rare. Of course such a state of affairs is deeply painful and humiliating to a man, whereas women, to the surprise of many men, often regard it as incidental and of little basic importance. Indeed, it is not uncommon for a woman to declare herself totally and passionately in love with a man of severely limited sexual vigor, and willing to court great risk in order to be with him, even though her own husband, for example, labors under no such difficulties at all. Perhaps such women treat it as a challenge to themselves, and their own sense of womanhood becomes ful-filled in meeting that challenge. Two women have, in fact, so expressed them-selves to me. And I know one young, beautiful, and intelligent woman in love with an invalid who has no control over his limbs or of his bodily functions, a man who in fact lacks virtually every normal physical capacity except speech; and I have seen her gaze into his face with total adoration. Men find this possi-bility completely bewildering, but women, I have learned, usually do not.

People who think of love affairs as nothing more than sexual adventures, and often casual ones at that, are therefore very much mistaken. On the contrary, these relationships are usually deadly serious and deeply meaningful. Perhaps one reason some people find this fact difficult to accept is that social convention has reserved such meaning for the presumably lifelong relationship of marriage; an affair is quite naturally thought of as a rival to this marital arrangement. Therefore, the only acceptable conception of extramarital love is a trivialized one that excludes every source of affection except sex.

In fact sexual intimacy is only one ingredient of a love affair and, to those involved, it is likely to be considered secondary. People have all kinds of needs that have little to do with sex: they need affection, recognition, a sense of self-worth, simple friendship, and the banishment of loneliness. Any of these can serve as a strong basis of a love affair. Whenever I have asked those with whom I have talked whether their relationships might have been possible even without sexual contact, many have said they would have, though it must be added that this view was expressed more often by women than by men.

*   *   *

Still, the rare case does occur in which a love affair rests upon sexual attraction almost to the exclusion of everything else. There are, in fact, men and women who have a strong and immediate sexual attraction to each other, often inexplicable, but sometimes instantly known to both of them. From what I have seen of this it does not fit the usual stereotype of physical attractiveness. Sometimes it is referred to as a kind of "chemistry" between two people, and the metaphor is apt, suggesting a strong but irrational action and reaction. This chemistry is sometimes lamentably weak between husbands and wives, who care deeply for each other and whose marriages are genuinely happy. I have even known a man, of unusual attractiveness and sophistication, who had felt no sexual attraction whatever for his beautiful wife in nearly fifty years of marriage, even though they had always, from mutual desire, slept together. Needless to say, he was a veteran of several love affairs.

I am convinced that the presence of such feelings, or the lack of them, is totally beyond the control of people, and equally beyond their understanding—something which should, by itself, be enough to exhibit the foolishness of those who want to condemn them. With the exception of Schopenhauer, who gave a metaphysical explanation of passionate love, hardly any philosopher has attempted a serious explanation. There is no comprehending *why* a given man or woman is swept up in a tide of sexual passion for just one particular person, and quite unable to muster such feelings for another with whom he or she might be genuinely and deeply in love, who is recognized as a better person in all ways.

One of the people with whom I spoke, an intelligent woman of exquisite beauty, had made herself the virtual slave of a man having no redeeming qualities whatsoever, even in her own eyes, except for a mysterious power to arouse sexual passion in her. This lovely person had never experienced orgasm in seven years of marriage to the best of husbands. Following divorce she had had a succession of lovers, many of them men of taste, refinement, and social position;

some of those affairs had been sexually and otherwise fulfilling, yet they had aroused in her no deep feeling. Only the crude and selfish boor referred to could do this, and he did it casually and effortlessly, sometimes causing this hitherto frigid woman (as she thought) to orgasm merely by putting his arm around her waist. He had this effect on her in spite of his lack of any appealing attribute, for he was sullen, without warmth, untidy in his person, incapable of keeping a responsible job, and, except for this beautiful companion, quite friendless.

We shall consider this specific affair in greater depth later on. Meanwhile, here is the description another woman gave of her passion for a particular man, the first in the forty-some years of her life to have this effect on her. She had been long but not always happily married, and was the mother of five. She was also a person of the utmost respectability, both within her wide circle of friends and in her church, in which she is active:

> I had never made love with anyone but my husband, and my sex life with him was not abnormal or lacking, at least according to what I had read and heard. But almost from the day I met Paul I found I wanted to be with him every minute I could. This had never happened with anyone else in my life. And what I wanted was to touch him and have him touch me; I wanted to do just everything I could imagine, and I didn't have the slightest shame or modesty about it. If I ran into him on the street, or stopped at his house to talk with him, even with his family there, I would usually go straight home and write him long letters, telling him all my feelings and saying things I had never in my life said in letters, and wouldn't dare say out loud, even to him. When we are alone together he talks the same way, and he seems to find it exciting. Even when we are with other people we both know what the other is thinking, and when no one else is around we do the same thing at the same time—we immediately take off all our clothes. We make love every way you can think of, and even though we are both quite bashful around other people, we never are with each other. If he calls me on the telephone I can almost see him at the other end, and he seems so close I can practically smell him. When I go to bed alone I think of him being there with me, and I cuddle down warm by myself or with my cat and sometimes I have actually "come" that way, just thinking about him and fantasizing. It is not that I am so crazy about sex. In fact I never thought much about it; I was a virgin when I got married, and couldn't describe any lurid experiences until I met Paul. He is much older than I am. He has a nice wife and home and even a granddaughter he dotes on. Most people might not think of him as sexy, but if he even asks me how I am or comments on the weather my impulse is to unzip his clothes. If we're alone but can't make love, because I'm having my period, then I make love to him. I certainly am in love with him, but I have never said so, except in my letters, and we have never talked about love or getting married or anything like that.

According to the longer account given to me by this person, from which I have excerpted only part, this intense attraction was mutually felt by her partner. But it should also be added that even though sex was woven into every aspect of that relationship, it was nevertheless meaningful in other ways too. It was not, in other words, "mere sexual attraction," if such an expression has any validity to begin with.

*   *   *

Probably the most common misconceptions of love affairs arise from the supposition so many people insist upon making that men and women are basically similar, or even almost identical, in their fundamental needs, desires, and impulses—differences here being simply the result of cultural conditioning. It is astonishing to me how many people want to *insist* upon this, as though merely saying it over and over is going to make it true, in spite of every indication to the contrary. Of course all these contrary indications are explained away as "conditioning."

The source of this supposition is ideological. It does not arise from experience or from thoughtful attempts to understand the ways that men and women react to each other. The ideology is that men and women are equal in their psychological capacities, or at least that differences in this area are certainly not attributable to gender. And that, of course, is true. To suggest otherwise would betray simple ignorance. But then "equal" comes to be understood as "same," so that one is not allowed even to suggest that men and women are, in very basic ways, quite different in their needs, desires, and responses. Any suggestion that they *are* different is dismissed as "sexism," and thus interpreted as a stupid and outdated attempt to compare the sexes invidiously and, presumably, to portray men as somehow superior to women in one or more ways.

Thus, it is common for people to note that women desire and "enjoy" sex just as men do, and to conclude from this, with only minimal reflection, that differences in the ways these desires are expressed must be entirely the product of conditioning. The trouble with such an attitude is not so much that it is false, but that it is superficial. It does not even begin to express the immense complexity of male and female sexuality. Men do, in fact, for the most part, have stronger and more clearly focused sexual desires than women, while women typically derive more actual pleasure from sex than men do. For example, many women are capable of several orgasms, with increasing pleasure each time, whereas men, and especially older men, are often capable of only one. But none of these observations is particularly important. People who possess strong ideological convictions, whether positive or negative, concerning the equality of the sexes, feel compelled either to insist upon observations such as this, or to dispute them, thus blinding themselves to the enormous complexity of human beings. Even to express these points in terms of the idea of "pleasure" or "enjoyment" is a gross oversimplification.

Anyone with the slightest sense of logic can see that equality of worth by no means entails identity or even strong similarity with respect to anything else whatever, and similarly, that strong and fundamental differences imply nothing at all concerning value, merit, or worth. Anyone who tries to understand the opposite sex by making the uncritical assumption that it is basically no different from one's own is certain to achieve almost no real understanding at all. A man who thinks that, beneath appearances, women are very much like himself, so far as all the impulses and feelings relating to sex are concerned, has no understanding of women, and has almost no chance of ever establishing deep and meaningful relations with them or, indeed, any kind of relationship at all that extends much beyond mere flirtation or, as often happens, boring and uncommunicative marriage. The same is true, of course, for women.

This has to be noted because, long ago, I concluded that the differences are fundamental and not the mere product of cultural conditioning. Men and women who become deeply and passionately involved with each other over a considerable period of time, whether married or unmarried, are usually sensitive to these differences.

I am going to try to advance the understanding of a love affair, as well as of marriage, partly by comparing and contrasting male and female sexuality. I shall, for example, describe men as basically egoistic and polygamous, while women are vain, and I shall offer suggestions as to why the sexes possess these traits. In doing so, I must repeat and insist that I am making no invidious comparison of the sexes, and there is nothing old-fashioned or chauvinistic in what I say. My analyses are, I believe, no more than the unbiased interpretations of experience, much helped and, I think, confirmed by the experiences that others have related to me.

6

Within the Halls of Ivy

If our elaborate and dominating bodies are given us to be denied at every turn, if our nature is always wrong and wicked, how ineffectual we are—like fishes not meant to swim.

—Cyril Connolly

What is usually thought of as the sexual revolution in this country began on the college campuses. If one were to pick a time and place, it might be the University of California at Berkeley in the spring of 1965. There the "free speech movement" of the previous fall culminated in the display of signs and banners bearing obscenities and slogans that were quite correctly perceived by the regents and others as an assault upon middle-class values. Before the spring was over, President Clark Kerr had submitted, then withdrawn, his resignation. In looking back on the whole episode, which now seems essentially silly, one wonders what the noise was all about. That is because the revolution succeeded, with a minimum of upheaval.

Probably none of the events of that spring were thought of at the time as having anything to do with a sexual revolution, but they nevertheless raised a simple question that was going to come up over and over again on every campus, and then beyond the campuses—the question, "Why not?" When a group of students at Berkeley named itself Freedom Under Clark Kerr and erected a banner bearing its acronym, they implicitly asked the question, "Why not?" It had no rational answer. Soon afterwards, students on several campuses demanded that dormitory rooms be accessible to visitors of either sex. Why not? Later, they demanded that men and women be permitted to live in the same dormitories. Why not? Then they sought permission for both sexes to live on the same floors of the dormitories without being expected to account to anyone for their comings or goings—and so on.

In 1966, Brown University made news when it announced that the student health service had supplied contraceptives to an unmarried female student. The student was, after all, twenty-one and entitled to make her own decisions. Why not? The next step was so obvious that it was taken almost at once: easily available contraceptives to any student anywhere.

It is doubtful whether any college has been able to preserve the norms of student conduct that were taken for granted prior to the sexual revolution, with the possible exception of evangelical schools where the students live in dormitories segregated by sex. Even Roman Catholic colleges seem to have yielded. At one of these, for example, an effort was made to maintain strict separation of the sexes in dormitories, and to lay down rules in keeping with the church's teachings concerning sex and chastity. But the students rebelled, asking why they should have to submit to such rules when the majority of students, living off campus, were under no such requirement. It was, of course, impossible to give a convincing answer to that. What generally happens, then, is that rules are set forth, and everyone is exhorted to honor them, even in the knowledge that they are easily and regularly disregarded.

One university president, ruefully taking note of all this, quipped that he had three main problems in administering the business of the university: "Sex for the students, athletics for the alumni, and parking for the faculty."

*   *   *

The basic features of any university make it a natural focal point of revolutionary change, and this is especially true with respect to changes that have taken place in the customary relationships of the sexes. There is first of all, of course, a large population of young adults, all of approximately the same age, many of them beyond even the loose surveillance of parents for the first time in their lives, and thrown constantly into each other's company. Few of them have ever been married, but they become involved in what can properly be called, and are by themselves sometimes called, marriage relationships. In fact relatively few emerge from college without having had one, and often several, such relationships. Around this institution of *de facto*—though informal and usually impermanent—marriage there has grown a fairly elaborate code of ethics.

There are, however, other features of a university community which nourish intense, intersexual relationships among its members, though less obvious. A university faculty, for example, at least within the liberal arts programs, comprises persons of considerable sophistication, most of whom are well read, widely traveled, and many are original and independent in their thinking. Such is, indeed, the very ideal of teachers of literature, philosophy, and the arts. These people often set their own standards and feel no discomfort if they radically depart from accepted custom. Professors are, moreover, sooner or later protected from economic insecurity by tenure, and thereby released from the strongest force inclining many others in the direction of conformity. In most universities a professor cannot be dismissed for sleeping with students. In some businesses, by contrast, an executive can be eased out of his job for mere eccentricity of dress, or his refusal to wear a necktie. A university would not wish to make an issue of a professor's involvement with a student, especially in the case of some well-known scholar, unless it had other very strong reasons for wanting to be rid of him—for instance, if he had a long history of attacking administrative policies. Still, the publicity such an effort might engender would cause considerable embarrassment, and, in any case, the effort would most likely fail. The dismissal of a tenured professor normally requires the concurrence of a faculty committee, and it would be hard to find any committee willing to concur in this—the more so since some of its own members might, if the facts were known, be subject to inquiry on the same ground. Universities therefore do not try to prevent such relationships among the faculty or between faculty and students, a task which is by its nature virtually impossible. Instead, institutions of higher education assid-uously try to keep them out of sight. This is considered "discretion," and a lapse from it is viewed with the same horror as, for example, plagiarism, or cheating in sports.

* * *

There is no doubt that the introduction of female students into hitherto all-male dormitories has elevated the quality of life there. A sophomore, who had spent his freshman year in a men's dormitory, described the contrast this way:

> If you change a light bulb for a girl, she brings you some cookies she's baked, or gives you a back rub. And the men are neater with girls around. They don't roam around in their underwear, and they are not as noisy and don't swear as much and don't fart in the halls. It's much better this way.

The idea outsiders have, however, that these changes promote promiscuity among students is entirely groundless, connoting as it does sexual intimacy with-out deep feeling, commitment, or lasting (if impermanent) devotion to one per-son. Students sleep with each other, but most of them do not "sleep around," with one person one night and with another the next. The room to which a student is assigned, the room listed next to his or her name in the student directory and for which rent is paid by parents, is very likely not the one the student, for all prac-tical purposes, occupies. There is much swapping of rooms, sometimes with combinations of byzantine complexity, yet serious dislocations rarely result. Most rooms are occupied, one way or another, and rarely by more persons than would be acceptable. Whether these persons happen to be of the same sex is a question the university prefers to ignore.

The student who more or less abandons his room in favor of another is almost invariably the male partner of the relationship, reflecting an unwritten rule of the student ethos. The basis for this is the very clear conception students have of the different sex roles. For a woman to move into the room of a man would either appear "tacky," or else suggest a stronger commitment on her part than she is likely to have, or want to appear to have. A man, on the other hand, suffers no discredit whatsoever when it is learned that his girl has allowed him to move in with her or, at least, to sleep with her regularly. Indeed, if anything, his status is enhanced by this fact.

The code of ethics that has emerged within student marriage relationships is fairly complex, and perfectly understood by all. For example, it is common knowledge who shares whose room; no other student would seriously contemplate trying to ingratiate himself with one of these partners, in the hope of sexual intimacy, unless there was some reason to suppose that the existing relationship was eroding. Therefore, the idea some persons who stand outside these institutions might have, that a female student thus involved might be a "likely prospect," is the very opposite of the truth. No prospect could be less promising. Existing relationships are respected and treated as inviolable, without thought or discussion ever being given to the matter.

*   *   *

Often, however, students feel a strong need to conceal such relationships from their parents, although this is far less common now than it once was. Sometimes the fear of parental discovery borders on paranoia. One student describes her feelings this way:

> I got involved with my history professor during my sophomore year, and I used to live in terror that my parents would find out. Gregg, whom I'd gone with in high school, used to come to visit on weekends sometimes, and I don't know where my parents thought he stayed; the question just never came up, and it didn't bother me. But this other was different. I used to think that Daddy would walk right into my room when we were there, even though that was hardly possible, since he didn't have a key, and anyway, I knew he was in Allentown. Once when we went to some meetings together every other man in the airport looked like my father, even the policeman who stood by the place where they examine luggage. We both laughed, but I never got over feeling that way.

Another student gives this account of a close call:

> I was practically living at Carl's fraternity, and his parents were coming up for Parents' Day. They weren't due until noon, so we thought there would be no problem if I got out of there by ten. But, to our horror, they arrived at nine, and before I was even out of bed they were standing right in his room! They didn't know I was there, because I was in the top bunk, frozen with fear, and all of a sudden his mother insisted she wanted to see where Carl slept, and was going to climb up to look, and Carl was telling her she didn't need to, but she was insisting, and I actually saw her hand come up over the edge, to climb up, when

Carl somehow pushed her away and got her to leave. After everyone was gone I just lay there for about thirty minutes, paralyzed.

Another disaster was averted at the last minute this way:

I thought I'd gotten my room all back to normal for my parents' visit when I suddenly realized my pillow was missing! There wasn't time to go get it so I stuffed a pillow case with laundry, and just that minute in they walked. And they never noticed.

Or, consider this unhappy but strangely comical experience:

I got pregnant my freshman year, and by the time Christmas break came I hadn't been able to go to any classes for weeks, I was so sick every morning. So I took incompletes in everything and went home. Of course I didn't dare tell my parents what was wrong. They would both have had strokes, and it would have been the end of college and everything else for me. But then before I'd been home a week my father began having all the same symptoms of pregnancy as mine, and everyone became very concerned! I thought it was hilarious, but maybe it also prevented people from guessing what was wrong with me, since no one suspected *he* was pregnant. Mononucleosis, everyone decided.

Then, to my absolute horror, my father made an appointment for both of us to see the family doctor, *together.* I felt trapped; I could think of no escape at all, and in my desperation I took fifty dollars with me, to *bribe* the doctor to keep the secret. But then I didn't have the nerve to offer him the bribe. He examined me, even poked around—and I was actually beginning to *look* pregnant, I thought—but he didn't seem to suspect a thing. Then he took a blood sample, which I knew for sure was going to be my death warrant, but apparently it didn't tell him either. Finally he decided we didn't have "mono"; instead, he said we had "vertigo," whatever that is, and gave us medicine.

My father recovered quickly, and a week later I went to Buffalo and had an abortion. To this day my parents do not know, and I'm sure they would murder me, even now, if they found out.

The inclination to smile should not overwhelm the perception of pathos in this story; for here was a girl, caught in a dreadful crisis and in desperate need of love and help, who was prevented by fear of reproach from turning to the very people she had always been taught to look to for protection, that is, to her own parents— people whom she perceived, correctly or not, to be more absorbed in their own ideas of morality than in the safety and well-being of one of their children.

The occasional attempt by parents to control the attitudes and behavior of their children by threat and remonstrance almost always fails, for students always have the easily available alternative of secrecy. For this reason, the threat of a father to his daughter to "cut her off," that is, withhold payments for educational expenses, is much worse than futile. In addition to failing in his purpose he alienates his daughter. Control of this kind ceases when a son or daughter leaves home for college, no matter who is paying the bills, and parents defeat themselves by thinking of payments as the purchase of influence or control. An only child from a very rich and influential family recalls her parents' attempt to break up her relationship:

> I got to know Spike over the summer, before I came to college. I'd known him for a long time, as one of the crowd, but we had never paid any attention to each other. Then one night he and I both stayed at a party after everyone else had left, and got to talking, and after that we began to see each other all the time. Eventually he suggested that we should make love, but I never had, and I was too scared to. He didn't make any issue of it, or bring it up again for a long time, and it was months later before we did, for the first time.
>
> My parents couldn't stand him and finally demanded that I have nothing more to do with him, or they would totally cut me off from everything. He came from a working-class family, and was several years older than I, but there was nothing else about him my parents could object to. But I would never give him up, and even when he is in Baltimore and we are separated for weeks at a time I could never care about any one else, even though I have lots of friends, and lots of them are nice men, even men my father would like.

Not all students are secretive. Male students, in particular, are often quite open with their parents, and sometimes female students are as well. Here, for example, is a verbatim transcript of the student's end of a telephone conversation with his mother: "Yes, Mother, I'm living with a girl here. . . . No, I won't be home this summer. I'm going to be living with three girls in Boston, and driving a taxi." But what is interesting about this student's report to his mother is what does not appear in it; for he and the student he was living with were in fact mere friends, and had never given the slightest thought to romance or intimacy. Their living arrangement was simply the practical outcome of their oneness of mind concerning when it was appropriate to study, when to play music, when to go to bed and when to get up, and so on. They were, in short, compatible roommates, in the most innocuous and traditional sense.

When parents do succeed in significantly influencing the behavior of their children in college, or at least their choice of more or less permanent companions, it is apt to be due to cultural or religious values still honored by their children rather than overt attempts at outright control, as illustrated in this account:

> Dave's parents said they were going to take him out of college if he didn't end his relationship with me, and in fact they did, by paying his way to Israel for seven months. I resented the fact that he hadn't even told them about me, as if I were some sort of untouchable, even though I had offered to convert to Judaism. When I first asked him what he would tell them if they found out, he replied he would just explain that I was some Italian girl he had picked up, and there was nothing serious about it. I resented that. His parents absolutely insisted that he must not think of marrying a non-Jewish girl, and this meant enough to him, too, that he capitulated.

Similarly, this condensation from a long and doleful account:

> Lisa and I fell in love when a student we both knew died. We found each other
> in the library, and learned that each of us was looking for the other, even though
> we hadn't known each other very well until that night, when we both felt so
> bereft and awful. We stayed with each other that night, then spent the rest of the
> spring together, day and night, and she was my first real love. I had only made
> love once in my life before Lisa, and that had been meaningless, but this was
> total.
>
> By summer I knew things were changing, though. When we visited her
> parents they were polite but cold, and I got the message that they thought I was
> nothing. Her father took me out to watch him drive golf balls, which meant
> nothing to me, and this was his way of being polite but letting me know where
> I stood. They told Lisa that I could never hope to be more than an impoverished
> professor some place, and they were very conscious about money and status. It
> all finally got to her, and my frantic efforts to make things the way they had
> been, by showering her with expensive presents I could hardly afford, had no
> effect but to make me feel worse.
>
> Her way out was to treat me as a nice friend. I spent the rest of the sum-
> mer in complete misery, and the couple of times I tried to phone her, her mother
> answered and said Lisa was out and she didn't know when she would be back.
> When school resumed in the fall I went around to Lisa's to get my sleeping bag,
> and it was still in the trunk of her car, where it had been left all summer, com-
> pletely moldy and ruined. It was sort of the final touch. My last year in college
> I withdrew from everything, didn't see many friends, and spent the whole time
> playing my piano, entering cynical thoughts in my journal, and composing my
> senior thesis—which I dedicated to Lisa.

*   *   *

The greatly increased freedom of contemporary college campuses, however, has
not eliminated loneliness in students and, in fact, has in some ways increased it.
Some feel a kind of pressure to try to do or be what they may be psychologically
or otherwise unprepared for. For example, one female student known to me, who
had never had a close male friend in her life, nevertheless ritualistically took
birth control pills, apparently from some felt need to be like her friends. The loss
of the dominant male role, once taken for granted, has tended to make some men
more timid with women, and sometimes even withdrawn. Men can no longer
assume that girls are eagerly waiting to be asked out. Even the expression "making a date" is archaic, and, in any case, it is likely to be the female student who
initiates things. One of the most beautiful students I have ever known, who, in
the college community setting of twenty years ago would have been the object
of constant attention from men, had never been invited out in four years of college. Having great beauty, a car, and a vivacious personality, she had enjoyed a
vigorous social life, but it was always, without exception, at her initiative—she
unabashedly telephoned any man who interested her and asked him out. This

kind of female student—fairly common nowadays—can be quite intimidating to a man, especially one of limited experience. If he learns, or even suspects, that his companion may be more sexually experienced than himself, then he can become totally awkward. The thought that he might compare unfavorably with some of his predecessors is often enough to guarantee that very result, and his response is apt to be a withdrawal to his books.

It is in response to this kind of fear and loneliness that students on two campuses known to me have organized what they call the "Screw-Your-Roommate Dance." The expression has no sexual connotation, and the event is organized as follows. A weekend is chosen, and each resident of a given dorm who wishes to participate is supplied with a blind date by his or her roommate. It is officially supposed that the date will be found thoroughly objectionable, though in fact every effort is made to bring together men and women who will like each other, often with confidential consultation on this between the roommates themselves. The dance is held in the lounge of the dormitory sponsoring the dance and recorded music is used for the entertainment. In the event that the couples do turn out to be quite incompatible, then embarrassment and humiliation are avoided by the supposition that this was, after all, precisely as it was planned, and both can laugh. If, on the other hand, they enjoy each other's company, as both secretly hope, then loneliness has been banished without great risk to anyone. The somewhat intimidating task of initiating the encounter has also been avoided by handing the responsibility over to a roommate. It is thus a fairly effective way of solving both problems at once, with fairly good results and a minimum of hurt feelings. Of course it is impossible to measure the overall success of this novel institution, but when I asked two different students to estimate the numbers of such couples who end up that night sleeping together, both thought that about twenty-five percent would be a good guess. Of course the remainder are at least left without feeling totally rejected.

*   *   *

Another obvious feature of every college and university is the existence of a predominantly male and married faculty together with, at least in most universities, a class of graduate students, both male and female, many of whom are married. But while the existence of such groups is obvious, certain features of their mode of life, the nature of their work, and their actual or possible relationships with each other as well as with students is much less obvious.

Most of the older members of a university faculty, it must be said at once, maintain a strict and often impenetrable reserve with respect to their associations with students. Relationships outside the classroom are limited to occasional office conferences and, perhaps once or twice a year, a picnic or a luncheon or dinner at the professor's house, prepared with the help of gracious wife (or cooperative husband). For such visits to a professor's home the students are likely to put on neckties or dresses for the first time in months. Conversation is invariably strained, running to such matters as athletics, the university dining service, or, with a bit of extra effort, national politics and current events. Students find these affairs deadeningly tedious, yet are flattered to be invited, and invariably speak well of the professor who has asked them. The professor often feels self-conscious or called upon to appear both learned and affable at once; he plays his role as best he can, and is relieved when the occasion is over and has "gone well."

This large group of faculty typically lunch with each other in the faculty club. They would feel exceedingly awkward venturing into the student dining halls, rathskeller, or student bar, and could never be imagined smoking the ubiquitous marijuana with students or listening to records in their rooms. Thus, they are relative strangers to the actual lives of students, about whom they are nevertheless sometimes profoundly curious.

The description just given applies also to a large proportion of the younger faculty members who are sober, scholarly, and, above all, shy. Indeed the quiet of academic life has always attracted this type, who are accordingly found there in large numbers.

But at the opposite end of the spectrum are professors, very few in number but well known to the students, who quite unabashedly importune their female students for sexual favors, sometimes blatantly offering high grades in return. Students are, for the most part, not outraged that such a proposal should be made, and they do not make an issue of it. Of course, a university's administrative officers would never publicize such a complaint even if it were made. They would instead just add a secret memorandum to the file of the professor in question. One student who did bring the matter up was apparently embittered that she had received only a "C," but the professor, while denying nothing else, denied only that anything more had been promised.

Of course the feeling would be different if a professor offered not a favor, but a threat—or, in other words, threatened to fail a student for refusing. Any student would plainly consider this coercion, and a professor who attempted it would surely risk losing tenure. No faculty committee would uphold such action, no matter how distinguished a scholar the professor might be. Indeed, such coercion would constitute a basis for court action by a student, the very last thing in the world any professor, or any university president, wants to read about in the newspapers. Such a lawsuit was in fact brought by a student at Yale.

*   *   *

Between these two extremes—stiff reserve, on the one hand, and blatant solicitation of sex on the other—there is of course a continuum. But to understand this we need to have a clearer picture of the unavoidable psychological and sociological relationships between all students and faculty.

To begin with, a professor who stands before students, often large numbers of them, is in some sense important. Of course this is never declared, but it nevertheless describes the psychological impact of certain professors. In a classroom he is in control of almost everything—what is to be discussed, when, and by whom. The setting itself somewhat resembles a theater with but one actor who may speak from a raised platform and, if the class is large, to ascending rows of students. Many professors in such a situation, and especially after years of practice, develop great flair and charisma, though in vastly different ways. One, for example, postures and pontificates upon his favorite subject. Another sits on the edge of his desk and mumbles. A third gazes abstractly at some indeterminate point on the ceiling and rambles. Styles differ. But in strange and various ways they sometimes produce a similar effect, to varying degrees, in the feelings of a few or more female students. Some of these students may sooner or later make this known: some will move to the front row, for example, while others will try to be the last to leave the classroom, and so on. For others the message is much less covert. Occasionally, the infatuation leads to a "confrontation," initiated by the student; that is to say, an outright declaration of feelings. The dangers inherent in this are quite grave; for even if nothing more ensues than a polite rebuff on the part of the professor, the psychological damage to the student can be considerable.

The solicitations of a beautiful undergraduate student can be quite overwhelming to the feelings of a professor, even one who has been long and comfortably married, as illustrated in the following account:

> I noticed the second week of classes that Lynn was sitting in the front row, only a few feet away, even though my seating chart had her towards the back of the room. A handful of students usually gather around me after class to raise questions, and Lynn was always among them, and always the last to leave. Soon we were walking back to my office together after every class, and soon after that, having lunch together, since the class got out right at lunch time. I started looking forward to this each week, even though these encounters were not overtly flirtatious, on either side, and our conversations were on perfectly innocuous subjects. I think each of us was flattered by the interest of the other. Eventually I was invited to dinner, off campus, at a restaurant I was to name. It happened to be within a day or two of my birthday, though no mention had been made of this. After dinner I was astonished to see the waitress bringing a cake, with candles, to our table! Gradually I learned that Lynn had researched my birthday in the library—thereby also learning, of course, that I was three times her age—and had baked the cake herself in her dormitory kitchen; that she had then taken a long bus trip to the restaurant and back, in winter, to leave the cake there with her instructions. I was thunderstruck. Afterwards she invited me to her room, which she shared with no roommate, and we talked alone for a couple of hours, about nothing in particular. I felt awkward, reading into her behavior what seemed to be its unmistakable message, yet appalled by what seemed to me the utter incongruity of the whole situation. The same source that had given her my birthday had surely also disclosed, for example, that both my children were older than she. The whole situation was at once exciting, uncomfortable, and very threatening.

It is not hard to understand the appeal of professors to students, in spite of the vast differences in age which may be involved. It is, for one thing, quite easy for a moderately articulate and charming professor to look very good in the ordinary routine of his work. Not only does he have things quite within his control, but he is the focus of attention for perhaps a hundred pairs of more or less admiring eyes. Within such an audience there are apt to be a few who are, whether silently or avowedly, infatuated. Nor does it always matter that the professor may be happily married, and even have children of his own who are older than they. To some this is a formidable damper, but not to others.

The obverse of this situation, that is, the evoking of similar effects in male students by female professors, seems to be rare, and this is probably not entirely due to the relative paucity of female professors. Still, it is not unheard of, and one such affair is known to have finally culminated in the professor divorcing her husband in order to marry a college senior many years younger than herself.

*   *   *

The final feature of a university community requiring attention is the existence of a class of graduate students. Graduate faculties are, for good or ill, predominantly male—an imbalance that is gradually being corrected everywhere, but is certain to remain for a long time to come. This faculty is also almost entirely tenured, making turnover slow, and also creating a justified sense of security in its members, whatever may be their lifestyle and values. Unlike undergraduates, a fair number of the male graduate students are likely to be married, and so their wives are added to the social milieu; and of course there are also sure to be female graduate students of considerable sophistication as well as, sometimes, wit and charm, most of whom are unmarried.

The relationships among faculty and graduate students are clearly and significantly different from their normal impersonal relationships with undergraduates. Often the former are quite close. In the first place, they have sometimes an intense intellectual interest in common. Thus professors tend to win disciples from among the graduate students—persons who dominate their seminars, assist them in whatever ways they can, even becoming officially recognized by the university in that role, and who otherwise become a fairly significant part of their professional lives. The solicitations inherent in such a situation are likely to be immense in case such a graduate student is female, attractive, intellectual, and above all, quite obviously filled with genuine admiration for her mentor. The situation is sufficiently frequent that it has received a common and very apt description, namely, "worshipful graduate student." A professor may be ever so conventional, reserved, and happily married to the best and most devoted of wives, but he can seldom be so lacking in ordinary human feeling as to be totally oblivious to these blandishments, effortlessly administered to his ego; and the ego of a professor, especially in those areas of creative scholarship that are at the center of his intellectual life, is likely to be very buoyant indeed.

A wife's reaction to the intrusion of this new person into her husband's life is apt to verge upon violence, especially if she is in middle age and has devoted herself mostly to home and the rearing of children. She can hardly fail to see herself comparing unfavorably with this student, both physically and intellectually. Added to this affront to her vanity is an acute sense of insecurity for her own future. Yet situations of this kind often present no great threat to a home if things are simply allowed to run their course. Certainly fierce jealousy, anger, and recrimination in these circumstances have never endeared a wife to her husband. On the contrary, they only make him feel misunderstood and attacked, and more than one husband has felt himself driven from his home rather than lured. In spite of the fact that, for a while, he feels swept away by a current of passion, usually the real and lasting love of such a man is for his wife, and this is the force that will make itself felt if given a chance. For a while at least, a professor and his student imagine themselves to be soul mates, but this is apt to be as chimerical as the intellectual content which they think their love so miraculously rests upon. The home that he has shared with his wife for decades has a meaning that is real and strong, in spite of appearances.

Still, the effects of a liaison between a professor and one of his worshipful graduate students is sometimes devastating. It is amusing to survey a gathering of scholars—of philosophers, for example, assembled for one of their annual conventions—and note the considerable number who have ended up marrying their graduate students, more often than not at the expense of what was an already existing and apparently happy home. In fact, it is not unknown for a professor to marry a succession of his graduate students, over the course of his career—something that enabled one seasoned departmental secretary to quip: "Professor Allen always sees his wives through to their Ph.D.s."

*   *   *

It would be a mistake, therefore, to think of the modern university community as a kind of microcosm. The interpersonal relationships found there, among young adults usually spared the necessity of toiling for a living, and tenured professors spared anxiety about losing their pleasant source of livelihood, are much more free and joyous than those found on the outside.

Still, in spite of changes that once would have seemed almost unthinkable, universities are now conservative places. The sexual revolution is long since completed, and the fundamental values that have always been attached to modesty, affection, and to fidelity in feeling are probably stronger there now than before. Certainly the relationships between students are more civilized and less childish than they once were. The mayhem of fraternity parties is largely a thing of the past. Men no longer plaster the walls of their rooms with pinups of nude women. The once ubiquitous graffiti of men's lavatories, expressive of lurid fantasy and often debasing of women, have disappeared. Such childish behavior as the panty raids of the fifties is now a thing of the past. The jokes so well known to earlier generations, puerile in character and degrading of women, are no longer heard. And even the most dedicated lover of the old ways can hardly maintain that the automobile—cramped, furtively parked in a dark, lonely, and sometimes unsafe lane, without real privacy or running water—was an ideal setting for the expression of affection.

Finally, let it be noted that most students are still deadly serious about marriage. Female students who are particularly devoted to this idea are described as working for their M.R.S., but they are not ridiculed for it. Nor can it be doubted that, unlike previous generations, students today are wiser about human relationships and about each other, and thus better prepared for fulfilling marriages. Their predecessors were somehow expected to wait for such wisdom until *after* they had taken that momentous step, meanwhile depending upon nature, romance—and ignorance.

7

The Ethics of Having Love Affairs

What we call "morality" is simply blind obedience to words of command.

—Havelock Ellis

What is "wrong" with having love affairs, if one wants to use this language of morality, is that they destroy marriages. It is that simple. Even when a marriage somehow survives the infidelity of one of its partners, it is damaged, often irreparably. The wound inflicted sometimes never heals. Sometimes one partner, or both, ends up marrying someone else, whom they love for the rest of their lives, but even then, the pain is likely to endure, especially when young children are involved. The deception of having an affair is almost always discovered eventually, and is always debasing, even while undetected. Few people can lie to someone they care about without feeling degraded.

Even a casual flirtation, because it involves deception, can snowball into a bomb of dreadful force, injuring not only husbands and wives, but children. Thus many divorced people can easily relate to the following account, told to me by a man of obvious strength and striking good looks:

My marriage was perfectly okay, and I never had any thought of letting anything spoil it. We had three beautiful kids, and a fourth on the way. Then I started playfully flirting with a good-looking woman where I worked. It was just a game, and we kept it that way for a long time. I knew the numbers of all the telephones around the place, and if I saw her walking near one, I would ring it, and we would say silly things—that sort of thing. We started having coffee together every morning, and then, after awhile, we began sipping wine in her office sometimes. Once, with what I recognized as a large hint, she arrived at work driving a camper. It eventually turned out that she wanted a serious involvement.

Her husband was not only boring, but controlling. I was lured into an affair, and it went on for a couple of years. It involved endless deception, which worked for a long time, but I hated it, and hated myself for it. Eventually, one evening, when I was supposed to be at a meeting, one of the kids cut himself, and my wife tried to phone me, thus learning that I had lied. When I got home, she confronted me with it and, caught off guard, the truth came out. It was the terrible turning point in my life, when everything began to come apart.

The affair itself was never worth much. I wasn't in love. Maybe my partner was. She had left her husband by now. I was only looking for excitement. We didn't have much in common. She had her friends, whom I couldn't relate to at all. She liked to take me to her social gatherings, where I felt completely out of place, just standing around with nothing to say to anyone. I think she only wanted to show me off. She eventually moved away, and we haven't tried to stay in touch. I don't even know where she lives.

My marriage never had any of that excitement, but it was a good marriage. My wife and I were very different. She became increasingly overweight, beginning with her first pregnancy, and we never enjoyed the same things. I liked going out with friends and dancing and that sort of thing, and she just liked staying home. Still, she was a good wife and mother, and I blame myself for everything.

Even though I have remarried, and have a wonderful wife and two beautiful daughters by this new marriage, I still wish I could have kept the first one. Certainly the affair I got into was not worth all the pain, and the good marriage I have now will never really cancel that pain and guilt. I have lost the love not only of my first wife, but three of my children. I tried to keep up a relationship with them, but it didn't work. We just couldn't talk. When I took them out to dinner and tried to make conversation, they just responded with a word or two. Mostly there was just silence, and I could feel their resentment of me.

I wish none of that had ever happened. It was stupid, pointless, and very destructive and painful to many people. My ex-wife has gotten very fat, has sort of withdrawn from everything, and her house is a mess. And I'll always feel the guilt about lying to someone I cared about. No one should treat anyone the way I did.

*   *   *

Love affairs are dangerous and destructive, particularly for married people. They risk not only the deep injury of eventual rejection, but the destruction of homes and damage to children. Even unmarried people, such as those in college, sometimes scrupulously avoid sexual intimacies, usually on moral or religious principles, and there is no doubt that they thereby avoid certain risks. Passionate love is strong, and sometimes explosive in its effects.

People who value safety, orderliness, and a certain predictability in their lives—especially married people of this temperament—are probably wise to avoid temptation and hold firmly to accepted values, drawing comfort from a socially approved premarital virginity and then monogamous marriage.

At the same time, no one should assume that everyone ought to avoid love affairs, or that even married people should necessarily abstain. Dangerous as love affairs may be, no one would suggest that they are without joy. In fact, the vehemence with which they are condemned from some quarters is indicative of how absolutely exhilarating they can be.

Nor should love affairs be thought of as casual and lighthearted, mere games that are easily entered into and just as easily abandoned. This idea, common to popular journalism, is closer to fantasy than fact. The idea that love affairs add spice to marriage, or that an affair can be a tonic to revive a faltering marriage, is simply naive. Love affairs are deadly serious, and the popular references to "playing around" are merely intended to belittle them by distortion. Perhaps life would be simpler if sex were not serious business. Certainly human relations would be easier and we would be spared a great deal of misery. But that is not how we were made. The most powerful passions in life cannot be made trivial.

In this realm we are where every person must decide for himself and accept his own responsibility. No one can tell another person what is and is not permissible with respect to whom he or she will love, and when or where, or under what conditions. No clergyman can make that decision for you, nor can any moralist, teacher, parent, or functionary. It is your decision and yours alone, to which you need answer to no one but yourself. Nor can such a decision be made by one partner in a marriage for the other; for to pass the choice to someone else—anyone else—is not to act correctly, but simply not to act at all. It is to relinquish all responsibility for one's decisions and actions with respect to the choice in question.

*   *   *

No ethic ever emerges in a vacuum. Every ethic, though it may be represented as the deliverance of God, is in fact a response to human needs. That moral rules are intoned with solemnity, and deviations from them regarded with frowns and ostracism, testifies to the depth of the needs which those rules protect and not to their exalted origin. For their origin is in the needs themselves, a humble beginning, but most certainly a real one. Of course it follows from this that moral rules which no longer help to fulfill human needs are rules that do not deserve any intelligent person's allegiance. Timid moralists and clergymen who have themselves become so acculturated to ancient ways and conventional rules as to make them the basis of their own emotional security recoil against such suggestions, with fear and sometimes anger; but they have nothing with which to oppose them, except the tireless and solemn iteration of the rules themselves, as though the mere repetition of some slogan were a confirmation of its truth and wisdom.

This book is written with the conviction of the unrivaled goodness of passionate love, in which the greatest fulfillments anyone can find are sometimes possible. Indeed, genuine and intense happiness probably has no other source except, perhaps, in the ecstasies of religion. Those who seek fulfillment elsewhere—in fame, power, wealth, or whatever—find nothing but substitutes for real happiness. Some people do, for example, find power in high positions, but it is a poor substitute for the warmth of genuine affection that is sometimes found in the arms of a lover. Similarly, some attain fame, but it, too, is a poor second to the actual understanding of the heart and mind that is achieved by lovers. Convinced of the helplessness and misery of mankind, the famed defense attorney Clarence Darrow concluded one of his extensive litanies about the wretchedness of life with the declaration that no genuine happiness exists anywhere—but then added, in parentheses, as if by grudging afterthought, "except within the warmth of the family circle." Cold and calculating, and steeped in the pessimism and cynicism that his life and career had fostered, even Darrow felt forced to concede this one possibility of happiness. It was a source that was withheld from him. His own marriage had ended in ruin, and he almost never alluded to it.

The happiness that is sometimes within the reach of lovers is by no means automatic, however. It is almost banal to point this out, for who but the romantic and sentimental is unaware that lovers expose themselves far more to misery than joy? All persons suffer—some more, some less—from illness, accident, loss, humiliation, and so on. But there is something especially poignant and seemingly unnecessary in the sufferings of lovers. They *ought* to be happy, so why are they so miserable? We like to imagine that it is some sort of mistake, that an adjustment here or there will restore everything, and sometimes, even, that a few well-spoken words or a renewed declaration of love will put everything back as it should be. Yet, in fact, the misery of those whose love is dead, particularly those still married, is profound and virtually immovable. Hardly anything is so heavy with sadness as a household in which the warmth of love has been replaced by a stolid acceptance of something else, whose whole value consists in the fact that it is less bad than the possibilities exposed by abandoning it. If you find yourself in such a household, you see the lines of sorrow that have replaced the glow of love in faces of former lovers. Here and there are half-completed projects, once started with zeal, and now pursued perfunctorily, often in the vain hope that someday things will get better, someday the kind of days once lived will return again. Children come and go with sullenness, for while they are not participants in the crumbling love their parents once felt, they nevertheless pick up the sense of something lost. They feel insecure and no verbal assurances can convince them that all is well. They know otherwise. A garden goes to weeds and projects in the shop or yard are left half finished; friends come and go as before, but only momentarily divert the sad participants in this unhappy allegiance. There is worse suffering than this, certainly. In fact, this kind of dead but still existing marriage is closer to the norm than we would like to admit. Most marriages limp, even those that are not crippled or moribund. Those that are vibrant are rare. But the kind of pall that settles over a dying marriage has a poignancy and sadness of its own, partly because of the hopes that seem so needlessly unfulfilled, and partly because the bitterness of it all seems so irrevocable. It is the kind of suffering that accompanies repeated hope in the face of utter hopelessness.

It is partly from a perception of the immense goodness, and the immense evil, that lovers can create, and partly, of course, for the protection of children, that civilized peoples everywhere have hedged the institution of marriage—and, to a lesser extent, unmarried love—with rules, prohibitions, laws, taboos, and customs which have ritualized marriage and erected obstacles to its termination. The home, it is thought, must by all means be preserved; and having no other means of keeping it intact, societies have resorted to rules and ceremony. Needless to say, this does not work. A society can, to be sure, render the legal dissolution of a marriage impossible, as has been done in some countries; but all this has ever achieved is the preservation of the thinnest outward appearance. A church can, of course, with much solemnity, formalize the state of matrimony, even declare it incorruptible and indissoluble; but this, too, only creates the outward appearance. Marriage itself can in no way be created by any priest or servant of the state. It cannot be preserved by them nor by any other power of heaven or earth, except in appearance. Nor can it really be terminated by them; they can at best only recognize what has already ended. Marriage is entirely the work of those who enter into it. Its successes, and rewards of rejoicing, the warmth and fulfillment it gives, are theirs alone. Its failure, and the inner desolation this produces, are theirs too. The rest of the world can look on, but only they will have the blessings if they succeed, and of the anguish if they do not.

*   *   *

There is, therefore, absolutely nothing wrong or immoral in the marriage relationships so commonly established between young people, especially those entered into at college, and society as a whole is gradually coming to realize this. Persons involved in such extralegal relationships should make no attempt to conceal them, and if this outrages their parents, then it is actually the parents who ought to be ashamed, rather than their children. The legality of a marriage relationship adds nothing whatever to its morality, and the absence of such legality takes nothing away from it. All that legality does is to suggest a greater permanence, being considered the expression of a stronger commitment on the part of the partners; but it by no means guarantees this. And it has nothing to do with the rightness or wrongness of the relationship.

The marriage relationships of students are in most ways not essentially different from the marriages of their parents. The motivations for them are similar, and their patterns are much the same. They differ mainly in that they are less public, depending upon parental attitudes, and there are usually no outsiders filling the roles of in-laws.

What leads college men and women to take up living together is not the desire for sex, as some outsiders sometimes suppose, for most campuses are already perfectly free with respect to sexual relationships. It is by no means necessary for students to live together in order to sleep together, for they can do that any time they wish. Just like marriage itself, the marriage relationship severely restricts the sexual freedom of its partners, for each is then accountable to the other in a way he would not otherwise be. Secrecy, too, becomes more difficult, since the whereabouts of each partner is apt to be known to the other or can, at least, be inquired about.

The primary motivation students have for entering into a marriage relationship is security. It is a word students almost invariably use when asked why they want to live together, usually in secrecy from their parents. However, the security of such a primary friendship is often purchased at the cost of many less important but more numerous relationships. The following, for example, is more or less typical:

> The reason Bob and I moved in together was for emotional security. I wanted to go back to our room and know he would always be there, and that's how he felt, too. It was going back to someplace that meant something, not just to a place to sleep and study and a roommate I hadn't even chosen. Even if we had a fight, I knew he would come back, because that was home.
>
> One night when Bob was hours late coming home I nearly went crazy. He was supposed to be back at ten-thirty, and it was nearly one in the morning when he walked in. He hadn't even phoned or anything. I didn't care where he was, and I didn't think he was with another girl or anything like that, but I felt neglected and abandoned when he didn't let me know, and then finally walked in just as if nothing in the world was wrong, and wondered what I was upset about. He had only been out with some friends, and that was perfectly okay, but he could have let me know.

To this account of an experience that is familiar to so many wives, the student added the following, which is not so familiar to people long married:

> The relationship lasted less than two years. We're still friends, but we don't live together. We found we had cut out all our other friends, without intending to. They all thought they had been put in second place, and I can see why. Seeing that the two of us were completely wrapped up in each other and never went any place except together, they just looked to other people when they wanted to go to a movie or a concert or anything. And I also think they were sometimes jealous. They knew we liked each other better than we would ever like them. Of course if everyone in college were living with a lover, then it would be different, but that isn't the way it is.

Accounts such as this, so banal and so typical of married life, do raise the question as to whether the presence or absence of legality in a marriage relationship has anything more than symbolic significance, and a fairly trivial significance at that.

In any case, in what follows I shall treat extralegal marriage relationships as marriages, since the problems arising in them are essentially the same as the conventional marriages; and when I speak of "husbands" or "wives," what is said can usually be understood to apply to the partners in these relationships as well as to legally united couples. The main differences between the two, so far as this discussion is concerned, are that nonlegal marriage relationships are usually (though not always) less stable or lasting, and they seldom involve children. Most important of all, these marriage relationships will never be treated as *love affairs*. This expression will be reserved for intense and passionate relationships between men and women, at least one of whom is already married to, or in a marriage relationship with, someone else.

8

Fidelity

*Those who are faithful know only the trivial side of love; it is the
faithless who know love's tragedies.*

—Oscar Wilde

There is a tendency among human beings to convert things that are truly good
and noble into something else, some counterfeit of the original, and then, quite
forgetting the noble thing they began with, to treat the imitation as that which is
good, even calling it by the same name as the original.

Patriotism is an example of this. In its original sense, patriotism is the love
for one's country; and if we think of such love in its true sense, as resting upon
the perception of the beauty and goodness of one's country, its institutions, and
history, then it is surely in every sense a good and inspiring thing. But, over time,
this originally noble idea has been doubly corrupted. The love that is embodied
in it has been reduced to a kind of blind and mindless allegiance, and the object
of such love has become no longer one's beautiful country, but the *symbols* of
that country, such as the flag or, worse yet, the instruments and weapons of war.
Thus a patriot is now thought of as someone who, without thought, displays the
flag of his country here and there and who can be counted on to support war and
the preparations for war. Quite obviously, this is not genuine patriotism, but a
counterfeit so skillfully done that virtually everyone is gulled into accepting it as
the real thing.

Another example is religion, which originally stood for the love for God.
Conceived in this sense, it can hardly be doubted that it, too, is a noble and inspiring thing, assuming (as some of course would not) that it rests upon a true perception of the goodness of God. At the hands of human beings, however, religion
has come to mean a devotion, often mindless and blind, to the *symbols* of reli-

gion, and to certain practices that have come to be associated with religion. Sometimes, in fact, it tends to deteriorate into a devotion to an *institution,* namely the church, and to the officials who administer the affairs of the church—a bishop or pope, for example—even when devotion of this kind is condemned as idolatrous. The corruption of religion becomes so complete that the counterfeit reduces the original almost to nothing, and millions of devotees imagine themselves actually to be religious, even deeply so, when in fact their devotion to the mere symbols of religion has made it impossible for them to be truly religious at all, in the original sense of the term. Thus they deceive themselves, their devotion to a counterfeit rendering them no longer capable of recognizing, or even of forming a very clear idea of, a genuine devotion to God. Nor, of course, do they deceive only themselves. If we see someone whose thoughts are much preoccupied with his church, who spends much of his life ritualistically observing the practices fostered by his church, and who venerates its priests or other officials, then it is difficult *not* to think of him as "religious." But this only shows how totally distorted the idea has become in the minds of most people.

The very same can be said of marital fidelity. Originally, fidelity meant faithfulness, which translates into constancy of love when we are speaking of the love between men and women. But like patriotism, religion, and other noble things, fidelity has been corrupted and replaced by a counterfeit. Fidelity in a marriage relationship has been reduced to mere sexual exclusiveness and, what is worse, this is thought of as more important than the constancy of love itself. Thus people see no contradiction in saying of some wife, for example, that even though she long since stopped loving her husband, she at least remained "faithful," in spite of the numerous infidelities on his part.

There are innumerable ways lovers can break faith with each other having nothing whatever to do with sexual inconstancy.

These points will be illustrated as we go along, but first, a few more general things need to be said.

* * *

The ethical factor in having love affairs is very simple, straightforward, and clear. It is expressed in five words, "Thou shalt not commit adultery." There is nothing to be said on the matter beyond that, so far as ethics is concerned.

But having said that, note how totally pointless it is. It is easy, indeed, for someone who has never been tempted, to say, "thou shalt not," for observance of the rule is for him as effortless as mouthing the words. It is very easy for those who are devoid of any romantic spirit to pronounce those words, and likewise for timid souls who, being tempted, and "committing adultery in their hearts," as it is said, are too shy or inept to act. So the commandment becomes for them a consolation. They can enjoy the self-congratulatory sense of putting temptation behind them when, in truth, they were incapacitated from doing otherwise. They are like children who are brave indeed with their tin soldiers!

The pointlessness of the rule is seen also in the consideration that it has probably never saved a single person from sin. The pull of romantic love exceeds the power of this rule by a power of ten. And people no longer believe, in case they ever really did, that God is ready to smite them for transgressing it. Someone who is romantically in love and feels the overwhelming need to act accordingly, may indeed refrain, even when circumstances and everything else impel him forward, but this is more likely because of the fear of discovery than simple respect for a rule. Usually (though not always) there are many reasons for not committing adultery, but the mere existence of a rule, even a very ancient and universal one, is not one of them.

There are, certainly, married people whose love for their partners is so total that they could not think of becoming involved with another person. They, in other words, are not tempted. But rather than being praised for their fidelity, they should be envied for their blessings. They have the ultimate happiness and no need to be faithless. They have every incentive not to risk what they have.

Instead, then, of taking flight into the neverland of ethics, let us focus upon the idea of human happiness and ask these questions: Why do people sometimes become involved in love affairs? Why are they so destructive? These are the important questions, and not one of them, it should be noted, is answered by intoning, "Thou shalt not. . . ."

*　　*　　*

A love affair results almost always from a marriage that has, in some sense, failed. Thus the affair is not the cause of the marital failure, but the other way around. It is important to nail this down, to use it as a kind of point of departure, for nothing ever gets solved by thinking of some outside third person as the cause of a wrecked marriage, even though this is, typically, how people look at the matter. People just say "he (or she) was faithless," and think that they have explained something, when, in fact, they have only managed to call attention to what needed explaining. And the result, as in the case of so many false and simplistic notions, is to foster more unhappiness rather than to remove or reduce it.

When a married woman becomes involved with another man, it is almost always because her husband has become, as she is apt to put it, boring. This means that he has come to take her for granted or, sometimes, to actually find ways to make her feel belittled. In courtship he was attentive and solicitous. His ego expanded almost to bursting as he found himself winning her admiration, affection, and lifelong commitment to him. No effort seemed too great; he would drive all day and all night to be with her, gifts were lavished upon her, everything else was moved to the background as he poured his energy into impressing her and winning her. But then, that having been accomplished, he soon relaxed, returned to his old pursuits and interests, reverted to his self-centeredness, and, in short, began to take her for granted. This he could now do, for the point of all his courtship has been achieved, the deal is done. His awareness of his wife verges now on the subliminal. He is likely to think of her when he needs things—affection, sex, whatever, or when he needs to show her off to associates he wants to impress—but there is no longer any point in giving priority to *her* needs. So he more or less disregards them or, rather, ceases to be aware of them.

If, now, she becomes the object of attention from someone else, who manages to make her feel beautiful, intelligent, creative, resourceful—whatever makes people feel good about themselves—then she is very likely to fall in love with him. A love affair follows, and the marriage is soon dead, even though, for various reasons—children, security, whatever—it may be kept legally intact.

The scenario is much the same in the case of the faithless husband, except different words are likely to be used. A husband who falls in love with someone else does not usually describe his wife as boring. He is more likely to say that she has become cold. He feels uncared about. All sorts of things can claim a wife's attention and divert it from him—children, for example, or her career, or some friend or circle of friends. A husband thus finds himself taking second place. When it is children that begin to absorb a wife's attention, then very often they become overwhelmingly important to him, too, so that raising them becomes a common endeavor, and the marriage may even be strengthened by this. But when other things, such as some female friend or friends, begin to play a very large role in a woman's life, so that her husband begins to feel that he has been relegated to second place, then he becomes very vulnerable to an outside woman who restores his sense of his own importance. She listens with admiration to his achievements and the important roles he plays in the world, while his wife has long since taken them for granted and is no longer impressed. He falls in love with her, because she adores him—and his wife, it seems, no longer does.

That is usually the pattern, the faithless wife describing her husband as "boring," and the faithless husband claiming his wife is "cold." Both, of course, miss the point. Their reactions become even sillier when their problems come to be cast into the framework of morality. The wife says that her husband "cheated" on her, while the husband is more likely to compare his wife with a prostitute—that sort of thing. Needless to say, such talk only promotes bitterness and warfare. It assuages a man's ego and a woman's vanity, but nothing more. It destroys any possibility of marriage based upon enduring love.

The destruction that follows sexual infidelity is made even worse by the felt need to cast blame on the outside person. The outsider, if a woman, is seen as a home wrecker or, if a man, as a womanizer. Epithets thus displace understanding. The outsider is *not* the problem, and nothing but the venting of feelings is achieved by focusing on that person and wallowing in morality. *Of course* she should not have gone to bed with another woman's husband, and *of course* he should not have gone to bed with another man's wife, but what is the point of going on and on about that? The problems that gave rise to this situation lie in the marriage itself. If the marriage is to be restored and brought back to life, then it is not going to be as a result of berating the third person and throwing moral epithets around. It will be restored only by a renewed appreciation of each other's needs and a concentrated effort to meet them. When this happens, love flourishes, and there is no need for any "thou shalt nots." Love affairs result from marital failure. They do not cause it. So a wife, however deeply she may feel betrayed, should direct her appraisals at herself, not at the "other woman." It is nothing but a distraction for her to concentrate on the wrongness and wickedness of someone else. She should instead ask, "Where did I go wrong?" And then she should try to come up with some answers to that. And the same holds, of course, for a husband. He must totally ignore the role another man has had in his wife's life, put aside his conceits and self-centeredness, and begin to pay attention to his wife's needs—all of them, all of the time. Love will follow in time, and with it, the happiness that both had counted on.

Our purpose now, then, is not to set forth a comprehensive ethics of marriage, but only the principles that pertain to *sexual fidelity*. And with the introduction of that term, we find ourselves involved with some large misconceptions.

The first, and probably the most dangerous, of these is that the ethic unique to marriage is completely exhausted by the concept of fidelity, or in other words, that morality in marriage requires the sexual exclusivity of its partners. Other rules and guidelines, it is supposed, are of a purely practical nature, some of which are of great importance, but none of them are considered strictly moral. This mean and trivial standard gives married lovers one primary rule: Thou shalt not commit adultery. The notion is cultivated in married couples that, so long as they heed this rule, the basic requirement of morality, at least so far as marriage is concerned, has been met; if the rule is ever broken, then morality has been violated. It is thought to be that simple. Adultery is, for example, the only ground that is universally considered sufficient for divorce. And here, accordingly, we begin to see why the goodness and well-being that marriage promises are so rarely found; namely, that the ethic governing it is so grossly oversimplified.

The second misconception has to do with the concept of fidelity. Infidelity is everywhere treated as though it were simply synonymous with adultery, illustrating once more the vulgarization of the ethic which seems everywhere to accompany its ritualization. Some persons look upon the wedding band as a kind of "no trespassing" sign, and upon the marriage certificate as a type of permit or license to make love, a right which must then have been lacking until conferred by that document! Yet, as we have already noted, the real and literal meaning of fidelity is *faithfulness*; and what thinking person could imagine that there is only one way in which someone can fail to keep faith with another? Faithfulness is a state of one's heart and mind. It is not the mere outward conformity to rules. There are countless ways that it can fail which have nothing whatever to do with sexual intimacy nor, indeed, with outside persons. It can be fulfilled in various ways as well, even in spite of sexual nonexclusiveness, though this is sometimes more difficult to see.

To illustrate this, imagine a man who has long been married to one person, a man who has never lapsed from the rule of strict sexual constancy, nor has he ever appeared to, and who could never be suspected of this by anyone with the slightest knowledge of his character. This man, we shall imagine, assumes without doubt the rightness of his behavior, is scornful of anyone whose standards are less strict, would not permit a violation of this rule by anyone under his own roof, and would consider no circumstances to mitigate the breach of it. So far, so good; he is, it would seem to most persons, a faithful husband.

But now let us add to the picture that this same man, being of a passive nature and having somewhat of an aversion to sex, has never yielded to temptations for the simple reason that he has had no temptations placed before him. His intimacy with his own wife is perfunctory, infrequent, dutiful, and quite devoid of joy for himself or his spouse. They are, in fact, essentially strangers to each other's feelings. In this light, the nobility of his austere ethic begins to appear less impressive, does it not?

But we are not finished with our description. Let us add to the foregoing that these two persons appear to the world as hard workers, but still quite poor. He works monotonously as a sales clerk in a declining drug store, we can suppose, while she adds what she can to the family's resources by putting in long hours assisting in the local public library. Appearances are misleading, however, for behind this facade of meager resources there are, unbeknown to anyone but the husband, and scrupulously kept secret from his wife, eight savings accounts, which have been built up over the years, each in his name only, and none containing less than thirty thousand dollars. At every opportunity—sometimes by shrewd dealing, often by sheer penuriousness, and always by the most dedicated selfishness—the husband squirrels away more savings, so that by this time the total, augmented by interest compounded over the years, adds up to a most impressive sum.

Has the rule of good faith been breached?

But to continue the description: We now suppose that the long suffering wife of this dreary marriage is stricken, let us say, with cancer, and undergoes a radical mastectomy as the only hope of saving her life. Whereupon whatever small affection her husband ever had for her evaporates completely. He turns sullen, distant, and only dimly aware of his wife's presence, finding all the comfort for his life in those growing and secret savings accounts. He never thinks of sexual infidelity, and congratulates himself for this, as well as for other things, such as his thrift.

Finally, let us suppose that his wife has always been a poet of considerable creative power, whose creations have never received the attention they deserve, least of all her husband's, he being only dimly aware that they even exist. Yet they are finally seen and sincerely praised by another sensitive soul having the qualities of mind necessary to appreciate them, and through his encouragement, we shall imagine, she is finally able to have a sense of meaningfulness in her life, hitherto found only meagerly in the lonely creation of poetic beauty. This same newfound friend is, moreover, oblivious to the scars of her illness; he cares only for her, and, unlike her husband, his love is sincere, impulsive, passionate, imaginative, and as frequent as conditions allow.

We could expand this story, but the point of it is abundantly clear by now. It is found in answering the question: *Who has been faithless to whom?* In that answer one finds not only the essential meaning of infidelity, which is a betrayal of the promise to love, but also, by contrast, the true meaning of fidelity.

There is no need to point out that the kind of faithlessness just illustrated has its counterparts in the real world. In fact, its essential elements are found in virtually every marriage, perhaps less exaggerated here and there, but nevertheless present. How many husbands, for instance, see no breach of faith in keeping their incomes secret from their wives, precisely as a means of control? It is astonishing how this type of marital infidelity sometimes evokes no real condemnation, not even from the church, whose sense of fidelity one would expect to be most acute.

Consider, for example, this true account:

My Uncle Tony came to this country from Italy in the twenties, with a young wife, my Aunt Carmella, but very few material goods. He found jobs in motion picture theaters, which were just getting started, and which were then called "photo plays" and, eventually, "movies." Of course sound films, or "talkies," had not yet been invented.

My uncle and aunt were poor but, nevertheless, they saved enough to move to the Catskills. Eventually, Uncle Tony had saved enough to buy a movie theater of his own. This was very lucky for him, because theaters were among the very few businesses that flourished through the long depression that started at about that time. In fact my uncle prospered and bought more theaters, finally owning a string of six. Still, he and Aunt Carmella lived as frugally as ever. They lived all their lives in the same simple house he had bought when they moved up from the city, and she either made all her own clothes, or bought cheap dresses. She was a simple, uneducated, and devoted wife who never had any idea of her husband's prosperity.

When Uncle Tony died, it was learned that he had left his entire fortune to Our Lady of Mount Carmel Church, except for a couple thousand dollars he left to each of his two brothers. There was about a million dollars in his estate, which was a very great deal of money in those days. Aunt Carmella was stunned. She received nothing at all except the house she was living in. She spent her last years, after her husband had died, impoverished and wretched. Uncle Tony, everyone thought, had simply tried to buy his way into heaven.

Although the abomination just described caused a great deal of comment among relatives, there is no record of its having been condemned by the church, in spite of the fact that a more perfect example of marital infidelity, in its true sense, would be hard to find. But worse than this, had it been discovered that this same man, or for that matter his wife, had just once been intimately involved with any third person, then *this* perhaps trifling situation would have been singled out, by the church and others, as an act of infidelity, quite deserving of strong moral condemnation. This is, to be sure, the usual way of moral rules. Starting out from a clear perception of genuine evil, they eventually degenerate to mere triviality, while evil flourishes as before, with about the same buoyancy as ever.

*   *   *

We have thus far been considering marriage as a relationship between a man and a woman, leaving out of consideration homosexual relationships, even though the partners in such relationships often think of themselves as married in every significant sense except the legal one. There appears to be no ethical reason other than mere custom for denying such couples the legal status of marriage, if that is what they seek, and many good reasons in favor of its legal recognition, but it would take us far afield to go into that question here. What is worth noting, however, is that the concepts of fidelity and infidelity have exactly the same relevance to homosexual relationships as to any other.

To see this, imagine the following scenario: An unmarried man—let us call him John—becomes increasingly involved with a young and happy marriage, which includes beautiful children. He begins to call fairly often at their house, and his attention is directed entirely at Suzan, the wife; husband and children are mostly ignored, though they are expected to be friendly and courteous. Suzan responds to his overtures with similar interest and growing friendship. Soon telephone calls become frequent, and are conducted in hushed voices when the husband is around. Notes expressing warm friendship, and the importance of this in each of their lives, are exchanged and, occasionally, expensive flower arrangements appear, addressed to Suzan, but often received at the door by her husband. They spend more and more time together, Suzan and John, and before long she is spending weekends with him at his cottage, to which her husband is never invited. When, on one such occasion, he expresses a desire to be included, the suggestion is rebuffed, with the observation that it would change—that is, spoil—everything. All these things take place with the husband's knowledge, no attempt whatsoever being made at secrecy, and mutual friends are quite aware of it as well. *But no one finds in all this anything very unusual or deserving of comment.*

Unbelievable? Of course. It is not that such things do not happen, but rather, that when they do, the utmost secrecy is maintained, and under no circumstances would a husband be expected to find nothing strange and threatening about this. Indeed, such behavior on Suzan's part would be seen by everyone to be astonishing and outrageous. It is one thing to have an affair, but quite another to do so in full view of everyone, including husband and children. The whole thing is almost unthinkable.

But now change John to Jane. In other words, suppose that the outsider is a woman, not a man. Now it suddenly becomes quite thinkable, and in fact, this sort of thing happens. And families are thus destroyed just as effectively as by any triangular affair.

And the question now arises: Why is *this* supposed to be all right? Why the condemnation of the one triangular relationship, and not the other, when the factors involved are the same, and the destructiveness the same? Ethically, there appears to be no difference at all between these two situations.

Clearly, our customs and rules with respect to marital infidelity have not kept up with the changing behavior. When we think of love affairs, we think always of involvements between men and women, and marital infidelity of this kind is quite universally condemned. It probably makes little sense to say, simply, that such infidelity is morally wrong, even though that is what nearly everyone does say. What does "morally wrong" mean here, other than being the violation of some customary rule of morality? What should, instead, be said of marital infidelity is that it is hideously destructive of marriages and, often, of much else—of the well-being of children, of reputation, and so on. This *does* mean something, for the destructive consequences are perfectly visible and obvious. So now the point should be made: Marital infidelity involving a third person of the same sex, whether male or female, is just as destructive of these things. And if, in the light of all this destruction, one wants to say that the one kind of infidelity is "morally wrong," then the very same judgment should be applied to the other; though it is probably better, just in terms of clarity, to point only to the destructiveness, and leave moral judgments aside.

* * *

When the effect of homosexuality on marriage is discussed, in magazines and newspapers, it is usually represented as homosexuality on the part of the husband. This is because of the persistence of stereotypes. Female homosexuality was, for a very long time, thought to be far less common than it has, in fact, turned out to be. Homosexual acts were, in England, a criminal offense, but the law applied only to men. Female homosexuality was apparently thought to be nonexistent. When women lived together it was far less likely to raise questions in people's minds than for men to do so. Even today, if a man appears in public in female attire, he is instantly the object of hostile attention and even disgust, and yet a woman can dress and groom herself as a man would and enter the best restaurants, or even appear in church, attracting almost no attention at all. Such behavior on the part of a woman is not necessarily associated with sexual orientation, as indeed, it should not be.

Men become aware of their homosexuality much earlier in life than women. Usually a boy discovers that he is different in adolescence. Women, on the other hand, are very likely to have married and had children before they become aware of it. This is no doubt part of the reason that homosexuality is still usually thought of first as being male homosexuality, even though everyone is perfectly aware that it exists in both sexes. It is not clear why it should typically emerge in the life of a woman later than in a man's, and of course there are many exceptions to this. Sometimes women discover it in themselves early in life, and men late. But perhaps the kind of acculturation experienced by girls has something to do with it. From a very early age, girls have impressed upon them certain expectations of womanhood, from their mothers and teachers, and these include marriage and motherhood. Boys too, of course, are made aware of certain expectations of manliness, by their fathers, coaches, scoutmasters, and so on, so perhaps this difference of acculturation in children does not account for much after all. My own belief is that the very clear difference in terms of when the two sexes discover their homosexuality is mostly biological, and not much a matter of upbringing.

In any case, the effect of this difference on marriage should be quite obvious. Homosexual men tend, with many exceptions, never to marry. Homosexual women, on the other hand, are very likely to marry, simply because their sexuality has not become apparent to them when that step is taken. Then, when it is discovered, their marriages are destroyed, usually by separation and divorce or, if not that, then by lifelong indifference or hostility toward their husbands. If a woman has young children and, perhaps, no property or income, and no good chance of gaining these, then she has strong reasons for remaining in a marriage and not disclosing her homosexuality to her husband, but the marriage is, nonetheless, dead. The husband may even go to his grave wondering what happened to their once warm and vibrant marriage, wondering how his wife could have changed so. She, in turn, continues to share the same roof with a man for whom she has a strong aversion. The whole thing is, in any case, profoundly tragic.

The following account is highly illustrative, throwing light on this aspect of human sexuality that is very insufficiently appreciated:

I had been married for twelve years, and thought my marriage was, in every respect, perfect. We had three beautiful children, and our household was filled with the warmth of love. It was inconceivable to me that anything short of serious illness, accident, or other natural disaster could ever damage this. Through all those years, I brought my wife flowers, occasional perfumes that she loved, we wrote tender notes to each other, hers as filled with love as mine, and we kept in touch when we were separated, especially for overnight. It was idyllic. My wife and children were my whole life and happiness, and I had no doubt at all that no greater or more lasting happiness existed anyplace else in the world. Her feelings seemed to be exactly the same. We lived for each other.

Then things began to change. I thought nothing of it when she asked me not to bring her flowers anymore. They were, perhaps, after all these years, an extravagance. She stopped using perfumes, and cut her hair short, which I also thought nothing of. She had, meanwhile, revived her interest in painting, was spending more and more of her time with artists and, especially, with her own female art instructor. I assumed that her apparently declining interest in me was due simply to her increasing interest in art, and that in time the love and warmth would all return. The thought that she was discovering her own "inner self," as she later described it, and that this inner self was lesbian, did not occur to me, although there were numerous hints. If we were in a restaurant, her attention was likely to be on the female patrons, especially if two of these were dining together. I had long been accustomed to her indifference to men generally, but now it became a positive disdain. She sometimes spoke enviously of lesbian couples she knew—and still the truth did not penetrate my brain. I believe that, still thinking in terms of the marriage we had had, I was subconsciously unwilling to confront the awful truth.

She began to spend more and more time away from home, especially evenings. She went by herself to see a film, about the trials and sufferings of a lesbian couple, and, as I eventually learned, she remained in her car for a long time afterwards, weeping. After many months of this, while I was becoming increasingly desperate, still not knowing what was happening, and sometimes almost out of my mind, she finally told me outright, and I was dumbfounded. The marriage, and all my happiness with it, was dead, completely dead.

But the most astonishing thing of all was the sequel to this. My wife left me, and I nearly died. Neither of us made public the reason why. Over the course of the next couple of years, however, I did confide these things to my closest friends, especially those far away—perhaps fifteen or twenty, altogether. And, with but a single exception, every one of these had exactly the same response, namely: *"The very same thing happened to someone I know."* Several said they knew of two, or even three, marriages that had ended exactly this way, and two astonished me by saying, *"The same thing happened to me!"* And from a psychologist, knowledgeable in this area, I learned that this is a fairly typical pattern of female homosexuality—late discovery, after marriage and often after children.

I still see her from time to time. We have remained outwardly friendly and cooperative. But she is an utter stranger, like the many people one knows only by name. Sometimes, these years later, when I look around the house and see the many reminders of her, I still find it hard to believe what happened. I still have a huge folder of her letters, as beautiful and touching as any love letters can be, and a box filled with the little notes she wrote to me over the years, but I never look at them. I don't really know why I keep them. The beautiful person who wrote them simply disappeared from the earth, and was replaced by a likeness.

9

The Fatal Attraction

Heaven has no rage like love to hatred turned;
Nor hell a fury, like a woman scorned.

—William Congreve

Every love affair ends badly. So, at least, declared Ernest Hemingway, and he was close enough to the truth to make this our point of departure. About the only way a love affair can end well is for its partners to marry. However, this is really not an end to the affair, but rather, an attempt to make it legitimate. Even when an affair ends in marriage (which is seldom) there is still tremendous unhappiness in the others who are affected—the abandoned marriage partners of the lovers.

Yet it need not be so. A love affair can end as decorously as any marriage. The fact that this is uncommon, either in a marriage or in an affair, should lead us to find out why, rather than merely accepting it as a fact of life. It used to be thought that divorce was an inherently tragic thing, usually laden with shame and guilt, but this assumption is no longer made. Given certain rare but right circumstances, divorced people can be friends, even magnanimous friends, overcoming their insecurities, and recognizing that their marriage, while once good, has just ceased to be so.

Sooner or later, *all* human relationships end, one way or another. The fact that these relationships have been good does not mean that they must come to an unhappy end. People have found ways of protecting themselves from the sadness of many endings. Of course it takes some doing. Nothing good ends well unless something has been done to ensure it. If simply left to founder, a marriage will end miserably. The same holds for love affairs. They always end. If merely left to take their own course, then everything goes to pieces. Persons who yesterday were lovers now suddenly find themselves the most implacable of enemies. This

87

is wretched enough, but what is worse, each is likely to be armed with appalling weapons, and the passion they once poured into affection is now suddenly diverted to mutual destruction. It is not merely sad, but hideous, gruesome, sickening, appalling, and most dreadfully effective.

*   *   *

Here, for example, is a description to show just how badly a love affair can end. Fortunately, it is not typical, but the element of explosive hatred is all too common.

The love affair I fell into certainly violated good judgment, but I don't regret it for that reason. Affairs are seldom expressions of good judgment. What I do regret is my own impetuous stupidity later on. Some lives were deeply damaged, not by the affair, which could have ended harmlessly, but by the way I handled minor crises, producing explosions of horrible strength. My partner, I must add, did no better.

It all happened long ago. Marie was half my age, and married to Mark, one of my own graduate students, who was assisting me when the relationship started. Never mind how it got started, except that she was a poet, and I was the only person around, not excluding her husband, who took any interest in that fact. We spent Wednesday mornings in a motel nearby, then I'd return to the university for my seminar, in which her husband was the dominant student. It gave me a strange feeling sometimes, perhaps a perversely pleasant one, to go straight from her arms into that role. He, at any rate, sometimes reminded me of Robert in *Madame Bovary* in his childish eagerness to throw us together. If I went to their house, he would usually leave so we could talk; and on one occasion, when I had to drive over to Fredonia to give an evening lecture, he virtually put her in the car with me to go along, though he could have gone too.

Maybe he was thinking only of her happiness. It was obvious that she was happy with me around, but I can't imagine why he never wondered how come. Maybe he thought we were discussing poetry.

The real mistake came when she took a longer, three-day trip to Illinois with me. Mark didn't know about that; she told him she was going to Toronto. My mistake was to ask my host there to confirm plane and motel reservations for us both. He wrote back that he had, but the letter came after we had left, and since it looked like something important, my wife opened it. A phone call soon came for me in Illinois, and I went limp. I confessed the whole thing. I could at that point have explained things away, for there was rather little real suspicion, and the affair would eventually have wound down with no real damage done. But instead, the greater detonations still lay ahead. Even now, when I look back on all that, I find it hard to believe what ensued. What had begun as hardly more than an ego trip for us both—a beautiful girl interested in me, and a professor interested in her and her poems—gradually became several stages of nightmare, each worse than the one before.

Having been discovered, my first reaction was totally childish. I conceived of the affair as a *grand amour,* laden with meaning and tragic overtone, and portrayed it in those terms to my wife—certainly the last thing in the world she wanted to hear. I should just have said that it was a trip, it was fun, and now let's forget it.

Meanwhile, Marie and I now seemed to ourselves beleaguered, and what had before been joyous now became deadly serious, sometimes tearful, and accompanied by a considerable imbibing of gin. We fell into each other's arms and clung there as if for dear life. Still, Mark saw nothing when solemnity settled over all our encounters and hands met and clasped tightly under tables, right under his nose. I didn't know whether he was trusting, or just blind; but I decided it wasn't just trust. Perhaps I should have felt guilty around him; but it was, after all, his wife, and not I, who was lying to him.

Even then it could all have ended quietly. It was over by the middle of the summer. My wife had, in spite of my idiocies, repaired the damage to our marriage and to her pride. When fall came and classes resumed I almost never saw Marie any more, except for an occasional lunch. The atmosphere was cold. Nothing remained.

Then fresh fires were ignited. Marie's marriage started coming apart. She moved out, then returned, and her parents descended upon them both in great consternation. Confession followed, and my complicities were disclosed. Soon after that Mark broke into my office in search of all the love letters his wife had written to me, and failing to find these, removed the considerable collection of her poems and a few other odds and ends. The next day both came to my office, in a towering anger, to seize those letters, by whatever means; but by good luck, they were not there.

The episode so angered me that I went to the police, culminating my considerable history of dramatic stupidities in these matters. But my sweet friend, now turned resourceful and implacable foe, countered with a tale of rape and extortion, filling this out with the lurid detail that only poetic imagination can contrive. The campus police, whose lives seldom rise to greater adventure than issuing parking tickets, gravely labeled the rape an "incident" and hastily distributed their "report" of it through the administrative offices of the university, none of whom bothered to mention it to me. During the next four months the rape report was further circulated through two additional faculty committees, still unbeknown to me. When summer came, and I was at long last told of these things, I was flabbergasted to learn that the latest such committee was eager to read all the letters Marie had sent me, the very letters that had, of course, prompted the break-ins at my office. These letters, as lurid in their expression of passion as the rape report had been in its expression of fury, were duly delivered into the hands of the members of this committee, to enliven their meetings and their insipid lives. But in the light of their contents the rape report was, these five months later, finally dismissed as a fabrication and, there being no more juice to squeeze from this wretched and rotting lemon, the whole matter was allowed to die.

Aristotle said that your true friend is someone who will not listen to lies about you. By this standard some of my friends did indeed show themselves to be genuine. Others proved themselves to be worms, willing not merely to listen to what they knew to be lies, but, with the aid of their wives, to fuel and oil the gossip machine for all the mileage they could get out of it.

Strangely, I do not regret all those things, painful as they were at the time.

The experience ripened my cynicism and nourished an undying contempt for the university, but it also enabled me to step outside the academic world in which I have spent my life and to see the administrative and academic mind in all its shabbiness, something that few who dwell in that sometimes artificial atmosphere ever have a good opportunity to do. I do regret admitting the affair when it was first discovered, for without that it could have been brought to an end and eventually reduced to a pleasant memory of just two people. But more than that, I regret turning over Marie's letters to that contemptible committee, virtually drooling to read them, and saying to me, in effect, "Let's have those letters now, for we can, you know, recommend a humiliating and ignominious dismissal." I wish I had had the courage to tell them, in the eloquent words that a great U.S. attorney general directed to the president of the United States, to go piss up a rope. I don't think I would have been fired, and I certainly would have felt cleaner.

*   *   *

Why did something that was evidently once meaningful have to end so badly? Part of the answer is given by the author of the account, namely, his own excessive reactions, which produced corresponding excesses on the part of others. But there is more to it than this, and some of the larger answers will unfold as we go along.

First, though, we need to define more closely what we are going to count as a love affair.

We have described a love affair, or what is sometimes euphemistically called an "affair of the heart," as an intense and intimate relationship between a man and a woman, at least one of whom is married or part of a marriage relationship with someone else. Homosexual relationships do not count as love affairs, as the expression is used here, nor do casual sexual encounters. A man away from home who sleeps with a stranger for one or a few nights is not involved in a love affair, because the relationship, though intimate, is not intense. Nor will we include platonic relationships in the definition, for no matter how intense these might sometimes be, they lack intimacy.

Most of the problems we are going to consider are those faced by lovers, whether they are married or not, although the most acute ones will usually involve a marriage. The main question at issue is: Why are love affairs so often destructive? Are they inherently destructive, particularly when they involve married people, as is so widely supposed? Must they necessarily destroy existing marriages? Other questions present themselves, which are seldom raised and answered in a serious way, such as why anyone, most especially married people, would become involved in affairs in the first place. This question is important in light of the simplistic assumptions that are so commonly made: for example, that involvement in an affair clearly indicates a failing marriage, "weakness" on the part of anyone who becomes so involved, or, worst of all, the moral failure of that person, and so on. Most analyses, in other words, simply presuppose that a love affair is superficial, deviant, and even unnatural—something that is shunned by those who are decent and upright and, particularly, by those who are devoted to their families.

In fact, a love affair is rarely superficial in the meaning it has for the persons involved. On the contrary, it seems sometimes to express far more natural human emotion than does lifelong monogamous marriage, which is surely a product of convention if anything ever was. Love affairs are not always merely fallen into, as if by accident, but ardently cultivated by people who are perfectly upright, wise, moral, and strong. That this is not always apparent testifies only to the power of convention to force even bold and creative people to conceal what is popularly made a subject of gossip, such concealment often passing under the euphemism of *discretion*. And love affairs are, by their very nature, quite easy to conceal, at least from a curious and prying public.

*   *   *

When people get married they normally enunciate vows which are typically administered by a clergyman. It would be natural for a moralist to treat these vows as though they formed the basis for an ethic of marriage. In fact they are apt to be regarded as the entire sum and substance of that ethic. The ethic of the relationship is breached if any vow is broken, and otherwise it is fulfilled. There is, to be sure, much more than this to a *good* marriage, for no marriage was ever made truly good and fulfilling merely by the observance of promises. Thus marriage counselors and others who take a strong interest in the preservation and improvement of this relationship quite rightly concern themselves with much more than compliance with vows. Still, the *ethic* of marriage must rest upon such vows, at least as a starting point.

Partners in love affairs, of course, make no such vows, and in the case of those who are already married the vows they have previously made have already been violated. Thus, anything which purports, as this book does, to be an ethic for love affairs will find its task to be extraordinarily difficult. We have to start from scratch. It is partly for this reason that the undertaking of this book is almost without precedent, and partly also because *any* ethic for love affairs has to collide with every other existing ethic for marriage. It is no wonder that the moment these questions arise moralists respond by saying "Thou shalt not," almost automatically and without thought. But we are not going to stop with that, or even start with it.

Instead, we begin with the fact that one person cares for and is intimately and passionately involved with another under circumstances in which some third person—a husband or wife, for example—might be thought to have a prior "claim," and a great potentiality exists that far-reaching harm may be done. Rather than just treating such a relationship as if it ought not to exist, and calling it an "infidelity" or some other expression of abuse, we will consider it possible that it should exist, or at least, that there is no reason in abstract morality why it should not.

Next we ask two questions. The first is: How can we minimize the power of such a relationship to cause deep and lasting injury to others? And the second is: Assuming that the injury to third parties can be reduced, how can the relationship itself be made good and fulfilling to its partners, such that, when it finally comes to an end, it will terminate with the least damage to their own emotions and stability?

Of course the first question can be answered quite easily by merely terminating the love affair. But this is often not possible and, even when it is possible, it can usually be done only at the cost of great damage to one or both partners. And it really is about time that we take this fact into account. It is time for us to stop treating lovers as automatically guilty in cases where at least one of them is already married, and society should stop looking upon them as deserving of whatever suffering they have gotten themselves into. Such a negative approach is almost always self-defeating anyway, for no proper marriage has ever been made good by the anguish or humiliation of either of its partners, whatever the cause. Thus a wife might, for example, discover her husband's affair and, with the instruments society gives her, she might smash it, all of which is very easy for her to do. But either she will no longer have a husband after that, or, if she has one in name, she will not have a marriage that is worth having. She will have destroyed something real, and what will have been saved is nothing more than an insubstantial appearance.

10

Male and Female

Woman wants monogamy
Man delights in novelty

—Dorothy Parker

It is not uncommon to find sex treated as though it were merely a source of pleasure, almost a form of entertainment. Thus people are likely to be thought of as pleasure seekers, and sexual activity is then thought of as differing from other pleasant activities mainly in its intensity. Looking at the matter this way, one can indeed wonder why people would choose not to be monogamous, since there is no very clear reason why sex with one person should be significantly more pleasant than with another. One should be enough. Sometimes when one's wife or husband is discovered to have had an affair the painful reaction is expressed in the question "What is wrong with me?" or "Am I not enough?", as though the whole thing were a mere quest for pleasure—pleasure which, it was thought, was already available at home.

Such a view is so superficial as to be essentially false; and, in addition to this, it so trivializes human nature and sexuality as to be a debasement of both. Sexual intercourse and the activities that normally accompany it are of course pleasant, but that is not why they are sought; and human beings do sometimes seek pleasures, but that is no real explanation for their behavior. The impulse to sexual intimacy expresses one of the deepest yearnings of any person, which goes beyond even the yearning to love and be loved. What sensitive and thoughtful people seek in their lives is not pleasure, but fulfillment and an inner sense of their own worth as persons. Even these characterizations are superficial, but they provide a far better foundation for the understanding of the love of the sexes than the gross oversimplification expressed in the idea of pleasure.

93

*   *   *

When someone is discovered—whether by a wife, a husband, or a lover—to be involved in an affair with someone else, the first reaction is likely to be shame and guilt, not unlike the feelings of an adolescent discovered masturbating. These feelings are as groundless in the one case as in the other; and worse than this, someone with such a sense of guilt usually has ways of expressing these feelings which seem appropriate enough to himself, but which are in fact frightfully damaging. The guilt and shame are made worse still when, as is often the case, they are combined with other strong and negative emotions, such as self-pity.

The reactions of men and women thus discovered are likely to be quite different, though not necessarily so. Thus a husband is apt to react with fervent declarations of love, not for his wife, but for the third person, declarations that are deeply felt and even, perhaps, accompanied by tears. He does not see that, even though his love may be real, his declaration of it, to the very last person on earth who should hear it, is no more than an attempt to mitigate his feelings of guilt. It is without a doubt the most inept and ill-considered behavior he could possibly display. What he should do is feel no guilt at all; and, if he does, he should either keep still, or pour his feelings into the ear of someone he can absolutely trust to keep his mouth shut.

What lies behind the feelings of guilt is quite simple. We all have been taught that adultery is wrong. Many believe it, in spite of the fact that there is no more basis for this than its iteration from one generation to another. Feelings are hard to shake off, even long after they are recognized to be groundless. The feeling that sexual infidelity is wrong is a perfect example of this. Human beings were not created by nature to be monogamous. On the contrary, monogamous love violates the natural feelings people have. A man who claims that monogamous love expresses not merely his own moral standard, which is common enough, or the norm required by his church, which is also common, but that it expresses his own feelings and inclinations, is either a hypocrite or is quite devoid of feelings in this area. A man, by nature, desires many sexual partners, and if custom or circumstances limit him to one, then his dreams and fantasies are filled with others. Hence the male preoccupation with the females he encounters: the constant flirting with waitresses, with female employees, with whomever he can view as subordinate or somehow beholden to him and thus, possibly, available. Most such behavior is inept, often childish and repellent, especially in the eyes of women, and it is almost never successful. But it cannot be said that it is not natural. What is unnatural is the cultural conditioning, the purely man-made rule of monogamy, which gives rise to this bizarre and pathetic behavior. Thus a man will unabashedly flirt with some waitress who is a perfect stranger to him, and who he knows is almost certainly destined to remain one. Even this knowledge does not extinguish his hope. The man can take this brief flirtation at face value, that is, as the expression of genuinely felt desire; whereas, on the woman's part, it is really an act, and even perceived as such, expressing no more than the hope of a good tip. And this is what it culminates in, an absurdly large tip, carrying the very simple message that the giver of it is every bit as glorious a man as he wishes to be thought. It is a small trip for the ego, a poor consolation for the ego trip that is really wanted and so vainly sought, and it is dearly purchased, not just in terms of coin, but in terms of the foolishness that the giver displays. But the price is never begrudged. The tip, indeed, is meant mostly to offset the otherwise inescapable image of the fool, and it does this, more or less, by being a large one.

*   *   *

However proper a man may appear—staunchly reserved in manner, speech, dress, and bearing—however scrupulously he may submit to the most refined demands of society with respect to his habits and appearance, totally succumbing to convention, there nevertheless is, or once was, a completely polygamous being behind that facade. By nature he is capable of siring a hundred or more children in a year, and nature, which seems sometimes to have no other goal than the proliferation of her creatures, has given him the impulses consonant with that power. Though inwardly proud of their power, men are not taught to be proud of the desires that accompany it. Women are likely to think of them as "animals" on account of these quite unselective desires, as though the stiff and contrived civilized man was somehow nobler. Good he may be, by conventional standards, but that monogamous man is not the expression of his true nature. It should be no mystery why men revert to such silliness in the presence of younger women, why in groups, as at conventions, far from the scrutiny of their wives, the childishness of each man reinforces that of the others, until before long an assemblage of respectable men, once reserved and innocuous, seems miraculously converted to a kindergarten. It is as though the sun's rising depended, in their minds, upon seeing, even if at a distance and for a brief moment, a young woman undress.

Sometimes the repressive force of society does succeed in producing what seems to be a monogamous man; in other words, a man who can sincerely say that he has no lively interest in "other" women, one who no longer dreams and fantasizes on these themes. It is even the misguided wish of some women that their own husbands or lovers should be so repressed. But such a man is also apt to be one in whom the sexual impulse itself has begun to fade. He has become an unimaginative and perfunctory lover, if still a lover at all, and frequently one whose energy has been directed to other outlets, as they are so aptly called. Thus, finding no longer any overwhelming enchantment in sex, he seeks his ego fulfillments in his business or profession, spending long hours at this and, quite often, with stunning success. Thus professors, whose teaching may require their presence on a campus only two or three days a week, sometimes spend each long day there, and even vie for committee work, sometimes only to escape the galling atmosphere of their home life. Their apparent dedication may be real enough, but its source not always entirely understood. Other men find outlets in hobbies— long fishing trips, endless hours in their gardens, or whatnot.

Society looks upon this type of man with approval, either for his industry or for his devotion to utterly harmless pursuits; but underneath it all is likely to be a very unimaginative and boring person. The following account suggests the serious impact this could have on a marriage:

> My marriage was perfect, from every standpoint except mine. Jack was kind, loved animals and children, loved his home, and was a wonderful gardener. He would spend hours in his garden or working around the house. No one in his family ever wanted for anything, and bills were always paid.
>
> Then what was wrong? He was boring. In the evening after supper he would just fall asleep, and he never did anything more exciting than work in his garden. He never gave me any gifts, even on my birthdays, unless someone told him to. We raised our children, but through all those years sex was a nothing, as far as I was concerned, and I don't think it ever meant much to him either.
>
> Then I met Norman, who was just the opposite, and had a love affair with him that lasted over ten years. Norman praised me, taught me the real estate business, gave me self-confidence, and encouraged me to take the regular training courses in real estate, which I did, and I became very successful at it. He would send me cards and gifts even when there was no occasion to, and as for sex, he taught me everything I know about it, and it was wonderful. There was really only one thing wrong with him, and that is, that for all those ten years he led me to think he was going to get a divorce, and he never did, and never intended to. Finally, when his wife had learned about us, I went to see her, assured her that I never wanted anything to do with her husband again, and I meant it. For a long time I hated him deeply, I'm not quite sure why. Now when I see him we say hello, and maybe chat, and that's it. There's nothing left.

It may seem to be driving the point home a bit too hard to say that, after having learned of his wife's affair, the husband described above committed suicide by turning a shotgun against himself in his garden; but it is true.

*   *   *

The suppression of the polygamous impulse in a man is, in any case, bought at a great price. Deep inside he is likely to think of no sweeter joy than a genuine love affair, for which he has ruefully abandoned hope. Any such man, whatever may be his worldly glory, is really pitiable.

When, some years ago, an enterprising man set up booths near the campus of a university in a large city, and hired female students to pose nude in them for the benefit of persons having a passion for photography who might want to take pictures, men came with their cameras. These were mainly for the sake of appearances, however, like the empty luggage lovers used to take with them to motels. All they really wanted to do was look. And, as it turned out, one of the constant patrons of these booths was a vice president of one of the greatest corporations in the world. He had every conventional blessing, but needed still the greatest blessing of all, and by this pathetic act came as close as he could to getting it.

*   *   *

Nature and human convention not only fail to coincide, in this realm, they are in clear conflict with each other. Nature summons a man to one thing, while custom demands another; and it is not at all clear why nature should stand condemned. Cultures may create their own prohibitions and induce men to heed them, but these are never going to eradicate the deepest expressions of our human nature. A clergyman may extract from a bridegroom the promise to forsake all others, but he cannot be induced to forsake his own feelings. The power of custom, and the general approval that goes with it, is, to be sure, sometimes astonishing. By it people can be made to do almost anything. They can be forced to bow down daily and pray, to doff their caps and bow to persons highborn, to leap to their feet in the presence of royal persons, to conceal their bodies on pain of mortification, or allow themselves to be blown to bits for their country, even to cling to a totally meaningless existence rather than expose themselves to taunts and ridicule. In the same way, custom can secure a uniform declaration that monogamous love alone is good, even that it is ordained by nature, which it most certainly is not. People can be made to believe this, associate it with the greatest approval, and reserve the deepest condemnation for departures from it. Thus a man who has never departed from the exclusive attachment to his own wife, and has perhaps not even permitted himself to think of doing so, is likely to congratulate himself inwardly, to feel that he has somehow lived up to some worthwhile ideal. No one can say why this is so, other than to point to the fact that it bears the stamp of religion and custom. Sometimes this strange custom is carried to an absurd length, as when it is suggested that ideally, a person should experience no intimate love for anyone even *prior* to marriage. This was once thought obvious. It no longer is. But it is also not yet seen to be utterly absurd. Thus one can still proclaim this as a moral precept, and while this declaration may be met with skepticism, usually it will not be greeted with laughter. Such is the power of custom, even customs that have been largely abandoned in practice. There are actually persons who feel a certain moral approbation for those few species of animals, such as pigeons and elephants, who mate once for life, as though even these were somehow heeding a precept of morality.

This conflict between the demands of nature and the demands of custom would be of little interest to anyone except philosophers if it were not for the fact that it generates negative emotions, particularly guilt and, to a lesser extent, jealousy. These are terrible not only in themselves, in that they are painful to their possessors, but even more terrible in their destructive power. The power of jealousy to destroy precious human relationships is well known. The similar power of guilt is not always so obvious.

*   *   *

There are two extreme views of female sexuality, both very simple, and each as absurd as the other. One is that sexual activity is pleasant, that men and women alike seek pleasure, are equally capable of receiving it from this source, and that therefore any differences in the expression of their respective sexual impulses must be due simply to the effect of cultural conditioning. The implication of this is that once such cultural conditioning is overcome, the feelings of men and women, and the behavior arising from such feelings, will be about the same. This view is sometimes implied in the remarks of feminists. More often, however, they interpret its denial as little more than another expression of male chauvinism. Persons who think like this are likely to maintain that the only natural differences between men and women are the obvious anatomical ones and that, inwardly, the sexes are the same. Some, indeed, quite illogically interpret the denial of this as rejecting a natural equality among males and females.

The extreme opposite view, which is now happily less often heard, is that it is a man's natural role to initiate, dominate, and command, while a woman's role is to follow, to submit, and to obey. The ramifications of this basic idea—which not very long ago was considered quite obvious even to educated women were exceedingly numerous and penetrated just about every area of social life. Thus, women did not, and many still do not, see any absence of balance in the thought that it is a man's place to provide, and a woman's to make a home. Until recently, the head of a household could only be male, and a homemaker could only be female. Sexual intercourse was naturally initiated by a man, and only very indirectly, if at all, by a woman. In fact, for an unmarried woman to initiate sex with a man was thought to mark her as cheap, whereas no such stigma has ever been attached to men for that reason. Again, men alone were, and indeed still are, thought capable of rape, or of forced sex. It is exceedingly difficult to think of any woman importuning a total stranger for sex except from some ulterior motive, as in the case of prostitutes.

Much of this conception of respective sexual roles has persisted, of course, and not all of it is absurd. What is absurd is the idea that there is some sort of natural master-servant relationship between men and women. It is certainly false to insist that men and women are by nature just alike, except for obvious anatomical differences, and that all other differences in their thoughts and feelings are the product of cultural conditioning. But it is equally false that there is a natural difference between them which implies a subordinate relationship of women to men.

*   *   *

To get a clearer view of this we should begin by noting that, while a man can, except for the restrictions imposed by convention, easily sire over a hundred children a year, and has every natural impulse to do so, a woman can usually bear only one. It is she, moreover, who will for a considerable time carry and then give birth to that one child. This is a fundamental and incontestable difference between men and women. It seems to underlie both male and female sexuality and sheds far more light on the basic ways men and women feel about each other and act toward one another than any considerations of cultural conditioning. In fact, much of what various cultures nourish and enforce seems to have its roots not in the thin air of pointless and arbitrary practice, but in the overwhelmingly important and unalterable differences just noted.

The constancy of a woman's feelings towards a man becomes, at least for the time being, quite fixed from the moment she marries him. Provided she has no misgivings concerning the wisdom and rightness of the step she has taken, then she also has little sexual attraction to other men, or at least none that she would be likely to act upon. This fidelity is deep and sincere, wrought not by custom and teaching, which are easily circumvented, but by her own nature. Consciously or otherwise—and it is probably true that she gives little actual thought to it—her deep interest is the security of the home that has thus been established, which means, the security of herself and the child who will eventually be born. Thus a woman who, immediately after marriage, should find herself sexually attracted to nearly every suitable man who crossed her path, would quite rightly wonder whether she was really ready for marriage. Others would put the same interpretation on her behavior. Nor does this merely mean, as some would have it, that she had perhaps not yet come to appreciate what was expected of her. To depart from conventional ways is one thing. To reject one's most natural feelings is very different.

A man, on the other hand, just recently married, has little such inner urge to fidelity, but the very opposite. Faithful he may be, but in his case, unlike that of his wife, this is maintained out of respect for the vows he has made, and his sincerely felt devotion to her. Whatever profession he may make to the contrary, the husband considers monogamy to be a restraint and a limitation; and it is no less a limitation if freely undertaken out of concern for something else he prizes, such as his own reputation, especially in the eyes of his wife.

*   *   *

The general rule that women tend to be monogamous while men are polygamous also applies to marriage relationships formed in college, but not, of course, without exception. In such relationships it is usually the female partner who genuinely and constantly cares for the man she lives with, who assumes the responsibility for birth control, who feels the greater sense of commitment, and who expects to be cared for. It is the female who waits, sometimes frantically, for the male to return after having been unaccountably gone and long overdue. Very often she will be the one to leave him, if the departure is intended to be permanent, but seldom otherwise. Many college men have ruefully described to me how their girls simply left them, once and for all. It was, on the other hand, almost invariably the men who had, as their girls usually described it, "slept" with someone else with no thought at all of ending the existing relationship. This account is characteristic of a man in such a situation:

> Joan was studying music in New York, and I only got to be with her on weekends. During the week away from her I sometimes slept with other girls, but not very often, and it didn't mean anything. One night I took Jan, who was singing at the Holiday Inn, home with me, and after we had had sex I told her she had to go home. She was outraged, but I hadn't agreed to anything more than that, and I just didn't want her there all night. Besides, Joan would be phoning in the morning, and I didn't want to have to lie to her. I didn't see that I had any obligation to let Jan stay all night, so even though she protested and said she absolutely wasn't going to leave like that in the middle of the night, I made her go.

Oddly enough, it never occurred to this man that the way in which he treated his casual friend was extremely shabby. He insisted that he had been honest with her, and supposed that he had thereby met any requirements of ethics. Of course comparable behavior on the part of women is not unheard of, indeed, some of the college women who shared their experiences with me had had a bewildering succession of casual sexual relationships. It was, however, quite uncommon for such women to have other lovers while being totally involved in a marriage relationship, whereas it was exceedingly common for men to do so—repeatedly.

It is in the light of this basic difference that many things concerning the relations of the sexes become clear, far more so than they would by trying, as is usually done, to account for every difference in terms of cultural conditioning. For example, regardless of her opinions concerning men, sex, and liberation, a newly and happily married woman is unlikely to be interested in casual sex with a total stranger. That sort of interest can usually be aroused only in women who have long since become disenchanted with their husbands or lovers and with their own conditions, women who feel they have been cheated out of something meaningful in their lives. Even these women are rarely roused to ardor by a man they know almost nothing about. On the contrary, they are likely to need assurance that their partner does in some sense at least care for or respect them, and that he is inspired by more than the mere thought of sexual gratification.

A man's interest, on the other hand, is sparked by the mere presence of any female of apparent buoyant health and appearance, particularly if she is young, or at least younger than himself. And a perfectly normal and otherwise decent man is prepared to satisfy this passion the moment an opportunity arises, particularly if his marriage is less than fulfilling. The casualness of a sexual liaison with an utter stranger is no inhibition to a man; on the contrary, it is usually an incitement to his ego.

*   *   *

No one should pretend that the descriptions just given apply without exception to all men or to all women. They are much oversimplified. Nevertheless, they express the basic truth.

Moreover, the claim that men are basically polygamous, and women are not, should not be taken to imply that lust is a uniquely male passion. Women lust after their husbands just as husbands lust after their wives, the basic difference being that men are more prone to lust after utter strangers and to act on those feelings. The following episode is surely one that most women would readily relate to. It was described to me by someone who was, at the time, living with her small children, separated from her self-centered husband and in the difficult process of divorce. Her story is perhaps made more interesting by the fact that, in addition to embodying perfect feminine loveliness, she was also the occasional assistant pastor of her church:

> The steps to the house were broken, so I got a carpenter I knew slightly to come fix them. I hardly knew this guy, but I had always been strongly attracted to him, even though he was married and had a family. As I watched him fixing the steps, I began to get an overwhelming attraction, though I don't think he suspected it, and after he had left, I was covered with sweat just thinking about him. I was shivering, and went out and mowed the lawn just to get this out of my system. A week or so later I poured some water on the floor and called him to say I thought the roof was leaking. That's how the affair got started. Pretty soon we were in bed a lot, after the children were asleep, and talking on the telephone whenever we could get away with it, without his wife finding out. But after a couple of months I broke it off. It was never anything but sex, and I could see that nothing was going to come of it in the long run. Neither of us wanted to get married or anything. I haven't really missed him, but it was pretty overwhelming while it lasted.

It was my good luck eventually to meet this man at a social gathering and I, of course, gave no hint of what I knew. Not surprisingly, he turned out to be, to all appearance, the most ordinary person imaginable, having nothing about him, so far as I could see, that would stir passion in an otherwise profoundly reserved woman.

*   *   *

It is not unusual to find the dining room of a motor inn filled almost entirely with men, traveling on business, dining and talking with each other, their minds entirely on work-related matters, and the conversations innocuous. They seem, and in fact they are, the models of probity and reserve. But if anyone imagines that this scene casts doubt upon the above descriptions, then he need only imagine that into this setting—one of ordinary, conventional men by themselves and lodged at an inn far from home—there should suddenly appear numerous young women, engagingly dressed, and distributed among these male patrons with ostentatious overtures of friendship and hints of availability. How many of these men would still find each other's company more engrossing than that of their new companions, whose very names might still be unknown to them? How many would resist the solicitations to sex? Some would, of course, but it is absurd to suppose that this sudden alteration of the scene would not evoke a profound difference in the feelings of these men. Desires of unbelievable force would be unleashed.

To further clarify this point, we need only to exercise our imaginations once more, this time by reversing things a bit. Imagine that these guests at the motor inn are all women—conventional, middle class, and mostly married—who are far from their homes and dining together, there being no men in sight at all except, perhaps, a busboy or two. Suppose as well that into this setting there should suddenly appear numerous men, who distribute themselves among the female guests and, with only the most perfunctory introductions or explanations, make overtures of friendship and invitations to have sex. It is not hard to imagine all of these women departing, in more or less acute discomfort, while it would be quite hard to imagine them rushing into bed.

You can, if you like, set this down to acculturation, but that would be naive. Set it down instead to a man's naturally immense fertility, in comparison to that of a woman, and to the accompanying primitive desires nature has given him. If acted upon, these desires—which no man creates himself and which are controlled only with effort—would require numerous sexual partners. A woman's basic desire, on the other hand, is usually not to have a great multiplicity of lovers, since a dozen men can make her no more pregnant than one. Her need is to beget and subsequently to nourish the one child at a time of which she is capable. For this she needs only one lover; but her need for him, and likewise her child's need for him, continues for years and even decades. None of that is compatible, so far as her feelings are concerned, with casual sex, which can only be self-defeating.

*   *   *

Although admittedly oversimplified, it must be stressed that the foregoing analyses are not intended to suggest that rationales underlying the behavior of men and women are conscious or deliberate. They probably never are. But neither, for that matter, are the sexual impulses themselves. We find ourselves impelled by these desires, without ever having selected them. Similarly, we find their manifestations unselected and far below the level of conscious, much less rational, choice. They are indeed neither rational nor irrational, nor, probably, are they morally significant, considered in themselves, though life would certainly be poorer, almost to the point of emptiness, without them.

Moreover, it must not be objected that the analyses have no qualifications or exceptions. The most characteristic exceptions are themselves instructive.

Thus, it is certainly true that not all men are polygamous. But those who are not are usually older men, long married, who have found ways to direct their sexual energies towards more acceptable goals, such as wealth, position, or professional recognition. Similarly, married women do sometimes invite casual sex, but these are usually women with grown children, women who feel neglected by or have lost interest in their husbands, and who, very often, feel denied the more interesting experiences of life. Many are simply bored with their domestic existence. What they seek is not just sex, but attention and an appreciation of themselves. It is apparent to any such women that their "womanness" is something deeply appreciated by men, something that can become an avenue to the appreciation of themselves as persons.

*   *   *

Each sex sometimes falls into curious and foolish errors by seeing the behavior of the other through its own eyes or, in other words, by supposing that sexual attraction expresses itself in much the same way regardless of one's gender. Thus, for example, a recently married woman is apt to feel shocked and hurt upon discovering that her husband's need to flit from flower to flower continues unabated. She mistakenly interprets it as a rejection of herself in favor of others. Still, it is severely condemned by society, and a recently married man is himself made to feel shame at overt and wholehearted flirtation, which, until a short while ago, he could have indulged to his heart's content. Therefore, men do conceal their passions, particularly from their wives or lovers, not only out of fear of hurting them but to escape a learned feeling of guilt. These feelings have most certainly been inculcated; no man by nature feels the least guilty about the most unabashed flirtation provided it can be concealed. Monogamous marriage was not instituted by nature but by society, and while it places rigid controls upon a man's public behavior, it modifies his inner life very little. Even if his feelings cannot be expressed in their most natural way, due to social restraints and customs, they will nevertheless find expression—in unabashed flirtation and pursuit if no one is watching, or otherwise in lurid fantasy. This is the primary reason why the casual conversations of married men sometimes seem to be so preoccupied with sex when these men are not in the company of women. This talk is an opportunity to express their fantasies and, quite pathetically, it is likely to be the only overt expression available to them. Young unmarried men, whose lives are quite free and polygamous, observe this behavior on the part of older men, this conversation and leering; they note with disgust the kind of humor and joke that moves older men to great laughter. It all seems so childish to them, which in a sense it is, for it certainly is not the behavior one expects from men of responsibility who cut significant figures in the world of business and the professions. Nevertheless, it is precisely the type of behavior one would expect from men of normal—that is to say, polygamous—sexuality, who long ago found themselves locked into monogamous marriage and have been closely watched most of the time. One has to remember that without vivid fantasy such men would, in a very significant psychological sense, cease to be men. When these fantasies have no hope of duplication in the real world, what on earth should we expect? It may be of little importance what young and unmarried men may sometimes think of the behavior of men who have been married for a long time, but it is of real practical importance that these men be understood by their wives. For these women to interpret their husbands' behavior and feelings as a rejection of themselves is grossly unfair and tends to undermine the genuine and total devotion their husbands do feel for them. What is involved here is not rejection, but rather, a man's realization of who he is.

A mistake made on the other side—a misunderstanding by men of the feelings and behavior of women—is even more common, quite stupid, and inexcusable. This mistake rests upon the supposition that women derive pleasure from sex just as men do, which is true, and that therefore, even taking into consideration the inhibitions created in some women by acculturation, they can be expected to have similar desires for sex, even casual sex. In other words, men project their own basic sexuality onto women, explaining differences as the product of cultural conditioning. Then it is supposed that all they need to do is identify those women who have managed to overcome such conditioning. Sometimes this expresses itself in their minds as a distinction between those women who "do" and those who "don't," which is as artificial as any distinction ever could be.

Thus a man, upon learning that a woman he knows has been involved in a love affair, is likely to direct special attention to her and even, sometimes out of the blue and on the spur of the moment, "proposition" her, that is, more or less obliquely suggest sexual intercourse. This absolutely never succeeds, and the suggestion itself is received with shocked astonishment. For example:

> One thing I had to put up with after my affair with Louise was discovered was the constant moralizing of one of my partners. This man is a stiff Presbyterian who would never dream of the slightest deviation from morality. I don't think he would rake his yard without making sure he looked all right to any passerby. Needless to say, he expressed grave doubts about my fitness to continue in the partnership.
>
> But then a strange thing happened. The annual conference was held in Philadelphia that year. I didn't go, but all my partners did, and Louise was there too. And do you know what this partner did? He propositioned her!

The same incredible misconception is expressed in this experience:

> I was involved with Lila, a lab assistant, less than half my age and hardly out of high school. One thing that was interesting was the way she came to be treated by other men when they learned about us. They all just assumed that she was fair game. They thought that if she would go to bed with me, then chances were she would go to bed with anyone. That was really incredibly stupid to anyone who actually knew Lila, who was a very quiet and proper girl and not at all easy to get to know. But lonely men thought they could just walk up to her any time

and start talking. Sometimes they began with some sort of remark about me—how I was married, comments about my age, that sort of thing—and then right away they would begin to boast about themselves, as if to invite comparison. Sometimes one of them would hang around where he knew she could be found, and as soon as she came by, just start walking along with her, uninvited. She didn't appreciate it at all, and in fact sort of liked some of these men, as friends, until they started acting that way. Mostly she was disgusted, and didn't understand it at all. I did.

The experiences expressed above illustrate a kind of impulsiveness and preoccupation with sex which, while very characteristic of men, is not characteristic of most women. Indeed, it is exceedingly rare for a woman to respond positively to a suggestion for casual sex, with the occasional exception of women who are embittered at their lovers or husbands or who are similarly disillusioned with their personal lives. Certainly there is no significant distinction between women who will respond positively and those who will not. Just as men are much the same in their sexuality (that is, polygamous), so are women much the same (that is, *not* polygamous). A woman's needs are significantly different from a man's, and one does not even begin to appreciate what these are by supposing that women seek sexual pleasure. They seek a far more significant fulfillment than this—and so, for that matter, do men. But men and women seek different things from each other, of which a great deal more will be said later.

*   *   *

That psychological orientations differ significantly between males and females with respect to passionate love seems beyond question. In fact, it would probably never be questioned if it did not seem to some, quite erroneously, to imply a subordinate status for women. Of course it has no such implications at all. But what has been widely doubted is that these are natural differences. Here it is claimed that they are, and that they are partly rooted in the totally different capacities of men and women with respect to siring and bearing children. The sexuality of men and women appears to be an almost metaphysical expression of these biological differences. That is to say, a man's responses are precisely what one should expect in the light of his capacities, and the same can be said of a woman's responses. These are characterized as "metaphysical" in order to avoid an otherwise inevitable misunderstanding. No man ever consciously reflects upon his immense fertility, and then decides to be polygamous. There is no thought or reflection about it at all; his sexuality is simply the nonreflective expression of that fertility. Similarly, no woman reflects much upon her vastly more limited fertility, amounting to the occasional production of a single egg in contrast to a man's daily production of a million seeds; nor does she decide in the light of this that her need is for a single and more or less permanent lover. The need is, again, simply the natural and unformulated expression of a basic biological fact.

These factors have influenced, in numerous ways, our fundamental conceptions of masculine and feminine nature, many of trivial significance but nevertheless revealing, and others more telling.

It has already been noted, for example, that women are never thought to perpetrate a rape, and any man who made such an accusation would not be believed. Nor would his claim become any more credible if it happened to be the case that he was slight of strength and build and therefore relatively defenseless in comparison with his alleged Amazon assailant. Relative strength has nothing to do with it. The accusation is absurd in the light of what anyone perceives as natural female sexuality, in contrast to that of a man. No one would doubt that a man of slight stature might be capable of raping someone twice as strong as himself, since all that is involved is a certain difficulty, not a basic absurdity.

Again, when the concept of a "home wrecker" is employed one usually envisions a female. No doubt this is partly due to the different roles society has tried to assign to men and women, and to sexual stereotypes that are hard to dislodge, but not entirely so. A man can, indeed, destroy a marriage by seducing another man's wife, but this is usually not how marriages are destroyed by third persons. A young mother whose husband is strong, resourceful, and a devoted spouse and father is an unpromising target for seduction by an outside male, no matter what he may have to offer. She already has everything of importance to her that he could provide. On the other hand, a woman long married whose children are grown and whose life seems to her somewhat empty easily yields to a man who offers her not primarily sexual pleasure, but rather appreciation of herself and her worth as a person. This is true even when there is no deficiency whatever in the sexual capacities of her husband. To a woman, sex is likely to be considered quite incidental in a love affair; not something withheld, to be sure, but at the same time something of secondary importance. An outside man, in short, does not destroy a home, though he may take advantage of its already weakened condition. Its actual destruction is much more likely to be wrought by the jealousy of the cuckolded husband, who feels belittled and inadequate, as well as deprived of something he thought was his.

A female home wrecker, on the other hand, is sometimes quite properly so-called—and this is said not in order to apply a different standard of conduct to women than to men, but rather to exhibit, once again, a basic difference in male and female sexuality. Thus, simply by the solicitations of sex, an outside woman can sometimes win over a devoted husband and father who until then had felt no deprivation whatsoever in his domestic life. His life need not be in any sense empty in order for this to happen; on the contrary, it can be one of rich fulfillment. Nor need his wife assume that she in any way compares badly with her rival. It may be as obvious to her as to anyone that the very opposite is true. Here, the appeal to a man's sexual nature—to his basic polygamy—is sometimes quite enough. It is for this reason that a woman, but not a man, can be aptly called a home wrecker, a term intended not so much as an adverse reflection on her as it is an indication of a man's vulnerability to the feminine blandishments. It is somehow supposed that everyone should know this, and that women, accordingly, ought not to exploit this male weakness thereby placing in jeopardy some other woman's home, a situation made even more precarious if there are children involved.

Other common notions bear out the same thesis concerning the natural differences between the sexes. Though a given man, for example, may have had many more sexual partners than a given woman, he is seldom referred to as promiscuous. Only a woman is usually so described. The reason is quite obvious; namely, that such behavior is thought to be more or less characteristic of a man, and hence no real fault, but uncharacteristic of a woman and not in keeping with her basic nature. Undoubtedly, the judgmental element in such assessments is unfair to women, but the distinctions involved nevertheless rest upon a correct perception. The same is true with respect to the idea of a "call girl." A male is in fact seldom referred to by the corresponding term *gigolo,* and very few men fill such a role—the role, namely, of providing casual sex to total strangers for payment. The idea of a "call boy" is inherently ridiculous because little demand for it exists, whereas the demand for women is so intense as to create the role itself even when this conflicts not only with clearly defined ideas of morality, but with the criminal law as well. Men are by nature polygamous, and this is concealed only by a veneer of convention. Women are not, and no modification of convention will make them so.

*   *   *

A "home wrecker" is thus always thought of as female, as someone who lures a husband and father from home and hearth with the thought of grabbing him for herself, the dutiful wife and mother being left behind to salvage what she can from the wreckage. Probably this stereotype is a reflection of another, namely, the notion that lust is a singularly male urge. A man is enjoined from coveting his neighbor's wife, but somehow no similar prohibition is thought necessary for a woman. Women are, in popular thinking, not thought of as lusting after men, or even after their own husbands. There is a common word for men who regularly act upon such lustings, namely, "womanizers," but no similar term has been invented for women who do the same, for again, such women are thought to be rare. That men, including men of the utmost reserve and respectability, should lust, at least "in their hearts," for women, is considered common knowledge, but women, quite contrary to fact, are not similarly thought of. Sexual harassment is almost always thought of as male behavior. If a woman accuses her boss of sexual harassment she is taken seriously. A similar accusation by a man against a female superior is met with automatic skepticism.

These ways of speaking do not rest merely on outworn stereotypes but on a basic difference between men and women. What needs to be emphasized, however, is that a marriage is seldom wrecked by what an abandoned wife thinks of as "the other woman." When a husband becomes involved in a love affair, and his marriage comes apart, then the third person, now thought of as a "home wrecker," is indeed one of the factors in the destruction; but she is only one, and usually not the most important one. The marriage was almost certainly unfulfilling to the husband in some respect and, very likely, this had little or nothing to do with sex. In one way or another, his sense of self-worth was not nourished in his marriage and, however superficially, it was nourished elsewhere.

11

How a Love Affair Starts

Where there's marriage without love, there will be love without marriage.

—Ben Franklin

People think of a love affair as a sexual adventure. Indeed, it is common to think of persons involved in an affair as having little, if any, other interest in each other.

It is, of course, sometimes true that adulterous love is almost exclusively sexual. It is the very meaning of adultery. But the mistake here is to suppose that married persons become involved in affairs just because they are seeking sexual adventures, and for no other reason. The result is that love affairs become trivialized and, more seriously, the real explanation of them is not understood at all.

Married people become involved in love affairs because their needs are not met in their marriages, and the unmet needs are very likely not to be sexual ones at all. Of all the many women who were willing, at my request, to tell me about love affairs they had been involved in, only one, so far as I can recall, described it in terms of sexual adventure. Having little to find fault with in her marriage, she was nevertheless overwhelmingly drawn to another man with whom she had almost nothing in common except the excitement of sex. The person who told me this story, in a casual and brief encounter, was a woman of great beauty, poise, and obvious refinement, and she described her affair this way:

There is nothing wrong with my marriage. My husband, an engineer, is impressive as a man and a perfectly wonderful lover. My attraction to Joe was purely physical. He is a "hunk." He never pretended to care anything about me, other than for sex, and that is exactly how I felt about him. My husband even knows all about that affair, which didn't last long, and it has made no difference to him. It is done and over, and he doesn't hold it against me at all. Our marriage is as good as it ever was.

109

I could not help hearing that account with considerable skepticism, both with respect to what she said was the quality and stability of her marriage, and her husband's lack of resentment. But even if we take it all at face value, supposing it to be undistorted truth, it most certainly is exceptional. Happily married women are not likely to become sexually involved with an outsider that casually. Men sometimes do, but even there, in most cases, their marriages are not all that fulfilling. And it is a rare husband indeed who could hear such an account from his wife without profound anxiety, resentment, and injury, and the injury would be very slow, if ever, to heal.

Indeed, it can be doubted whether the sort of thing just described should even be called a *love* affair. The more poetic expression, "an affair of the heart," is even less appropriate. Many, and probably most, adulterous lovers find great joy and satisfaction in each others' arms, but this is seldom what drew them into their affair. What was responsible for this was, quite simply, unmet needs at home, of the everyday sort that have been described.

Women who become involved in sexual infidelity almost invariably use the same word to describe their husbands: *Boring.*

And what is it to be bored by someone? It is, essentially, to be ignored. The boring person is aware of your presence, but of little else. Your thoughts, needs, and feelings do not even enter his mind.

Thus, suppose you are in the company of someone of uncommon intelligence and wit. He has, we can suppose, a vast knowledge of something that has always been of great interest to you—a knowledge of art, perhaps, or legal theory—whatever. His words flow, his understanding of the subject is genuine and deep, he injects witticism into his talk at appropriate points—he holds forth, in short, in perfect form. But, we shall suppose, he shows not the least interest in anything you try to inject into the conversation, even though you, perhaps, know more about the subject than he does. So he bores you to death! But the only thing that makes him boring is that, while he brilliantly displays his own gifts, he is totally unaware of your need to be a participant here.

That is the essence of boredom—to be treated like someone who does not count. And this is what drives married people, women especially, into extramarital affairs. A husband may be ever so dutiful and, in the ordinary sense, devoted, and yet he is boring. His wife always knows where he is, and he always comes home at about the time he is expected. He is always there. The family bills are paid, without demanding explanations; he is a gentle and loving father of their children; and in short, he fulfills every conventional expectation of the good husband. He is even all right as a sexual partner, even though he may ignite no great passions in his wife. There is nothing wrong with him at all—except, he is boring.

And what that means is that he is more or less unaware of his wife's ordinary, day-to-day needs. Some of these may be trivial, vain, or even silly, but there they are and, so far as any response from her husband is concerned, she may as well have, for a companion, a wooden post.

What, then, happens when this bored wife encounters a man who seems to admire all kinds of things about her and, as she soon learns, appreciates her talents, even though these may be small, is sensitive to her every change of mood, listens to and responds to everything she says—someone who, in a word, is never boring? What happens is that she falls in love with him, the kind of love we are calling romantic love. And this, in spite of the fact that he may lack every quality of the good husband. He perhaps offers nothing in the way of security, has an eccentric lifestyle, is not very dependable, and, above all, is already married to someone else and has no intention of changing that.

Men who become involved in love affairs almost never, unlike women, describe their spouses as boring, but the underlying reasons are much the same. They feel unappreciated or, which is about the same thing, unloved. Their wives do not seem to miss them when they are gone, do not rejoice in their achievements, seem to lack compassion for their defeats and frustrations—in a word, they do little to meet the day-to-day and ordinary needs of their husbands. The word men are likely to use to describe their wives, contrasting her to some newfound love, is "cold."

But this comes to much the same thing. These men describe their wives as cold for much the same reasons that women describe their husbands as boring. Both feel unappreciated. Probably the reason so many men, unlike women, choose a word like "cold," with its sexual overtones, is that men seem to have more of a sense of guilt about sex than women do. This does not, of course, mean that they are less prone to sexual infidelity than women; indeed, the opposite is true. But a husband whose adultery is discovered is far more likely to view it in grand and dramatic terms, to weep tears of guilt, to wish forgiveness, and so on. Women seldom act that way, and, of course, not all men do, but they are more likely to, because they are far less likely than women to take sex for granted as sort of a fact of life, and are thus far more prone to shame. This seems to be a basic, though not unexceptional, difference between men and women, and one that does little credit to male intelligence.

Much of what has been said so far is perfectly illustrated by the following story, told to me by a young and attractive professional woman, who is also a gifted writer, over a luncheon. Her marriage fits the common notion of family stability, but something quite different emerges from beneath that conventional surface:

> I've been married eight years, and we have all the good things—a nice house, with a picket fence and gardens, and lots of friends. We go out regularly for dinner, by ourselves or with others, and in the summer we have friends over for cookouts, like everyone else. Ben, my husband, is strong and good looking, makes more than enough money for both of us as a contractor, and I have a good income too. We both get along fine with each other's parents, and, in fact, mine think that Ben is just perfect for me. We have no children, I have miscarried twice, but I have not given up. I do want children.
>
> Before we got married, while I was doing graduate studies, Ben drove to the university almost every day, a round trip of nearly two hundred miles. Usu-

ally he just kept me company there while I studied. He has never had any interest in anyone else. I always know where he is, without having to ask, and I always know when he'll be coming home, at about the same time every day. He is a completely loyal husband.

There are things in this marriage that others never see, however. For example, Ben does not like touching anyone, even me, and does not like being touched; it makes him very uncomfortable. We don't make love very often, and it is meaningless to me, though it seems just fine for him.

Ben's all-consuming interest is deer hunting. He reads *Field and Stream* avidly, but little else. He spends all the time he can in the woods, both in and out of hunting season, tracking deer, collecting antlers and deer skulls, even going out at night to search out the deer and see what they are doing. He scrupulously obeys all the hunting laws, and when the hunting season comes, it is as if he were suddenly transported to another world. He can hardly sleep, and as the season approaches, he spends days in preparation of equipment and hunting garb. During the season he launders his clothes several times a day and takes three or four showers, using a special scent-free soap, and scrubs his hunting boots with soda—the rituals are endless.

I view this obsession with bewilderment. It means nothing to me. My interests are in poetry, literature, and writing—things about which Ben has almost no knowledge or interest. I did write a magazine article about his devotion to deer hunting, and he of course read that, and seemed grateful to me for writing it.

After these many years, we get along all right, but didn't always. We got to quarreling a lot, and it got worse and worse, until I finally left for two months. We tried counseling, but that only seemed to make things worse, by reminding me of all our problems.

Meanwhile, before that temporary breakup, I had become involved with a painter, Bill, a divorced man quite a bit older than me and with a son in high school. Bill is a warm, affectionate, and tender lover, unlike Ben, and a fascinating person. He loves music and literature, is an excellent cook, and loves all the things I love. In fact, I find in him everything that I do not find in Ben. I take pride in my looks, select my clothes with care, wear nice jewelry, and I like perfumes. Ben never notices any of these things. Bill never fails to notice them. Ben never telephones me. Bill calls every day, just to talk, and listen.

Still, Ben is where all my stability is. He is not unkind, and certainly not abusive. He provides the basics of home life that I need, and I care about him deeply. All that is missing, basically, is that he just takes me for granted, hardly aware at all of what I am thinking or feeling, even when we are alone together. I am to him like a maintenance-free vehicle that never needs oiling. If I say I would like a glass of wine, he is apt to just set out a bottle and a glass and walk away; it would not occur to him to pour it, and look at me. We might as well be in different rooms. When he went out for beer one time I asked him to bring me a light, mild one. He returned with the darkest, most awful beer you can imagine—it was as if he hadn't heard me. At one of our cookouts he was terribly solicitous of one of his male friends, checking every few minutes to see just how he wanted the steak cooked and garnished, but then when it came to preparing mine, he said nothing, as though I didn't matter. He is hardly interested at all in what is going on with me. When I undertook a recommended but unorthodox treatment for infertility, hoping to avoid further miscarriage, he simpy scoffed and belittled the whole effort. Communication is much of the time minimal, and he is even evasive about things that don't matter. When I came home once to find the smell of marijuana, he flatly denied that he had been smoking, even though it was obvious, and wouldn't make the slightest difference to me anyway.

Ben has known about my friendship with Bill from the start. I made no attempt to conceal it. But, of course, he does not know the intimate nature of it. After I had left for those two months, I made it a condition of my coming back that he accept that friendship, and he agreed. Since then, we have preserved a stable marriage. Bill sometimes comes to our house, and when he does, Ben always leaves. There is no apparent animosity there, but there is also no pretense of friendship. Bill and I never make love at my house, and I didn't see him during the two months of separation, either. I find that I love them both, Ben for the stability, and Bill for all the other things. If Ben were to become ill for a long time, and perhaps terminally so, I would take very good care of him, and do everything I should, and if he died, I would miss what we had together; but I do not think I would miss him emotionally. I think Ben must have some idea of what is going on with Bill and me, but he never says anything about it.

The idea expressed in this last comment, incidentally, is quite common on the part of adulterous spouses; namely, the belief that the husband or wife "must know." I believe that it serves to relieve the feeling of guilt. If the husband or wife *knows* what is going on, and does not object, then that is tantamount to permission, is it not? So there is really no deception or betrayal after all, is there?

The foregoing story is significant in that it embodies something that would be widely considered impossible. Most persons would say that my confidante should choose, that she cannot have it both ways. Some would even declare her conduct to be immoral. And indeed, I have said that an affair, even when not discovered, is fatal to a marriage. And that claim is perhaps even true in this case, if marriage is considered to be a relationship based upon profound and lasting love, for that kind of love is missing here. Still, it is worth noting that a marriage, of sorts, is kept together in the situation described and, what is more significant, part of the reason for its survival seems to be the very infidelity of the wife. Or, expressed otherwise, the marriage seems to hold up partly because one of its partners finds, outside the marriage, what should be in it.

*   *   *

Often people are astonished by the partnerships that are formed in love affairs, and the contrasts they present to already existing partnerships. Thus, for example, a man having the most estimable wife, one who is not only lovely and devoted but who possesses every quality that stirs men with love and desire, such a man is found to be deeply involved with a woman who has few of these qualities, who is in every sense a lesser person. This often happens, and friends wonder why. Even more common are instances in which a woman of the kind just described, graced with youth, beauty, and intelligence, and already well married to a man of comparable or even more impressive worth, becomes totally involved with a man who is physically and otherwise unattractive, intellectually unimpressive, crude, unemployed, and uninteresting. The idea of sexual appeal seems inadequate in such cases, and yet other explanations seem even less so.

*　　*　　*

The following account, for example, is so paradigmatic that I could almost predict, from one sentence to the next, what the author of it was going to say as she talked to me. In it are contained the elements that typically (though not always) lead a woman into an affair, namely, boredom, a neglectful husband, and an outsider who pays attention to her. This affair was also typical in its outcome, namely, abandonment of the affair. It illustrates perfectly how, contrary to popular opinion, sexual gratification is not necessarily the motive for an affair:

> There is only one way I could describe Ken—he was a sweet son of a bitch. I don't know why I ever got mixed up with him, except that I was bored. I had been married about five years, and now I was home all the time with the baby while my husband was away studying at the university. There was really nothing wrong with Carl, my husband, except that he took me for granted, and sometimes he found fault with me for little things that didn't really matter. One minute he would be telling me I was a good mother, and things like that, but I didn't really believe him because the next minute he would be telling me how badly I did everything. He didn't seem very aware of me, even when we were together and talking with each other all day. Maybe I envied him, because he had an interesting life while I was supposed to just stay home and take care of the baby and make supper when he got back.
>
> Carl comes from a very important family, and knows some of the most influential people in Boston, while Ken, the man I got involved with, wasn't much. In fact he was quite bad, and I knew it almost from the beginning. He was four or five years younger than me. I never found out whether he even had a job. He certainly never had any regular job when I knew him, or showed any interest in getting one. He spent his time playing pool with his friends and playing his guitar. But he did have lots of friends. And he was fun. The first time I met him, at a bar where there was dancing, I asked him if he wanted to dance, and he didn't; but he spent the rest of the evening dancing with other people. Then when the bar closed he came over and started talking with me. He told all kinds of jokes and outrageous stories, and paid more attention to me than Carl had in ages. He didn't ask to take me home, either to his place or to mine, which surprised me a little; but he did ask for my telephone number, and I gave it to him, and told him I was usually alone all day.
>
> Actually, I didn't see Ken again for a long time; then he started to telephone me all the time. He would just call up any time of the day and talk and tell crazy stories, and he would play his guitar and sing to me on the phone. That went on for maybe six weeks.

Things weren't getting any better at home. It seemed as though I was either alone with the baby and bored, except when Ken was telling jokes and singing songs to me on the phone, or else I was being criticized or ignored by my husband.

Finally, when Ken called and suggested that I meet him at a party, I did. It was only the second time I'd ever seen him, but he said he wanted to see me all the time, and even suggested that I go live with him, even though he knew about Carl and the baby. It was all so ridiculous; but we kept on seeing each other quite often, in bars and places, for a couple of hours at a time. We never went to bed together, not until quite awhile later. He seemed to like being with me anyway. He made me laugh with his outrageous stories, and he was pretty good with his guitar; no one had ever sung songs to me before.

Then one night I did go home with him, and stayed all night. It wasn't especially good, as far as sex was concerned, but that didn't make any difference. At first I didn't tell Carl I'd slept with Ken, in fact I told him I never had; but then a few days later I did tell him, and he just about went crazy with jealousy—even though he had told me of an affair he'd had after we were married, and I hadn't gone to pieces. The very first thing he wanted to know was whether Ken was better at sex than he was! And even though I told him he wasn't, which was true, he couldn't get over all this, and we had to split up, so I left and moved in with Ken.

That only lasted two and a half weeks. It was exciting at first, even though the sexual part of it wasn't anything special, but then it got to be less exciting very fast. I went home and told Carl what a bad person Ken was, which was true, and Carl knew it too. In fact, Carl was convinced that Ken had tried to kill him, by fixing his car so he'd have an accident. I never really believed it, but Carl seemed to. Anyway, I went back to Carl and the baby, and I guess things have been better since then.

I guess I was in love with Ken then, for a little while, but, as you can see, sex didn't have much to do with it. Ken never was very good in bed, and I wasn't very good with him either. There had never been anything wrong with sex at home. I don't think I ever came with Ken, though I almost always did with my husband.

What there was about Ken is that he was observant. It wasn't so much that Carl found fault with me. Even when he wasn't finding any fault, and everything was all right, I usually had the feeling that he was unaware of me. Ken wasn't like that. Ken wasn't much good, and I did hear lots of bad things about him, but he noticed me. Sometimes, when I just wanted to talk, and didn't want to dance or anything, it was as if he had read my mind, and he'd say, "Do you just want to talk?" That had never happened before. Once when we were watching television, and he was very interested in it, I was getting bored by it, but I didn't say anything or let on. Then suddenly he turned and said to me, as if he'd read my mind again, "You're bored with this, aren't you?" He was kind and gentle, and observing of how I felt and what I wanted. My husband had never asked at all; he had always gone ahead and done what he wanted, and I was expected to just go along with it. When Ken played his guitar for me, I always had the feeling he was playing to me, trying to please me with his songs, and not just showing off. Even if having sex with him wasn't very good, I had the feeling he cared about me there, too. Actually, sex has never been a big thing with me. I'd be perfectly happy with just once or twice a month, so whether Ken was good at that or not didn't matter much.

But Ken wasn't really a good person. People told me he'd been arrested for stealing, and it seemed to me it could be true all right. He always had lots of friends, but none of them did much, except play pool and drink beer.

Eventually I learned that Ken had boasted to his friends about our affair, and told them personal things that I never supposed he would tell anyone. Some of these stories got back to my husband, and I knew they had come from Ken, because no one else would have known without him telling them, and they were true. So I had lots of reasons to hate him, and not want to see him ever again. He stopped showing up. I never asked him to stop, but he did. Sometimes I'd call him up, and we would agree to meet, but he would never show up. Sometimes I would go out looking for him, all over, but I never could find him, and his friends would never tell me where he was.

That all happened over a year ago, and I haven't seen him in all that time. I really don't know what I would do now if I saw him again—if I looked up now, for instance, and saw him sitting right over there. I keep telling myself he wasn't good, because he wasn't. He was a son of a bitch, and it's just as well that I never see him again. I have even been warned by other women that he is no good. But still, I don't know what I would do if I were to just run into him some day.

Of course I could not help thinking, upon hearing that final wistful comment, that I knew exactly what she would do.

*   *   *

A man's interest in a love affair is apt to be quite different from that just given, and there is little mystery about it. While women who become involved in an affair are likely to describe their husbands as boring, men who are similarly involved seldom describe their wives that way. In fact, such men are often deeply in love with their wives. It is just this fact that is least understood by wives. They think—reading their own feelings into the matter—that their husband's passionate love for another woman is a rejection of themselves, and the first question to cross their minds is, "What is wrong with me?" The answer can easily be, "Nothing whatever." Because a wife does want to believe this, she may find it difficult to believe that her husband's other relationship can in fact be a serious one. Her very use of the expression "playing around" is intended to trivialize it. It is incomprehensible to her that any man can be sincerely and totally devoted to his wife, and in every way fulfilled in that relationship, and yet be seriously and passionately involved with someone else. She is especially pained if the "other" woman is seen to be a lesser person—someone who is incurably silly, for example, or otherwise lacking in charm, wit, and intelligence. It is this failure of understanding, a failure that is almost guaranteed by the contrasting sexualities of men and women, that elicits the most destructive responses in women and is the real cause of many broken marriages that are conveniently blamed on affairs.

Of course, the same is true of those marriage relationships between men and women where no legal marriage exists, with only this difference: that the partners in such relationships do not feel the same degree of inhibition about entering into other love affairs. It is, nevertheless, more often men who do this than women. When such relationships are described to me by students, for example, it is extremely common for the female partners to describe the hurt and pain they felt when they discovered that their men had been "unfaithful," sometimes during a period of enforced absence. Men, on the other hand, tend to boast of such double relationships, something female students very rarely do. Here, for example, is a fairly typical description of such a double relationship:

> My girl was a premed student and a year ahead of me, so she went off to medschool while I stayed behind to finish the last year of college. She was close enough that we could spend weekends together; but pretty soon I got tired of being alone the rest of the week. So I found a new friend, Pat, to come stay with me sometimes, though we never talked about living together, the way I'd lived with Judy, my med-school friend.
>
> I wasn't in love with Pat, although we liked each other, and I never changed my mind about wanting to marry Judy when we could. But Judy learned about Pat, and it got awfully messy. I thought that if she could meet her, and see that it really didn't mean anything, then maybe things would be all right, and so the three of us actually had dinner together. That was all rather strained, but it went all right. But afterwards, at a party we all went to, there was an awful scene between the two girls, and Judy went off in a rage. The next morning, about seven o'clock, there was Judy on the phone demanding that I tell her whether Pat had spent the night with me, in spite of the fact that we had long ago promised each other that we would never pry or ask questions like that, and Judy had not forgotten that agreement. She never asks those questions any more, but things have never been the same with us as they used to be, in spite of the fact that Judy knows perfectly well that neither Pat nor anyone else means anything to me compared with how I feel about her.

This brief account is illustrative not only of the points just made, but also of the male ego. It is fairly common for a man who is sure of the affections of two or more women to want to bring them together somehow, even when this would seem to violate all wisdom and prudence—as, for example, when he is married to one of them and having an affair with the other. Such behavior on the part of women seems far less common, for reasons that will become apparent as we go along.

*   *   *

In a love affair, a man seeks not only sexual adventure in its superficial forms—though he does most certainly seek this—but also a kind of fulfillment of the ego that women do not easily comprehend. This is why, for example, a man is eager to have his affair known, particularly to other men, but sometimes even to his wife, or to a woman who fills the role of wife to him. A man unabashedly exhibits his lover, sometimes going to considerable expense to do so, provided this can be done without great risk—such as the risk of losing his job or of having to explain himself at home—and sometimes even in full awareness of great risk. A man particularly loves to be envied for his love affair, envied by other men who can perhaps surpass him in some things, but not, he hopes, in this. To be sure, the desire to be envied is not uniquely characteristic of men; but the seeking of this kind of envy seems to be. When a man displays affection in public it is likely to be, at least partly, *because* he is in public and can enjoy the stares of the curious, the hamstrung, and the envious; whereas, if a woman permits herself to exhibit affection in public, it is *in spite* of the attention this attracts, never because of it. What is involved here is, quite simply, male ego. Indeed there are few men who do not relish the thought of being seen, not with an adoring female, but with two. This is, by the nature of the case, almost impossible to realize since in such circumstances each woman feels belittled by the presence of the other; but wealthy men have been known to stage such appearances, when travelling around, just for the sake of what they think is a stunning appearance.

The lengths to which men will go with this kind of exhibitionism is sometimes astonishing, even bizarre. Here are three examples:

(1) I had spent eight weeks of the summer at a conference for graduate and post-doctoral students, and before it was over I thought I was in love with the director. From the day we got involved with each other, and he discovered how I felt, he seemed to want to attract as much attention to us as possible. He always talked about me when the rest were there, and hovered around me whenever others would be watching, and on the last day, when quite a few of the people were taking pictures for souvenirs, he wanted to be sure that everyone got a picture of "us." I thought it was all sort of embarrassing.

(2) Seven of us students rented a house together, and I eventually became infatuated with one of the men, but I kept it to myself, mainly because he was already living with one of the women and had been for a long time. One night, though, we were alone, and I sort of seduced him. The next morning he called the whole house together, around the kitchen table, and made me "confess" the whole thing. I felt mortified, but he said that it was important for me to do it, so that the woman he was living with would understand, from my own mouth, that I was the one who seduced him, and not the other way around.

(3) We were on an archaeological expedition, and I started having an affair with one of the men. One night he insisted that we sleep together on the balcony. He didn't suggest it or ask me, he just insisted, and even tried to drag me out there, but I absolutely refused, and got very angry. It was worse than pointless, because this was in Tunisia, which is a Moslem country, and people there have some very strong feelings about men and women, and about sex, and public display.

Doubtless each of the men in these episodes would have a perfectly rational-sounding explanation for his behavior. The first, for example, might say that he merely wanted as many pictures as he could get, as reminders, or something of the sort. The second did, in fact, have an explanation—that he wanted to protect his relationship with someone else—and it is very likely that he actually believed this himself. The third would perhaps say that he was only pursuing a bit of bravado. In truth, however, every one of them was probably just showing off or, in other words, giving a lift to his ego. The second, for example, was saying, in this clumsy and roundabout way: "All of you please note that this beautiful woman finds me quite irresistible." It is a very heady feeling for a man. Of course women are also capable of being just as silly, but usually not in this way.

* * *

Women, perceiving this male egoism and flamboyance, are apt to be repelled by it, to regard it as childish, and to attach little significance to it. However, such a reaction fails to understand what is most certainly a driving force in male behavior. To condemn male egoism is partly to reject men as such, for this is what they are; and it has its counterpart, as we shall note shortly, in feminine vanity.

In fact the buoyancy that is provided to the male ego by a love affair does more to fuel that relationship than does sexual intimacy. Therefore, it is a distortion to think that a man's sole or even his primary motivation for such a relationship is sexual pleasure. A woman who cares for a man and tries to express this only through sex, perhaps in imaginative ways, can still fall very far short of fulfilling any deep need of his. It is, in the last analysis, what he thinks of himself, and what she encourages him to think of himself, that is crucial. Sexual intimacy is itself only an expression of this, for what a man thus seeks is not so much pleasure, but to be pleased *with himself.* He finds almost no price too high to pay for this. A man's fondest notion of himself is of a powerful, inexhaustible lover, and one of his bitterest thoughts is that he compares badly with someone else in this respect. Nothing so totally robs him of the zest for life, nothing makes his spirits sink as does the sense of sexual inadequacy—not, it must be stressed, because he feels himself thus cheated of sensuous pleasures, but because of the overwhelming affront to his ego. Absurd as this may appear to the intellect—and to the minds of women it sometimes seems so absurd as to be unbelievable—a man's basic happiness rests very much upon the power he believes to be lodged in his penis, the power to achieve and to maintain a strong erection, when needed, often, and at will. The threat to this power is a psychological threat of immense proportions. Women often learn with astonished amusement that a man is deeply concerned even with the size of his penis, and profoundly anxious not to compare too unfavorably with other men in this respect. And men, for their part, are sometimes as astonished to learn that women pay almost no attention whatever to this and, more astonishing still, that they are not even terribly concerned with a man's sexual prowess, that is to say, with the strength and durability of his erections. Usually a man's very first question, upon learning of his lover's intimacies with someone else, is whether that person was "better" than he is—a question which, in the sense he intends it, is not likely even to arise in her own mind. Even a man of immense worldly reputation, one who can truly regard himself as noteworthy and celebrated, will ask that very question of a woman with whom he has sexual relations, even though she might otherwise be virtually unknown to him. Thus an undergraduate student relates her encounter with a well-known television news personality:

> After his lecture a lot of us went with him over to the Commons, where we all sat around him and talked for quite awhile. Eventually he started flirting with me, and I found that pretty exciting, since he's not only famous, but very attractive. Then just before he left to go to the Towne House he kissed me, in front of everyone. After I got back to the dorm I thought about that for quite awhile, then went and telephoned him. He knew who I was, and asked me whether I wanted to just come and stay with him that night. So I called a taxi and went over there. The next morning I told him I was more or less living with a student, and all he said was, "Is he good?" Then no sooner did he see the expression on my face than he asked, "Is he better than me?" I was so amazed, and embarrassed, that someone like that would be asking me those kinds of questions; I didn't have any idea what to say.

What astonished the author of these remarks would surprise very few men, for it is the question every man raises in such circumstances, at least in his own mind. No man can bear the thought of being a second-rate or a third-rate lover, and he can never truly love any woman who allows him to entertain that thought of himself. From which of course it can rightly be inferred that a man's love for a woman is, initially, far less of a love for her than for himself. This does not mean that his love for her must be insincere, for it certainly need not be. It only means that genuinely passionate love for her cannot lack that basis. With his own conception of himself and what he perhaps childishly but nonetheless unavoidably thinks of as his own masculinity securely in place, he can love unabashedly and quite unselfishly. In fact, on these terms no sacrifice for her is excessive in his mind. He profoundly needs this sense of sexual security, and will love totally the woman who fulfills it. Without it he cannot love at all, in any true sense of the word. He can only love dutifully, merely going through the motions of it, and keeping up the appearance, meanwhile salvaging what he can of his damaged ego and, characteristically, seeking the fulfillment of his ego in other realms, such as wealth or power, or else in someone else's arms. Still, whatever may be his triumphs in the world, they will be but consolation prizes for his true yearning, which is inadequately expressed as the love of women. In truth the love of women evolves from his self-love, his conception of his own power and strength, which is directly and finally proved to him by the simple fact that he can maintain a strong erection. One can dismiss this as absurd; one can note, with truth, that it ill befits our conception of human dignity or even human rationality; and there are men who, in defense of their own egos, will deny it, professing a far nobler conception of love and family devotion in their own case. Nevertheless, it is true; and a woman who understands this seemingly childish but, in fact, overwhelmingly important part of the male psychology need never find herself unloved by men.

*   *   *

Of course it is not only in erotic love, but everywhere, that the male ego flourishes or is defeated. Thus the deepest wound that a man can suffer is an assault upon his sense of self-worth; and even the mildest affront is deeply felt. No man can tolerate a "put-down" without resentment, nor can he care deeply for anyone who delivers it, however innocuous it may seem to that other person. However meager may be his skills, talents, and natural endowments, they are nevertheless cherished by him. His feeling for any woman who totally appreciates them and encourages him to glory in them can rise to adoration. These attributes need not even be important ones; it is important that they are his. A man does, for example, take pride in his association with an important company, a university, or whatever group confers status upon its members; but he cannot really glory in this since it is an accidental association which can be lost and must, in any case, be shared with others, including some who cut an even greater figure there. However, he can truly glory in the qualities of his person, qualities that tend to fulfill his image of manliness. This is why men so dread baldness, even though it is nowhere considered a real fault and even though, significantly, it seems to have no effect at all on the attentions and affections of women. Similarly, a man who is very strong and tall glories in these attributes, and can be a foil for a woman who encourages him to do so. A man who has a powerful swimming stroke, or a great presence before an audience, as in the case of a gifted teacher, or a singularly dense and handsome beard, or any similarly insignificant but deeply personal quality that forms part of his self-image never tires of reminders of such things, particularly from women he cares something about. If, on the other hand, he conspicuously lacks some such quality, and is acutely aware that he does, then he can hardly bear reminders to that effect. If any woman should appear deliberately to produce such a reminder precisely in order to sting him, even if only playfully, then his instant hurt and resentment will dampen his affection for her until such time as the wound has healed or compensation has been made. This is the power of the "put-down," and no woman should indulge the perverse pleasure of inflicting it without an appreciation of its effect—something which, incidentally, the victim does not dare betray, for to do so would only make him appear as childish as he has already been made to feel.

However, in the last analysis, his sexual power will, in his own mind, contribute far more than any personal attribute to his sense of power and masculinity. And, ridiculous as this may seem, perhaps even to himself, the clearest demonstration of his power is the strength, size, and duration of an erection. No man can harbor a passionate love for any woman, or care very deeply for her, who cannot elicit this response, no matter what other wonderful things might truly be said of her. Nor can he fail to care for someone who does effortlessly bring this about, whatever may be her shortcomings. Despite the other forms of love human beings may be capable of, this is the key to passionate love so far as any man is concerned, and it is, perhaps, the strange and incongruous foundation of the most tender and intense feelings that can be evoked in men. It is not surprising, therefore, that a "put-down" in this realm—or in other words, a woman's deliberate and mischievous reminder to a man that he fails here—can irreparably shatter any possible affection he could have for her. Not only will he cease abruptly to have any interest in her but, if possible, he will never want or try to see her again, unless with the hope of redeeming himself. For even to see her would remind him afresh of that awful blow to his ego, thereby depressing his spirits once more.

*   *   *

Does an explanation for the dissolution of marriage relationships emerge from these remarks? Certainly not. These founder for numberless reasons, of which I have hinted at only one. Furthermore, I have said nothing of any special needs women have which are often left unfulfilled in marriage, and always at great cost. Hence, it would be singularly simpleminded to suggest that what is so often misleadingly called "sexual incompatibility," as men like to think of it, is always or even usually the cause of broken marriages. There are strong and happy marriages, especially in families with children, in which erotic love has only a minimal place. There are wretched marriages in which neither partner finds fulfillment, even though sexual problems do not arise. A marriage relationship has many ingredients, of which passionate love is only one; and that one is sometimes not necessary for lasting success, and is surely never sufficient for it.

What has been said does, nevertheless, call attention to one common cause of estrangement between men and women which is particularly important because it is almost always misunderstood. It is simply a woman neglecting to build up her husband or lover, most likely because she mistakenly assumes that he does not need this encouragement. Thus, what often happens is that she takes little notice of those qualities and virtues he treasures in himself, though he seldom alludes to them. His skill as a conversationalist is seldom remarked upon; she rarely recognizes the way he has with children, which others never fail to note; his natural superiority over colleagues, including those who have risen faster than he, tends to go unmentioned; his aplomb and presence before an audience, which has always been a source of gratification to him, is taken for granted; and above all, his sexual prowess, to which his thoughts turn many times in the course of a day, receives no attention or comment from her, even in moments of passion when he would expect her to be quite overwhelmed by it. He is, in other words, taken for granted; and while he has not the slightest reason to doubt that she really does see him as he sees himself, namely, as a man who has every reason to take pride in his powers, he is reduced to *asking* her in order to receive the assurances he so desperately craves.

A man in such circumstances doubtlessly has no ground for complaint, and when he feels ignored he is probably capable of seeing for himself just how childish his expectations are. Nevertheless, there they are, and they are in fact unmet. Now we need only to imagine the impact upon him if, after perhaps years of unfulfilled expectations, there suddenly appears on the scene another woman. She is impressed by him, and makes known to him, in many unspoken ways, that she delights in his company. He is made aware of the fact that the qualities he considers so dear to himself, namely, just about all of the qualities he has, are seen by her as well to be not only admirable, but unique. This man will experience an almost compulsive desire to be with this woman—often and alone—no matter how obviously foolish it may appear, and no matter what the apparent consequences might be to things in his life that he greatly values: his family, his work, and perhaps even his reputation and standing in the eyes of persons whose opinion he greatly values. Needless to say, the consequences are apt to be serious.

This kind of comment, for example, is quite common:

> There was nothing wrong with my marriage, and the thought of ending it had never entered my head. The children were happy and doing well, my job was going far better than I had ever expected, and we all enjoyed doing things together as a family. But the marriage was almost wrecked over just one affair, the only one I ever had, with a divorced woman who worked for the same company, and sometimes worked with me. Whenever we were at the same desk she always seemed to be paying more attention to me than to what she was supposed to be doing. If she had a chance to touch me she did. We began to see each other after work, always in public places, and she would comment on how tall I am, not once, but fairly often. Sometimes she told me that I have beautiful eyes. I don't think I have, particularly, and no one else has ever said so. It seemed to her that everything I did was remarkable. She admired my photography. She even thought I sang well. And I don't think it was all flattery. She seemed to mean it. I ended up spending almost a week at her house, when my wife was gone, and that nearly finished my marriage, because she made me feel like the greatest man who had ever lived. My wife never learned about it. But I decided I'd never have the kind of relationship with her children that I had with mine, especially her son, so finally nothing came of it. It all ended with a certain amount of bitterness, but I am glad now that it ended. I already had a perfectly good marriage, and beautiful kids.

However, many stories that begin much the same way do not end on such a comparatively happy note. What often and almost typically happens next is a total distortion of everything in the minds of both husband and wife, distortions that only fuel the discord and soon render hopeless any salvation whatever. He, for example, begins for the first time to speak of their "incompatibility," as though this had some clear meaning to him; and then, surveying the disintegration setting in around him, he lapses into self-pity, weeping sometimes when alone, and perhaps sometimes when not alone. From a hidden motive, which is his own sense of guilt, he frequently declares his devotion to his wife—a devotion which he finds coldly unappreciated by her. What he does, in short, is just about everything that is stupid and inept, and he thinks about everything except the simple truth that might possibly help put things back together.

For her part, his wife hardly does better, and she has a clear target for her frustration and resentment, namely, the other woman. Imagining, perhaps, that this other person in her husband's life might somehow, and in spite of appearances, be more alluring, she is likely to try, needlessly and pathetically, to compete. Now, suddenly, she begins to speak of her husband's immaturity—something she actually believes and can easily document. She nevertheless fails to see that this is characteristic of all men, for his childish needs are simply the needs men have, but which become conspicuous only when they are woefully unmet. Before long the feeling of utter rejection takes over, and she is finally able to salvage her pride as well as her sense of worth and desirability as a woman by an unreserved hatred for her estranged husband, and utter scorn for the woman whom she sincerely believes is responsible for her plight. In short, like her husband, she does everything that is inept, and believes everything except the homely truths which might, at one time, have saved things.

It is really appalling that things like this happen; but it is more appalling still that anyone should think they might be prevented by moralizing, distributing praise and blame, and by mouthing such idiotic slogans as "Thou shalt not commit adultery," as though that were the source of the trouble.

12

Vanity and Sex

Vanity, for which one reproaches the fair sex so frequently, so far as it is a fault in that sex, yet is only a beautiful fault.

—Immanuel Kant

The female counterpart to the male ego is vanity. In fact these two, egoism and vanity, have much in common, both being expressions of self-love; but there are differences in their expression, which justifies distinguishing them from each other.

It is not, for example, as characteristic of women as it is of men to take great pride and gratification in their sexual prowess, though they are deeply concerned with something quite similar, namely, their attractiveness, which originally means their attractiveness to men. This is not to say what would now everywhere be recognized as absurd, namely, that women do not derive sensuous pleasure from sex, just as men do. Nor is it to suggest that women consciously go about trying to lure men. The expressions of vanity are far more subtle. Women apparently derive even more sensuous pleasure from sex than men, but just as physical stimulation is not the primary concern to a man, in comparison with his need to be pleased with himself, neither is it the primary concern of a woman. Her deeper, largely unconscious concern is her ability to rouse men to ardor, partly through sexual allure, which is intimately connected with beauty, and partly through feminine blandishment. In short, a woman needs to be desirable in the most literal sense.

Thus, few women become overly concerned with their capacity to make love with great frequency, or with many men, or to sustain such a performance for any considerable length of time, all of which capacities are apt to be a source of great pride in a man. Although talk of this nature among men is common and expected, any woman who spoke in such terms would seem quite strange to other women. Again, no woman is concerned with the sheer size of her sexual organs;

125

no thought whatever is given to this; and she is not likely to have the least idea or interest about how she compares with others in this respect. Yet, a man's concern about his sexual organ is genuine, and it can even become an obsession in case he has misgivings on this matter. In a locker room men, without giving it much thought, are apt to make instant and furtive comparisons, which is an expression of the male ego that women learn about with amusement and almost with disbelief. The aspect of a woman's sexuality that compares with a man's profound concern for an erection of impressive size and duration is probably her capacity for multiple orgasms, which is quite difficult for most men, especially as they grow older. Here, certainly, is where female egoism would express itself, if it were comparable to a man's. Yet women attach little significance to this, are almost never known to boast of the sheer numbers of successive orgasms they achieve, and are not utterly distraught if none is achieved at all, even over a long period of time. They may indeed believe, and quite rightly, that they are thus deprived of something intensely pleasurable, but they do not feel particularly lessened as women, nor is any heavy cloud cast over their very existence.

What a woman needs most is appreciation of herself, the showing of an interest in her special talents and virtues, particularly on the part of a man. The most obvious expression of sexual allurement is, of course, physical beauty; and this is an aspect of a woman's self-image about which she is likely to be especially sensitive, even though she might be quite lacking in it. This is not to say that a woman preens herself and bestows such fastidious attention upon herself and her dress with even the remotest idea of the seduction of men, any more than a man's preoccupation with his sexual prowess means that he deliberately seeks self-glorification. Nevertheless the connection is too obvious to question. A woman, if there is a full-size mirror about the house, will scarcely walk past it without quickly turning herself this way and that, in close scrutiny, to note once more the graceful lines, even though she may already have done this less than an hour before. Loveliness that is evident to the eye is of immense importance, and is augmented in every possible way: through an endless variety of cosmetic preparations; clothing of every shape, color, and pattern that the imagination can devise; experimentation with hair styles; and so on without end. A woman can form an almost lifelong attachment to a hairdresser, and become distraught if circumstances compel her to find a new one. A fashion designer with taste and imagination wins the adoration of the women of two or three continents. The closest counterpart to this on the male side is a magazine editor who includes in his pages artful pictures and centerfolds of women that fuel the fantasies of men by giving them, if not real embodiments of their dreams, then at least the pictures of them. Editors who have, under misguided conceptions of female sexuality, tried to make a similar appeal to women with pictures of nude men have had little success. Soldiers and sailors never tire of sexual fantasy, constantly stimulating it by their talk, their jokes, and the pictures and books that pass from hand to hand; but their female counterparts in the armed services spend no time at all at anything like this. Their concern is instead with their looks.

Nor, of course, do women stop at visible appearance. The nose, too, must be considered, and therefore an indescribable array of scents is made available to them, and eagerly and dearly purchased. Even the auditory impression they make must be right. Thus a man may have a voice that is unique to himself, perhaps harsh and rasping, or it may be excessively deep and heavy, or so high in pitch as to be mistaken for that of a woman. None of this matters much, nor is it considered a fault, with the occasional exception of the male voice that is indistinguishable from that of a woman. A woman, on the other hand, whose voice is rasping or harsh, or that resembles a man's, or that is booming or coarse, or that is shrill, is thought to be embarrassingly handicapped. And this, for no other reason than that it falls short of the loveliness that a woman craves, however beautiful she may appear to the eye. Obesity in a man, though unattractive, is not considered nearly so bad as it is in a woman; such that, for example, it is seldom a reason for rejecting a man's application for employment, or even high position, though it is frequently sufficient for rejection of a woman. It simply violates the unspoken conviction people have that it is part of the role of a woman to be lovely, which is to say, alluring. The feminine obsession with looks, with what is most aptly called *attractiveness,* carries well beyond a concern for her own; she must know how others look as well, and how she compares with them. Thus a woman will leave a social gathering with a fairly clear idea of what every other woman there was wearing and with what taste she had prepared herself, while her husband is unlikely to have formed the least impression of these matters, except in the case of such female guests as aroused sexual fantasy by their attire. These he will have noticed as he stepped into the room. And while the locker room is for a man the place for furtive comparison and speculation concerning another's sexual prowess, a restaurant or lobby has the corresponding function for a woman. A woman can, indeed, spend an hour or more without boredom in a busy lobby making rapid assessment of every female person who comes by, all of whom are strangers to her, inferring at a glance the degree to which others have fulfilled their, and her, need to be lovely, that is, in the last analysis, to lure and attract, even though in doing so she is unlikely to have any such interest consciously in her mind at all. Again, her eyes are drawn, as if by a magnet, to shop windows, where ornamentation in the form of clothing and jewelry is displayed, and she revels in moving from shop to shop, not considering at all that hours spent at this are an incursion into her time. A man, on the other hand, is usually content to look more or less like other men or, at any rate, to look about the same from one day to the next, which to most women would seem unbearably pallid and monotonous.

*   *   *

What is especially significant in this connection is the attitude everywhere displayed concerning age. Age significantly beyond maturity is quite generally thought of as a kind of natural misfortune for women, while the attitude is significantly different towards older men. It is usually assumed that this is but a reflection of culturally inherited prejudice, deserving to be corrected as soon as possible, but it is doubtful whether this is the whole truth. The difference in attitude is probably due in part to the fact that a woman is usually past child bearing when she is fifty, whereas a man can normally sire children long beyond that age. In any case, a woman beyond the age of sixty is usually thought of as being, in an unflattering sense, old; and while she may be loved and esteemed for her inner strength, character, and achievements, she is rarely thought of as beautiful except in some perhaps admirably extended sense. On the other hand, a man in his sixties, whose hair is gray if not almost gone altogether, can very easily be thought of, not as old, but as "distinguished looking"—an appellation that is rarely applied to a woman of comparable years. And while a man of thirty might feel fairly uncomfortable in the company of a woman of fifty or sixty, and acutely so if he were thought to be romantically and intimately involved with her, a woman of thirty is usually in no similar discomfort if found to be involved with a man twice her age. If he is in fact distinguished, and appears to be, then his age, which is sometimes inseparable from that enviable quality, can appear as a positive asset. Youth in men, moreover, conveys to the mind the image of excessive vigor, egoism, and a lack of sensitivity to feminine needs, whereas age in a man is likely to suggest precisely the tenderness, gentleness, and concern that women find overwhelmingly touching. To some extent that impression is correct, for older men are quite conscious that they lack some of the enviable power of their youth, and are likely to seek to ingratiate themselves in ways that are, in fact, vastly more effective, even devastatingly so.

*   *   *

All this is quite obvious, and the description of it could occupy many more pages, but we have come now to the point of considering its significance with respect to passionate love between men and women. First, let it be noted that it would be a gross mistake and an oversimplification to suggest that superficial expressions of vanity such as we have described are the sum total of a woman's concern. They surely are not, except perhaps in the case of a woman of extreme shallowness. At the same time it is surely true that a woman is not likely to care deeply and lastingly for any man who totally ignores these qualities, any more than a man can truly adore a woman who is oblivious to his concern for his own sexual adequacy. There is much more to a woman, and to a man, than these things; and yet it must be stressed that there *are* these things. They do not disappear merely upon being described, and even correctly described, as silly or childish or, as is now fashionable, nothing but the effect of cultural conditioning.

In her relationship with a man, a woman's deep concern is not with being roused by him to great pleasures, whether sexual or of some other kind, nor with being showered with the world's goods. These things, into which men sometimes pour much misguided energy, do nothing to enhance her image of herself. Gifts stir the greed that she shares with men, but do little for the kind of vanity that is more characteristic of women. What a woman craves is what she herself is likely to describe as an interest in herself as a person. She does, after all, spend much of her energy and means trying to enhance her appearance. Somehow what she is trying to do has got to meet with some positive response for her to feel a sense of fulfillment.

Thus a woman is "put down," not by aspersions on her strength, for example, in which she takes no pride, but on her attractiveness, about which she is likely to be sensitive even though she may have little in which to rejoice. Though she may be quite aware that her eyes are too small or her teeth slightly misshapen, she will interpret as a stab any deliberate reminders of these—things which, incidentally, go quite unnoticed in a man, even by himself. A woman who is quite unattractive delights in whatever appreciation can be bestowed upon the qualities she does possess, compensating for the rest with other virtues and allurements, such as tasteful clothing and jewelry, for which she inwardly craves notice.

But of course appearance, though it is the most conspicuous and incontestable expression of feminine vanity, is also only the surface of it, and there is hardly a woman of any sensitivity who does not positively ask, from those whose affection she seeks, for an appreciation of herself. If, for example, she is talented as a writer, then this must be noticed, even though she may have no aspiration as an author. It is a talent that is nevertheless *hers,* and her vanity craves notice of it. Or similarly, if she has a melodious voice, or a painter's skill, or any talent whatever that is in some way uniquely her own, then she will never fail to respond warmly, at least inwardly, to whomever appreciates it; and that person, in turn, will appear in her own eyes as someone of sensitivity and taste, someone capable of appreciating, as she does, things that have genuine worth—to wit, his own talents and creations.

So important is this to a woman that she will sometimes appear to belittle her own physical beauty, which may be considerable, in her desperation to be seen beyond this surface. She wants, as she might express it, to be appreciated for herself or, whimsically, for her beautiful soul, expressions for which a literal reading can give no clear meaning but which are perfectly understandable to anyone with the least inkling of feminine vanity. A woman will sometimes sigh audibly, and be overcome with visible rapture, merely upon hearing, possibly for the first time in her life, an admiring comment on, say, the shape of her mouth; but far beyond this is her inward and outward response to the suggestion that someone is aware of her inner beauty as well. No woman can dislike any man who sees her that way, and who sincerely conveys this—indeed, this is a vast understatement. Her impulse will be to glory in his affection, whatever may be wanting in his own personal qualities, his intelligence, strength, resourcefulness, or whatever. He, at least, "understands" *her,* which is something precious and, alas! quite rare.

*   *   *

Marriage offers the possibility of the most lasting happiness a person can find, and is also probably the commonest cause of deep and lasting unhappiness. Most marriages fall somewhere between these extremes, however, in what can be called the humdrum. There are many married people who spend their lives together, raise their children, enjoy, more or less, the same things, eventually rejoice in their grandchildren, and so on, but who have long since ceased to be lovers in the full sense of the word. And there are others who, while remaining legally married for life, and even sharing the same roof, have long since lost all affection for each other. Their marriage, to the extent that it can be called such, is held together only by the most banal considerations—economic security, for example, or medical insurance coverage. Thus many long-married people would find something resembling their own situation in the following account.

> I was nearly thirty when I got married and my husband was twenty years older. It was the first marriage for both of us. I knew that we were different. I'd been to college, and he had gone only to eighth grade, but I assumed he would change. He did, but only in the sense that our differences became even greater. He tends to look at the dark side of everything, and always to expect the worst, and that got worse. A hint of bad weather is for him a portent of a storm. News of a friend's illness, however minor, is seen as a death knell. He pretty much keeps to himself, and communication between us, which was never good, has become almost nonexistent. He doesn't know what I am thinking and feeling from one day to another, and is not interested in knowing. I write short stories and poems, but he has never asked to read any of them. I just do this for myself, as a way of sort of talking to myself. I have never tried to publish them.
>
> We have two children, now grown up and gone, and while we were raising them the marriage was all right. We shared that interest, and both of us took it seriously. But there were tensions, even in child rearing. He tended to put himself between me and the children. If I disciplined one of them, by sending her to her room or something like that, he would sympathize with the child instead of supporting me. When one of them took the car without our permission or knowledge, he minimized it as not mattering much, since there had been no accident. We just didn't see things the same way.
>
> We haven't slept together for years. Sex was never good, and one could hardly call it lovemaking, from my point of view. The worst was one night years ago when I had fallen asleep on the sofa and he came in and forced himself on me. I felt raped, and indeed, I had been raped. That is when I moved to another bedroom and I have not been in his bed since then.
>
> I became involved in an affair about six years ago, with a man whose wife was as controlling as my husband was indifferent. It lasted about three years, until he moved with his wife to another state. We even spoke at times of marriage, but it was not feasible. My husband would never have let me go and, among other things, my lover would lose his medical insurance coverage if he got a divorce.
>
> During those three years we made love whenever we could, and it was wonderful, as it had never been with my husband, but that was not what kept

the affair going. We were held together by our mutual misery. I could tell him about mine, and he told me about his. We still correspond, secretly, but never see each other anymore.

After he moved away, I developed a serious problem with alcohol. It came to be, for me, like a warm hug, and I needed it very bad. I would drink, always by myself, and write my stories and poems, just for myself. Finally I got arrested one night for driving while drunk. I had reached rock bottom, almost lost my job, and what little else I had in life. But it cured me of drinking, and I haven't had one now for over a year.

My marriage means nothing to me. Going home to my husband is almost like going home to an empty house. To those who know us, I'm sure we seem more or less like any typical married couple. I do the cooking, he loves his gardening, we share meals, and so on. But there is nothing between us. We'll never get divorced, though. Even though our children are grown up, we would not want them to witness that, and besides, the world does not have anything better to offer either of us.

*   *   *

In the light of all this, one can appreciate the considerably different role that sex is apt to have in the attitudes and feelings of lovers. Indeed it is not a great exaggeration to say of two lovers that, while they seem to be engaged in essentially the same thing, namely, lovemaking, they really see themselves as involved in something that is quite different from what the other intends, all quite unbeknown to each other. Thus the male partner envisages himself as making a stunning impression of animal power. As we noted before, he is essentially trying to confirm an ideal image that he has of himself. His partner, on the other hand, is in a general way seeking the same thing, but the image she has of herself is quite different. The notions of strength, power, and vigor are not at the forefront for her. Instead, the notions of desirability and seductiveness are. Thus here, as everywhere, she wants to be noticed, appreciated; ideally, she would like no aspect of her womanness taken for granted, and nothing about her can be of such slight significance as to be worth no comment at all.

The clearest indication of the truth of this is the relatively minor importance women attach to the sexual vigor of their partners. The discovery of this usually shocks men, for a man imagines that a woman is carried away by his sexual prowess just as he is himself, and even that this is her chief interest in lovemaking, namely, to determine how good he is at it. Men are sometimes surprised to find that their partners seem to have no particular inclination to look at them when they are undressed, even the first time. A man's physical and sexual prowess, and the stunning impression he might imagine he makes on his lover when completely disrobed, for example, make virtually no impression at all upon her, provided he is not in some obvious way grossly deficient. She has almost none of his tendency to scrutinize and assess. In fact, her love is likely to be unaffected even by sexual impotence on his part, provided she regards it as more or less temporary and, above all, something which she can enable him to overcome. Sometimes even that kind of optimism is not needed.

Consider, for example, this story from one of my former students:

> Dan and I left college when we were both juniors. He was bored with it, and I had to get away and prove to myself and, I suppose, to my parents, that I could do things on my own and didn't have to be just like everyone else. We went to California and lived in Sausalito, more or less like a commune with another couple, and eventually got married there. At first I thought that Dan and the simple life were all I wanted, but I became dissatisfied. We made our living washing dishes and that sort of thing, but Dan's parents also sent us money, which greatly incensed my own parents, who had cut me off completely because of what they called my "lifestyle."
>
> I began to get involved in love affairs. Not many, and I didn't get much out of them, certainly not what I wanted, whatever that was. Some of them were pretty strange. For instance, one summer I went to live in Minneapolis for several weeks with a couple I'd known for a long time. They were married, and I fell in love with both of them, and I think they did with me. I mean, we would all three sleep together and everyone make love with everyone. That finally ended, but we're still friends.
>
> The only time, though, in all those three years when I was really in love was with a man in California who couldn't do anything. He had even been declared incompetent, for health reasons, to ever be able to make his own living, so he was going to be on welfare for the rest of his life. I don't know what was the matter with him; I suspect it was something psychological. He could hardly make love at all, in the physical sense. But I don't think I'll ever be in love with anyone the way I was with him. He was tender, and he made me feel like a woman, and all I wanted to do was be with him, every minute I could.
>
> I'm still married to Dan, legally, but I haven't even seen him for nearly a year, and I doubt that we'll ever go back together.

*   *   *

It is in the light of observations like these that we can appreciate the vast ineptitude of many lovers, both men and women, frequently even the cases of those who have been lovers for half of their lifetimes. We can also see at least part of the power of sex to destroy, not only marriages and families, but also lives and reputations, as well as its power to bless lovers with what are beyond a doubt the sweetest and most intense joys that human beings are capable of. The happiness that sometimes begins and culminates here far exceeds any other that is possible, and so, too, does the misery.

People sometimes suppose that a lack of sexual fulfillment is a medical or psychological "problem," as indeed it sometimes but quite rarely is. Far more often, the boredom of married lovers—and they have to be married to be so bored, for otherwise they would soon cease to be lovers—results from their being on two different tracks. They then complain of an inability to communicate with each other, and of feeling uncared for. We have already considered female ineptitude in this area. It can be described tersely as arising from the mistaken notion that her lover is in some literal sense bestowing affection on her, when in fact he is always at least in part, and sometimes almost exclusively, seeking self-glorification. This is why he is then so totally vulnerable, and can be deflated and feel inwardly emasculated by even a word or the subtlest "put-down" that suggests that he is not being seen in that light. Male ineptitude can be just as complete, however, and in the light of a certain male blindness is probably even more common. A woman can be rendered shortsighted by her vanity, but a man can be completely blinded by his ego, which virtually overwhelms any genuine awareness of his partner.

Consider, for example, a husband who, we can suppose, cuts a great figure in the world. He is big, athletic, strong, graceful, good at tennis and sailing, witty in conversation, and talented at making large quantities of money. No man could fail to look at him without envy, and no woman, we can suppose, without covetousness. Fine; but now let us suppose that he has not in weeks offered more than perfunctory comments on his wife's activities, noting only such things as that the coffee is good, that the garden she cultivates is doing well, and that sort of thing. The concentration she bestows on her dress, the combinations she considers each day, are wasted on him. Worst of all, he has not in months appeared to notice any personal qualities—her graceful figure or lovely ankles, the quality of her eyes or smile, none of these things. Having conceded all these qualities long ago, he sees no need endlessly to repeat what has already been said, there having been no significant change. That she is, let us suppose, a writer of some skill, whose stories and observations occasionally appear in newspapers, receives only incidental comment which must, moreover, usually be prompted by her in order to be forthcoming at all. He seems wrapped up in himself. He is glad to declare his love for her, but he never says why, and always appears to be talking more about himself than about her. She thus gets the feeling that she is loved, not (as she puts it) for herself, but as a thing, an ornament, an attractive and interesting object to exhibit to the world, as though she were but another possession. In bed he is magnificent—that is, in his own eyes. Every dream any man could have of sexual vigor and strength is in his case abundantly realized. He is a veritable stallion, and is overwhelmed with the self-glorification of a great plumed bird, spectacularly spreading himself. They, at least, have no sexual "problems," so far as he is concerned, and she, though strangely unsure of herself, concurs.

What could possibly be wrong with this? Nothing, she reassures herself, and she throws herself more than ever into those roles in which she can imagine herself envied, into the circles of the rich and locally influential, with the tried and true means of extracting attention: by expensive dress, house, cars, sailboat, whatever.

Such a marriage is profoundly vulnerable to stress, and unwinds predictably when this same wife encounters a man who, by all her standards, she should consider of little account. We can suppose that he has little aspiration beyond improving on his guitar, he is perhaps younger than she, and that he lives in an atmosphere of slovenliness such that his own needs can hardly be met from one week to another. Yet, instead of talking and glorifying himself, he listens to her and hears what she says, sometimes what she tiresomely pours out. He reads what she writes as avidly as she does, and does not need to be asked to say that it is frightfully good, that it expresses something of her own personality, wit, and talent for imagery—things she has never heard at home. And best of all, he means it! He thinks of himself as no great lover, and in this he is certainly right, yet there is no aspect of her that he does not seem to adore, almost as though every cell and hair of her body were incomparably precious; and in this, too, he is sincere. If his sexual prowess is not impressive, at least *he* is expressive, leisurely, attentive, and, above all, entirely aware of his partner.

A husband like the one we described earlier, having learned of such an affair, would probably call his wife something he had never called her before, namely, cheap. It is quite likely, too, that she would in the end forsake her lover and return to him abjectly with many reminders to herself of her blessings. In truth she would not be returning to her husband, but to the appearance of her husband. She would be returning to her security, which is worth a great deal, even if purchased at such a high personal cost. Genuine love and affection, even when rather feebly bestowed, are very precious. It is doubtful whether anything in the world is so completely good. But when it must compete with the need for simple security it has little chance. A wife who is the victim of emotional neglect will console herself with the thought that life is not always "romantic," that one must sometimes settle with it on its own more or less generous terms. Many marriages survive on these terms—on the terms of physical security, orchestrated and routine affection, community status, property, a deep interest in one's children and their aspirations, and a fundamental lovelessness. There are many ways of describing this, but none is better than the single word *pathetic*.

* * *

What has just been described is in one degree or another so common as to seem almost normal, though the rebellion of women against that image of normality, which has been gathering force for some years, is certain to change it. And of course the image does not at all fit the increasingly common type of marriage relationship where no formal or legal marriage exists. These are easily dissolved long before the point of monotonous lovelessness is reached, simply by one of the partners walking away, answerable to no one.

Still, the expansive, garrulous, self-centered husband is so familiar as to be virtually a prototype, and the soft-spoken, unfulfilled wife who has somehow come to terms with the world is hardly less so. Marriage, even stable marriage, often has many things to hold it together even when there is abysmal failure on both sides of the kind we have described. Men, for example, often compensate for their lack of ego fulfillment by hurling themselves into their work, and many a stunning career has been partly fueled in this way. Such men are likely to look with disdain on those free souls who lack that incentive, who seem, in their eyes, to have no ambition. And such a husband is totally flabbergasted, though seldom awakened, if one day he discovers that his ever dutiful and faithful wife has fallen totally in love with such a worthless fool. Wives also find compensations, often of a kind which tends to stabilize a marriage—for example, an involvement in their children's lives and aspirations, and sometimes in such things as home, garden, and pets. Such a wife is then likely to feel betrayed and cheated upon discovering that her husband has become infatuated with some shallow and seemingly witless woman. "Cheating" is, indeed, a word she is likely to apply. Surveying the destruction, it is no wonder that one or the other, depending upon which has been "unfaithful," wants to declare "Thou shalt not," when what is really needed is a heightened awareness, on the part of each, of what the other is and needs. Such awareness or sensitivity is not, however, something that the ordinary conditions of life call upon anyone to develop to any great degree. People by nature look first to their own needs, and the normally competitive conditions of life certainly do nothing to moderate this self-interest. Lovers, however, though they are still selfish, are not competitive, and the lessons learned in the hard world do not serve very well to nourish the kind of passionate love that can be lasting.

13

The Cultivation of Love Affairs

Disguise our bondage as we will
'Tis woman, woman, rules us still.

—Thomas Moore

There is a certain type of man, and likewise a certain type of woman, who is prone to love affairs. That banal observation would not be worth recording were it not for the fact that neither fits the popular stereotypes of such persons. Of course not all lovers fit the descriptions I have in mind, and there are very significant differences between men and women in this respect; but assuredly most fit them.

Men of this type are sometimes unflatteringly called "womanizers," a word almost never used by such men themselves, though sometimes by their wives or lovers. It is misleading, for it suggests an excessive, exploitative, and indiscriminate interest in sexual gratification, when in reality that is rarely the chief interest, and almost never an exclusive one. In fact, most men who become involved in numerous love affairs are already married and, whether as a consequence of this or not, they are apt to find sexual relations with other women, and especially with young and unmarried women, quite difficult, even sometimes mildly frightening, or impossible. In this area a man's fear of sexual impotence, however slight, produces that very result with merciless effectiveness. It is in fact very common for a love affair involving a married man, whether young or old, to limp along pathetically at first, so far as sex is concerned, however filled with passionate devotion it may otherwise be. Usually, with the passage of time—a few weeks perhaps, sometimes several months—a man's fear, impotence, and ineptitude are overcome, and the two lovers might with some justification think of themselves as the champion lovers of the world. This is what almost invariably happens after so halting a start. But until it does there is likely to be long and deep depression on the part of the man—but not, interestingly, on the part of the woman, except to whatever extent she might consider herself somehow responsible for such failure; namely, by being unattractive. Sometimes a man, confronting this sickening deflation to his pride on the occasion of his very first love affair, will rush back to the familiar bed of his wife, filled with passion and undoubted sexual power, leaving his lover totally dejected and cast aside. It is, however unwitting, a cruel thing for him to do, and more than one man has thus had driven home to him the truth that Hell has, indeed, no fury like a woman scorned.

*   *   *

Nor does the kind of man who easily falls into a love affair, and often a staggering succession of them in the course of his life, fit the popular conception of male dynamism that is conveyed by the media of popular entertainment. It is rare indeed to see on the screen a love scene suggestive of sexual intercourse which is not absurd, except sometimes in the case of sophisticated foreign films. The picture of a swaggering male, youthful, strong, exuding vigor and sexual prowess, overwhelming a woman and winning her love by the sheer power of his masculinity, is the picture of a lover who has exceedingly few counterparts in the world. Occasionally, to be sure, some women will in their speech—at a social gathering, for example, when conversation runs to such matters—declare themselves to be overwhelmed by this type of man; but they seem to be expressing a conventional attitude that has been produced by acculturation more than any actual felt need. Women whom I have heard expressing themselves in such terms have, so far as I have been able to ascertain, usually had no significant affairs at all in their own lives.

Contrast the popular conception with this account, which is much closer to what is typical:

> I had never loved any man until I was nearly thirty. In high school I had sometimes gone to dances and things, because that's what everyone did, but I didn't enjoy them, and sometimes I just turned down invitations and stayed home. It is sort of funny, then, that the only man I have ever been completely in love with should have been a married man.
>
> We both work for the state, in the same office, and although his job is much bigger than mine, I don't actually work for him. The way it started is that we bumped into each other on the stairs one day, and got to talking, about ordinary things. After awhile I found that I would sort of watch when he came and went, and sometimes arrange to run into him on the stairs. After that had gone on for weeks, nothing more than talking, usually on the stairs, one day he kissed me there, just in an ordinary friendly way. I don't think it meant much, certainly not to him. Pretty soon we were going for a walk after work about once a week, then eventually, weeks later, we would walk together after work several times a

week. We just talked. There was no romance, but we got to know each other better and better as weeks went by this way. Sometimes we would go over to my house, and even though there was no one else there, and we sometimes were in my room alone, we never did anything, except just talk. Then finally, after several months of this, I decided I wanted him to make love to me and I told him so, and took him to my room just for this. But I was scared to death. He had never seen me with my clothes off, and I was afraid when he did he wouldn't like me. I was awfully nervous. He wasn't at all. He knew how nervous I was, and told me we still didn't have to if I wanted to change my mind, and it would be all right if we both just got dressed and forgot about it. But I didn't want to change my mind and I didn't. That's how our love affair got started. It took months. But it lasted over two years, and was very strong. I don't know whether anything like that will ever happen to me again as long as I live.

This account does not give us the picture of a loose, promiscuous woman, nor of an aggressive, dominating male. Nor do the men that women actually become passionately involved with very often fit that stereotype, however fervently it may be coveted by men. The man in most love affairs involving married people is often significantly older than the woman, for example, sometimes twice or even three times her age. Young men may look in astonishment at this fact, but they simply have not reflected on the almost universal basis for love affairs. Instead they naively assume that a woman's love rests upon the perception of masculine beauty and power. In short, they project onto women their own feelings about men.

Male inconsiderateness has the same effect upon the young as upon the more mature. The following description of a student marriage relationship is essentially the same as many descriptions of marriage itself, though, luckily, these relationships are easier to terminate:

I had a three-month affair with Alan, which began by our talking to each other from our dorm rooms. But even though I thought I was in love with him for a while, and I felt bad when it ended, it never really got going. We made love whenever we were together, but we never communicated. He never said anything when we were making love, never asked any questions, and we always did exactly the same thing. Whenever we got together it was just assumed that we would make love, his way. I never came once in those three months. I finally thought I might just be missing something, so I tried sleeping around, started buying *Playgirl* magazine, and things like that. But when I finally found Harry I realized that what had been wrong was my choice of partners, not me, because he was just the opposite of them.

The contrast between the popular notion of love affairs as nothing but exciting diversions and what is closer to fact is also nicely illustrated in the following account in which a woman compares her feelings about two very different men:

For a while I was going back and forth between two lovers. Brad is a student like me, twenty-one, which is four years younger than I am. Gil is a professor, forty-one, which is sixteen years older than me, and he's married and has four children. In fact, one of his sons is Brad's age. But there has never been any question about who I'm in love with, and that's Gil. I would never be with Brad if I could be with Gil. The fact that he is married has never mattered to me. Actually, there's a certain kick to loving a married man. But I've always hoped that someday he would get a divorce and marry me, which is what he says he intends to do when all his children are old enough.

Brad is like most men, more interested in impressing himself than doing much for me. Sometimes he would get up in the morning and complain that our lovemaking had messed up his beautiful hair. I can't imagine Gil being concerned about such things. And Gil always smelled nice. Brad never cared whether he did or not. Gil was nice to my cats, and Brad hardly knew they were there. He didn't even know they were females. If Brad did something nice, like fixing my car, he liked to have me think that it was because he was a man that he could do things like that, but when Gil did something nice, you had the feeling he was just being nice. They are very different people.

I was attracted to Gil from the minute I saw him. All the girls were. But I never got to know him until one day when I dropped a table on my toe. It was awfully painful, and I went into Gil's office, and he held me in his arms. I don't think he even knew my name at that point. Maybe Brad would have done the same, but it would have been different. After that I started inviting Gil to go for walks and things, and we got to know each other.

What really attracted me to Gil was his sadness. He seemed so miserable, and I wanted to bring some happiness into his life. I don't think his wife had loved him for years. He eventually left her and lived with me, for over a year, although he was still married to her. He never let me meet his children, and that made me feel bad, but we didn't have any other problems. For a long time the sex was a failure, but that didn't matter much to me. He said it was a medical problem, and that he hadn't made love to his wife for years, and he was having it treated; but I think it was more an emotional one. I wanted to help him with that, too, and I was sure I would be able to, and that in fact turned out to be true. He became a marvelous lover.

I don't know what our future is. I still have never met his children, which makes me feel as if he's ashamed of me or something. And of course he is still married. But I don't think I'll ever love anyone so much.

That this young and beautiful person should make the kind of choice she did should not be surprising, except perhaps to people whose ideas in these matters have been too much influenced by popular films—usually directed, of course, by men, who may be more gifted at filmmaking than lovemaking.

And finally, the tendency to stereotype those who become involved in affairs as "weak-willed" men or "loose" and irresponsible women is not the product of observation, but rather of the wishes of conventional persons who would prefer to categorize people than to think about them. Partners in love affairs or marriages are, of course, *supposed* to be exclusive. Accordingly, departures from this *must* be symptomatic of some character fault. Alas, such is the extent to which some people ever think on matters of this kind.

* * *

A man does not win a woman's heart by how he manages to appear to her—as a man of great power, stature, greatness, brilliance, or preeminence of any kind—but by how he makes her appear to *herself.* This explains the sometimes incongruous couplings we often see—a woman of great beauty, status, and intelligence totally in love with the simplest of men, someone having none of the qualities of strength, good looks, and power that are associated with masculine appeal. A rather good observer of human nature expressed this point by noting that "a woman doesn't care if you're the president of the United States—witness Jackie. Or the Prince of Wales—look at Di. And look at Fergie, whose marriage to Prince Andrew was pretty brief."

Examples like this do drive home the point. Jacqueline Kennedy was the wife of a youthful president of boundless charm, the envy of the world, a man whose power reached around the globe, and yet there is every indication that the marriage was unfulfilling to her, and her feelings for him were located somewhere between emotional indifference and quiet hostility. He was absorbed in his own boundless ego, while she was left to feel like a decoration, a role that, because of her own legendary beauty, she could fill very well. After the death of her second husband, Aristotle Onassis, she spent the last years of her relatively short life with a man virtually unknown to the world, a balding and portly gentleman quite devoid of those masculine virtues associated with male charm. Although her relationship with him was decorously kept from the public view, she seems, by the accounts of those who knew them, to have been quite in love with him. The explanation given by one of these is revealing: "He made her feel like the most important person in the world. Jack was all caught up in politics, and Onassis only wanted a trophy." A woman's sense of self-worth is not much enhanced by the adoration bestowed on someone else, even if that other person is her own husband. On the contrary, it makes her feel even more like a mere ornament to him.

In this example we see, I think, the general picture of many failed marriages, and the example is made all the better by the fact that it would be hard to imagine a man who, by popular standards, could be considered a more enviable "catch" as a husband—youthful, charming, *and,* the president of the United States. By contrast, we recall a relatively obscure man, whose name is no longer remembered, who, until his young life was extinguished in a car accident, managed for over a decade to charm one after another of some of the most beautiful women in the world. So great was his success in this that he gained international fame as a charmer of women. Yet there was nothing about him, in the way of good looks, wealth, or stature that anyone would think of as attracting a woman's attention. When asked by a newsman what was the secret of his notorious success in these pursuits he responded, simply: "Women want you to, uh . . . be nice to them."

*   *   *

Men who become involved in serious and lasting love affairs almost always have one thing in common, particularly if they are married. Their chief characteristic is that they are quite genuinely caring persons. When women describe their utter devotion to such men, the very same words constantly recur—such words as *observant, considerate, attentive, interested in me,* and, most of all, *caring.* Often they will declare, with fervor, and in the face of what would seem to be evidence to the contrary, that "he really loved me." This seldom means that they were showered with gifts. Contrary again to a common notion, gifts or other material considerations are apt to have no place at all in such a relationship and, when they do, they are apt to be from the woman to the man rather than the reverse. No woman is flattered by the thought of being a "kept woman," and the thought of receiving anything *in return* for pleasure is suggestive of the most demeaning status a woman can have.

There are exceptions to this, but usually women desire to be cherished, not overwhelmed, and certainly not bought. This means that things concerning themselves in which they take deep pride and, even more, things in which they take little pride, are to be noticed and appreciated. I believe that this kind of appreciation on the part of a certain kind of man is usually not insincere. There are men who genuinely love women, who love to be in their company, and who, without effort, make their companions feel very good about themselves. The power of this is quite overwhelming, for it touches upon a need that almost all women have to some degree, and which some of them feel quite desperately.

*   *   *

The considerateness of which I have spoken melts not only the hearts of women who have long been married to self-centered and thoughtless husbands, but also the hearts of the young and inexperienced, and therefore seems to have more to do with certain differences between males and females than mere differences of age. This is illustrated by a sophisticated college girl of eighteen, the only child of a very rich man, who is in love with an older and impoverished son of a working man:

> I'll never love anyone the way I do Spike, even though my parents abominate him and have threatened all sorts of things if I don't break off from him. When he is staying over with me I go back to my room to find that he has done all my laundry or washed the dishes and things like that, though I never asked him to, and he sometimes brings me flowers he can hardly afford. When we take showers he rubs my back for me, and when he wanted to make love the first time and I was too scared to, because I never had before, then he didn't even bring it up again for several months, but just waited until I wasn't scared anymore. When he learned that I had "mono" he dropped everything and hitchhiked all the way from Baltimore to come stay with me and take care of me.

Mixed with that description, however, was this revealing aside:

> Once when I had been separated from Spike for several weeks I learned that he'd made love with someone else, so I did, too, out of sheer fury; but for me it was awful.

A similar description of male tenderness is given by another coed:

> Dave was a clown. Some of the girls thought he was a buffoon, and would watch aghast at some of his antics; but I just watched him with immense pride, that he was the man I loved, and the only man I've ever really loved. No other man had ever treated me the way he did; the others just expected me always to want to do whatever they happened to want. But Dave would get up and take my puppy out in the middle of the night, if puppy needed to go out, without my even asking him. If I was sick, he would bring me dinner from his fraternity, even though this was against the fraternity rules. One night when I couldn't sleep he stayed up with me all night. We were together all the time, day and night, and sometimes I didn't get more than three hours sleep, and wasn't tired at all, though I had been used to sleeping ten or twelve hours sometimes.

One man offered the following description of himself, which is paradigmatic of an extreme form of the sensitive and caring lover, and illustrates, moreover, why the pejorative term *womanizer* is really not appropriate. This is the kind of person who is likely to puzzle casual observers, who find it difficult to reconcile his "way with women" with his visible attributes, for the source of this description certainly would not fit anyone's conception of Don Juan:

> I have always liked females, young or old, it doesn't matter. I don't mean that I am crazy about sex, because even though that is important, it has never been the main thing for me, and in fact it doesn't have anything to do with my feelings about some, maybe even most, of the female friends I have had. If I get on a bus or plane I find that I always sit next to a female passenger if I can, even when I have no intention of talking with her. I just prefer the company of females. For a long time I didn't even notice that this preference extends to everything, even the choice of whom I'll sit next to, but it certainly does. If I am playing games with a group of children, I find that it is almost always the little girls I throw the ball back and forth to, without even thinking about it, and it is these girls that I want to teach some new game, or whatever. In stores I find that I strike up conversations with the clerks if they are female, but I usually find little to say to male clerks. But I honestly don't think I flirt; certainly not with waitresses and people like this, the way other men do. I just like to be friendly with female people, and they almost always smile back and show that they like me, even before we have said much.
>
> I was always like this, and when I grew up it bothered me, because I knew I was different from most other men in this way. In fact I don't like being with men, the way other men do, and I'm terribly uncomfortable if I am expected to make the kind of talk they do. I can't stand to hear men make jokes about

women. With women I can talk about anything, and it is pleasant and relaxed. I finally decided not to let this bother me, because I couldn't see that it had ever done me or anyone else any harm. And when I saw the "gay rights" movement, and how these people were dead sure nothing was wrong with them, even if they were different, I decided that at least I would rather be the way I am, and in fact I am glad.

I have had a lot of love affairs, but I really have cared about every one. I don't think I was ever just interested in sex. I have never seen a prostitute. If I did, I would probably want to make friends with her. I just think of female people as angel-like beings. I think my religious training had something to do with it (I was a Catholic), but also I had very gentle parents, and that was the way my father treated women.

I have sometimes been in love with two or three women at once, and sometimes in bed with that many in one day. But I have never asked a woman to have sex with me. I do just the opposite. For example, as far back as I can remember, even back in high school, I have sometimes suggested to a friend, before I went home, that if she would like to get all ready for bed, I would tuck her in, with the promise that I would not try to have sex with her—a promise I have always kept. That tells her that my interest in her is not just sexual, which is true. Usually the next time, or maybe the time after that, I get in bed too, when she seems to be ready for that and wants me to. But even then, the first few times, I usually do not have sex with her; in fact, I usually make it clear that we will not, and I stick with that, too. That way everything is relaxed and comfortable, and no one has to be fearful or anxious. That way a woman feels that I am interested in her, and not just in getting something from her. In fact, I once had a fairly long friendship with a woman, sleeping with her often, and we never had sex. I would have liked to, but she had too many problems about it, so I never pressed it or made any issue of it.

It seems to me that most men are awfully stupid about women. They talk loud and brag and sometimes suggest sex as though it were sort of a game, a way to have fun. I have never in my life seen a woman respond to that. They usually just make an awful face. But then I get to talking with them—more than that, I listen to them—and they discover that I like them and I am interested in how they feel about everything, and it is really true; I am not putting that on. Almost every time, after a while of just ordinary friendship, I can, if I want to, sleep with them to my heart's content. Of course women like sex, but that is not really the way to put it. What they really love is to be loved, and I have always found that the easiest thing in the world to do.

Men like this can fail in numberless respects—by being physically quite unattractive, balding, no longer young, utterly unattainable by virtue of being already thoroughly married, and defective even in the most elementary qualities of reputable character. Such men still, astonishingly, sometimes totally overwhelm the hearts and feelings of women of beauty, youth, intelligence, and utter respectability. Psychologists may have explanations for this, perhaps very good ones, but it is too near the norm to be considered strange or aberrant. It is, on the male side, almost a standard ingredient of every deep and lasting love affair.

*   *   *

The type of woman who is prone to serious love affairs similarly fails to fit popular stereotypes. For instance, she is almost never blatantly sexy, as is so often imagined. The somewhat overpowering woman, of broad hips and large bosom, loud voice and unrestrained vocabulary, has no appeal whatever to men except perhaps in a barroom. She may be someone to play games with, someone to try to get into a bed with, but no one to fall in love with in a thousand years. Indeed, women who fall into love affairs are not, for the most part, even singularly alluring. They look and act like women everywhere, and could in no way be picked from a crowd.

These women are sometimes described, in the literature of popular psychology, as "needy." This would be unobjectionable if it were not for the implication that there are women, or men, who do *not* have deep needs of whatever kind are referred to. A better description of these women (and men) might be the term *unfulfilled*. They are dissatisfied with themselves, their lives, their backgrounds, their husbands or lovers, and sometimes with several of these things and more. Women who fall in love with men other than their own husbands or lovers, and often with the husbands of other women, are exceedingly likely to be those whose need for genuine affection—which includes an appreciation of their womanness and an attentiveness to their moods and feelings—has been left unfulfilled. In the case of older women, they are almost always taken for granted by their families, and especially their husbands, whom they may dutifully love, but for whom genuine warmth of feeling has been nearly extinguished. In the case of very young women—university students, for example—they are likely to be those who for some social or biological caprice were more or less friendless, or felt themselves to be so, when growing up. Such women may have been too tall, for example, and painfully conscious of it; possibly they were ashamed of being awkward, overweight, or poor. Some may have been excessively controlled by their parents, subjected to a severe upbringing, thus receiving more unwanted guidance and manipulation than genuine affection from their family members. And even when these painful things have all been finally left behind, the feelings and needs are still there, perhaps never to go away at all.

*   *   *

The following is the account of a woman quite clearly lacking in the kind of fulfillment I have referred to. Many elements of it were almost standard parts of the numerous stories I listened to:

> I got married when I was only sixteen and already pregnant. No one could have been less ready for it than either of us, but we wanted to get married, and didn't have much choice. That marriage lasted eight years, and I had four children. But I can't remember anything good about it, and in fact the last few years were pretty bad, sometimes even violent.

Stan, my husband, was boring. He didn't have a single serious interest, and in the eight years we were married, I once counted that he had worked at over thirty jobs. He never got anywhere, just moved from one job to another like it, usually in restaurants. At home he was either reading comics or watching TV. He was so unaware of what was going on in the world that he didn't even know what "Watergate" meant, after six months of the Watergate scandal. He worked all kinds of hours, would sometimes come home late with some of his friends and sit up with them, then sleep until two in the afternoon, and go back to work again.

Except for the children, that marriage was simply empty. Stan never gave me credit for anything, and if I ever had any idea that seemed to me a good one, he would usually put it down. For instance, I wanted to go back to college and get a degree in social work, and in fact I did eventually go back, after my divorce, and did very well at it. But Stan just laughed at the idea, and implied that I couldn't possibly have the brains to do anything like that. I knew I was smarter than he was. Once we worked for the same company and I advanced faster than he did.

I really knew nothing about sex, and neither did Stan. In all those eight years I never got anything out of it. I would just submit to it, and I actually thought that was all there was to it. I always just felt like a thing. Eventually I became the master of excuses. Avoiding sex became a game, and I got very good at it. I once managed to hold him off for over four months! I was always glad when Stan worked the second shift, because that meant it would be easy— he wouldn't even get home until long after I'd gone to sleep, and I wouldn't have to invent an excuse. I don't know why sex was so bad. For me it was just a bore. But Stan was no good, though he apparently thought he was. His idea was just to get in bed and screw, and that was it. He never thought of me, and I guess I never expected him to.

When I finally left him I expected to feel guilty, to feel I had failed or something, since I'd been told that one always does. But I never did. I sometimes wondered when all the guilt was going to begin. I guess I just had no feelings of guilt or anything else by then.

The above description of former husbands is so common that one is led to wonder how many husbands in unbroken marriages it would more or less fit. There is no way of knowing, but I believe that many marriages limp along unbroken to the very end, held together by things other than affection. The female partner in such an alliance is likely to fall in love with a man similar to the one about to be described. This man, not rare but at the same time rather unlike most men, fairly typifies the kind of man who is never without female companions:

I didn't have any love affairs until I met Ben. I wasn't looking for them, because I had already had all I wanted of men, and I certainly wasn't interested in sex. But I never knew there could be men like Ben.

The only way I can describe Ben is that he is a perfect human being. He is very big and strong, an enormous man, about six and a half feet, but a completely gentle person. He runs an automobile repair shop, which may not make him sound like much; but he's also about the only person in town who reads the

New York Times all the way through every day. He reads *everything,* until he figures he knows all he needs to about that subject, then he learns all he can about something else. And he's patient and thoughtful. He once dropped a small car part into a drum full of water, by mistake, and I watched him, fascinated, while he patiently fished around with his hand for about an hour to find it, whistling all the time. He could have just dumped the water out. But he said that it gave him a chance to think.

When I had his baby he was there all the time, and was very caring. I think that during most of those six years he would have done anything for me—except get divorced and marry me. But he was always perfectly honest about that too. He never led me on. And I would have done anything for him, too. I once lied for him, though he didn't ask me to, and still doesn't even know I did. You have to tell the public assistance office who the father of your child is, but I lied, just for Ben's sake.

What is so wonderful about him? Everything. He is always noticing me, paying attention to me; I can be talking about the weather, and he listens as if it were the most interesting thing he ever heard. Stan never noticed me, and sometimes didn't even seem to know my name—he would just refer to me as "she." Even when I'm not talking Ben is always watching me and noting everything. It is as if there is nothing he'd rather be doing than looking at me. I've had five children, starting at sixteen, and with my clothes off I look like an old woman, with all the stretch marks I just hate, and sometimes I just feel like a cow; but Ben makes me feel like the most beautiful woman in the world, like the centerfold of a *Playboy* magazine! Maybe this is why I would do anything for him, because I just want to please him.

Actually he flirts with every woman he sees, and I don't think he even knows it. I could even see my *mother* falling head over heels for him; it's just the way he acts around women, and he doesn't mean anything by it. He makes everyone feel good. My husband only made me feel like a nothing. I'm sure neither of them acted the way they did on purpose, but that is the way they make you feel, anyway.

It was from Ben that I finally learned that there is more to sex than just having somebody screw you—though it took months for me to learn this, even with him. I had never come with Stan, in all those years, and it must have been six months before I finally did with Ben. I just didn't even know anything about it. But he gradually taught me everything. The way to describe him is that he is caring. He is tuned in to me. He makes it his business to know just what I like, and he tries to please me. And he is always different; he always alters things just a little, so in all those six years it never seemed the same twice. For instance, one time he would light a candle, and we'd make love in the soft light. Another time he'd leave the door ajar just a little, to let a little light in. Or he would leave all the lights on. Or we would make love under the Christmas tree. He was always imaginative and inventive, and, what is most important of all, he makes you feel like the most desirable and beautiful person in the world—even me. I hate to look at myself in the mirror sometimes, but when Ben is there I forget all that.

The affair isn't what it used to be, but we seem to keep going back to each other. Sometimes he has been gone as long as two months without even telephoning me, and I've finally had to go look him up. He is a good father for our son, when he is there, but we never know when he is going to be there. One night I walked into a restaurant and there he was with a girl in her twenties. She didn't know who I was, but Ben offered a friendly wave as they went out. Seeing that kind of thing hurts, but then, he never did let me think he was ever going to marry me or anything, and we didn't have any agreements or understandings anymore.

He is a perfect person—intellectually, physically, every way. I never expect to find anyone else who is.

While the above account is typical—so much so that sometimes I was able to anticipate more or less what was coming next—it should not suggest that men and women are very much different in their need for fulfillment. Men are no less in need of appreciation than women, though it is of a somewhat different kind. There is, however, this difference: a man is in a much better position to do something about his needs, whether by finding personal fulfillment in business or public life, for instance, in case he has a talent for these, or in the initiation of love affairs, in case his talents lie there. A woman, however, even today, and in spite of the sexual revolution, must sometimes more or less wait to be noticed, and the wait can be uncertain and long.

14

The Language of the Eyes

Why does the lover hang with complete abandonment on the eyes of his chosen one, and is ready to make every sacrifice for her? Because it is his immortal part that longs after her; while it is only his mortal part that desires everything else.

—Arthur Schopenhauer

There is one fairly subtle characteristic of both men and women who are prone to love affairs. Since it is rarely noticed and, to my knowledge, it has never been specifically pointed out by anyone else, it should be well worth describing here.

Quite simply, the characteristic is that these people *look* into the faces of others, and into the faces of each other. This behavior on the part of a woman, when directed towards strangers, is sometimes regarded as flirtation, though in fact it is not really noticed much, because it is usually subtle and normally unconscious on her part. It is less often thought of that way when observed in men. In any case, it is probably the surest, and at the same time the least noticed, mark of true love, simply because it is unfeigned and seldom even conscious. For someone to look at you, to look into your face, with animation and interest, when you are speaking, for example, or even when you are not, and when there is really nothing to be looking *for*—this is one of the most utterly disarming and totally genuine signs of devotion that any person can display.

If you point your camera at two lovers, you are likely to find, when the snapshot comes back, that one of them is looking appreciatively into the face of the other, or indeed, sometimes both are; though normally people look in the direction of the camera when exhorted to pose for informal photography. This mannerism is not, of course, confined to partners of love affairs, but is sometimes—though alas! rarely—discovered in married persons, even occasionally those who have been married many years. It is, far more than words, gifts, kisses, or other learned behavior, the token of love *par excellence,* precisely because it is un-learned, usually unintentional, and even unconscious.

It is also quite overwhelming in its effects, which are often far out of pro-portion to a cause so seemingly trifling. This is especially noticeable when glances are exchanged between strangers. Consider, for example, this specimen of a fairly commonplace experience:

> The day I arrived to start my new job at the university, I walked into the depart-mental office and the secretary looked up at me as if overjoyed at the sight of this total stranger, before I had even said hello. We had lunch the next day, and before long were having lunch together every time I was on campus. She learned, the second time we had lunch, that I already had a wife. Maybe that's why it was never much of a love affair, but we're still good friends, and I think we like each other more than either of us wants to admit. She just doesn't want another woman's husband, and I don't want her telling me so.

Or this one:

> If you ask about the very beginning of that friendship, it was when we started out in line to board the plane. I was walking ahead of Joan, whom I'd never seen, and I held the door open so it wouldn't just go shut in her face. She looked at me in astonishment, as if I had done the nicest thing in the world, though I would have done the same no matter who was behind me; so would anyone else. I sat down next to her; she told me about the gay holiday she had just been hav-ing in Boston with her dentist husband; but forty minutes later, by the time we landed in Rochester, she had told me all about her love affairs and her problems at home. We got in her car, she took me to her house for lunch, then to my office, and we were good friends, the very first day.

Or finally this:

> I remember seeing a woman, over fifty years ago, from a taxicab. She was stand-ing there; the cab was stopped for a traffic light, and during that entire brief time we stared into each other's eyes. I would have gotten out if my mother had not been in the cab with me, because that lovely woman and I virtually fell in love in those couple of minutes. The way we gazed into each other's eyes said everything that needed to be said. I remember it vividly, after these several decades.

None of these accounts is of much interest, so far as their content is concerned, but a philosopher can scarcely fail to note that in each case a significant chain of events began, or might have begun, with nothing more than a look exchanged between two strangers. I suspect that most love affairs, perhaps nearly all of them, begin in no other way.

One of the persons I interviewed, still in her twenties and divorced, had known a staggering number of lovers. The accounts she gave, over the course of our several talks, were mind-boggling, and somehow scarcely seemed to fit the demure manner and beauty of the person before me. I realized that she was uncommonly attractive and subtly flirtatious, but at first I did not quite see how I had come to this conclusion. Before long I realized that her face radiated pleasure every time she looked at me, which was often. Each time we parted, even though our talk had been candid and reserved, she would invariably steal one last smiling glance over her shoulder. I believe she responds exactly that way to every man who crosses her path. On the night preceding our first interview she had received profound declarations of love, by telephone from the other side of the continent, from a man she had met less than a week before. Her whole life was like that. This drove home to me the power of the eyes, of simply looking at someone; for quite some time, I was not even aware that she did this, though I was quite conscious of the fact that I liked her and felt comfortable in her presence.

The power of the eyes, whether merely to quicken interest in the case of strangers or to convey profound feelings in the case of lovers, is partly due to the fact that such expressiveness is not deliberate. It is quite unconsciously and therefore quite honestly given as a sign of genuine love, and is, equally unconsciously, interpreted as such, at least tentatively. Therefore, its message is likely to overwhelm every other feeling or doubt, and to supersede every explicit avowal. Precisely because little actual thought is given, beyond bare and almost subliminal awareness, to the fact that someone who is cared for very much is looking, perhaps even gazing, into one's face, for this very reason no defense is erected against it. The message "I love you" goes straight to the heart and feelings, and comes directly from an identical source, without thought, and hence without doubt and guarded response. Such behavior is, moreover, in no way unnatural or rude, so long as it is a look of friendship or even enchantment, and not one of curious scrutiny. Hence, such looking can sometimes, in the case of lovers, become excessive to the point of becoming starry-eyed, without making the person who is the object of it self-conscious or uncomfortable. It has this latter dampening effect only when it passes from looking to scrutinizing, at which point the person being examined begins to have precisely the feeling no lover can abide, namely, that of being a mere object or thing.

*   *   *

On the other side of this phenomenon, you can feel no more total rejection as a person, nor one against which you are so helpless to protest, than to find that someone lacks even enough interest in you to bestow a look. It is, quite literally, an expression of your total worthlessness in his eyes. To be in the company, perhaps the sole company, of someone who treats you this way for any considerable time is to experience an acute discomfort and ineradicable resentment, even though perhaps no unfriendly word is spoken and no overt gesture of hostility is ever made. One would rather be confronted with actual verbal abuse, to which at least a response can be made, than to be treated as worth less even than that.

One man I spoke with, for example, had had only one love affair in his life, and that one had not been very successful. He was a man in his thirties who had never married, who had involuntarily spent his nights alone, and who desperately craved the company of women. Nor was there at first any apparent reason why he should have to endure loneliness, for he was attractive and had a flourishing, even sometimes glamorous career as a photographer. Yet on the one occasion when I saw him in the company of a woman I noticed that every time she spoke he looked down at his hands or at the table, any place except directly into her face. This mannerism was, I am sure, the result of shyness, and not due to a lack of interest, yet its negative effect was decisive. The language of the eyes was simply one he could not speak, even ineptly. Whether or not this is what isolated him in his loneliness, it surely was a contributing factor.

A simple experiment of the imagination, however, will easily convince us of this power that the eyes possess. Suppose, for example, that you are at a social gathering—perhaps at dinner—and you find yourself seated next to an attractive stranger who directs not a single glance at you throughout the entire evening. He (she) converses, responds to your questions, shows no lack of awareness of your presence—but your eyes never meet. Now imagine the very same situation, with the single difference that this person is constantly looking your way; and even though he (she) perhaps says nothing to you in the whole course of the evening, you can hardly look in that direction without finding those eyes already upon you.

Which of the two would you approach after dinner? Which might you subsequently telephone or write to? Which, indeed, can you imagine yourself falling in love with?

*   *   *

There is no more perfect measure of the emotions than the eyes. The most subtle modifications of feeling are recorded there, in changes so slight that the most sensitive camera or artist could hardly capture them; yet they are recorded instantly and unambiguously in the mind of a beholder, often without any conscious awareness of the message he has received, which was probably transmitted in the same unconscious manner. Even dog owners soon learn to read the silent language of their pet's eyes, detecting every shift of feeling—fear, anxiety, adoration, hunger, discomfort, whatever. This also accounts for the discomfort one feels when in the presence of a complete stranger whose eyes are obscured by dark glasses. A whole and rich area of communication is thereby cut off, creating deep uncertainty. We have learned to depend on it, most of all to know just how we stand in the attitudes and feelings of others, for we know that these signals are far more reliable than words. Hence it is into another person's eyes—and not, for example, into his mouth—that we normally and almost instinctively look, in case we look at him at all, for we have long since learned the subtle but unambiguous language they speak. Words can be uttered without meaning, but it is quite impossible to feign and dissimulate with the eyes, for one can never check to see what has just been said. You see your own eyes only when you are staring into a mirror—precisely when you *cannot* dissimulate, for then you have no one but yourself to lie to.

The power of the eyes is rarely appreciated except by such persons as hypnotists. That is why most of us so easily and nonreflectively believe what is conveyed through another person's eyes. If a professor finds that an attractive or even moderately attractive student has her eyes fixed upon him most of the time, perhaps with a hint of deep interest or admiration, then he will hardly fail to glance her way each time he fancies that he has expressed some interesting insight, or combined his words rather well, or in some way managed to look good, just to see how his performance has registered there. He may be totally unaware of this, and not even clearly aware of her apparent fascination with him, but any teacher with the least capacity for self-appraisal can test it out for himself. In fact experiments have been conducted to confirm it. Thus it has been arranged, without the professor's knowledge, that the students on one side of his classroom will exhibit interest and attention whenever he happens to be on that side of the room, and exhibit indifference or boredom whenever he is not. After a few class meetings it is found that the professor is almost always on the side of the room first referred to, but has no idea why. If asked to explain his predilection for that side of the room, he responds, sincerely, that he just happens to prefer it, or that there is more light on that side, or something equally naive.

It is because the eyes are honest that most of us fall victim to their power. But the power itself is wielded sincerely and benignly, except in rare and almost aberrant cases. In fact, it is hard to use that power malevolently or to exploit, just because dissimulation is so nearly impossible. You really do not harm a person by telling him that you despise him, if that is the truth—or at least, you harm him far less than you would if you told him the opposite, which you cannot do with your eyes, if that is not so. And you certainly do not harm the person by telling him that you love him, if you speak the truth, and if it is your eyes unmistakably conveying this to him. Nor is there much danger that exploitative people might fancy that they have here an instrument for controlling others for whom they have no sincere affection. For not only is it difficult to lie by this means—especially over any period of time—but there is, in addition, an almost unavoidable and sometimes profound effect upon the gazer himself. In other words, to look appreciatively into the face and eyes of another person is, in truth, to gain an awareness not only of that person's beauty, which is sometimes not apparent with a casual glance, but to become aware also of that person's mind and soul; that is to say, of the thoughts and feelings underneath. It is quite hard not to love someone in the presence of such perception as this and, what will by now be even more clear, such love is almost sure to be reciprocated twice over. Surely this is precisely how the whole of humankind would have been created had we been the work of gods who were poets, and not merely gods.

15

Rules for Husbands, Wives, and Lovers

He who lets the world, or his own part of it, choose his plan of life for him, has no need of any other faculty than the apelike one of imitation.

—John Stuart Mill

Different people, in different ways, become drawn into the ethical problems surrounding love affairs, depending upon their various roles—whether, for example, one is a married person, an unmarried lover, the third person within a triangular relationship, a friend, a counselor, or whatever. We shall be concerned, however, with only three such classes of problems: (1) those arising between a husband and wife when it is discovered, or suspected, that one or the other is having an affair; (2) those arising between unmarried lovers or the partners in a marriage relationship when a similar discovery is made; and (3) those arising between lovers or partners in a love affair as a consequence of the fact that at least one of them is married to someone else, or has a previously existing marriage relationship, whether legal or not.

The first two groups of problems are very similar and will in fact be treated as essentially the same, but both of these are very different from the third group. That is to say, there are very serious ethical and practical problems resulting from a married person falling in love with a third person, or having an affair, but these problems do not result merely from the fact that this person is legally married. They arise from something closely connected with this, namely, that he or she has an existing marriage relationship, and hence a prior commitment of greater or lesser degree. The fact that the marriage relationship has a formal or legal foundation is an almost extraneous consideration, for as we have seen, marriages are made by the partners themselves, not by laws or ceremonies.

Thus, when a husband or wife falls in love with an outsider, and becomes involved in an intense and passionate affair with that person, there is almost certain to be deep injury and jealousy on the part of his or her spouse. But this is due to the presence of a marriage relationship rather than a legal marriage. The difference here is, at most, one of degree. Thus the problems will be much the same for a couple of students, male and female, who live together and more or less make a home together for themselves (even if only in the room of a dormitory) in case one of them falls in love with an outsider. The main differences are that the legalized marriage is apt to be older, will involve property and often children, and will be more difficult to dissolve because of the legal obstacles.

The third class of problems is entirely different, however, because it involves all three parties associated in the love affair itself, namely, the partners plus at least one outside person. But here, again, it does not make much difference whether one or both of these persons is legally married to someone else, or whether one or both has only a marriage relationship with someone else. In either case, the difference will be one only of degree. If, for example, a wife falls in love with a man other than her husband, then she and her lover may have certain problems that result from the existence of a husband in the background. But the problems will be much the same, though usually less acute, in case a woman, such as a female student, makes a "home" with someone to whom she is not legally married and then falls in love with a third person. The fact of formal marriage exacerbates the problems we shall be concerned with, but it does not really create them.

*   *   *

Monogamous or exclusive devotion to one person, sometimes lasting a lifetime, can sometimes be the ultimate fulfillment and provide the greatest happiness that we are capable of finding. Such fidelity by no means guarantees such happiness, however, and is, in fact, quite rare. Still, even when this falls short of total fulfillment, it can be a firm foundation for security, both for children and for the partners of that exclusive relationship. Even students who live together as marriage partners without any formalized marriage are usually motivated by a search for security even when they have no definite expectation of eventually getting married. In this case the security sought is emotional. Each knows that the other, who is deeply loved, will "be there" at the end of the day. One is relieved of the need for anxious speculation regarding the whereabouts of the other person or what he or she might be doing. Hence there is more than a day-to-day kindling of affection, for feelings that flourish one day can fade the next. Living together, on the other hand, implies a constancy of feeling similar to the commitment of marriage, though certainly of a lesser degree.

There is a price to be paid for this security, however: Such people usually come to assume a proprietary interest in each other, especially if they become legally married. Each is apt to assume that the other has in some sense become *his* or *hers,* so that not only can demands be made which would otherwise be resented as intolerable and absurd, but ways of treating each other become allowable which otherwise would not even be contemplated.

For example, a husband finds no impropriety in snatching a letter from his wife's hand if he is curious concerning its contents—something he would not dream of doing to anyone else, nor to her before she married him. Or a wife feels perfectly free to inquire about her husband's whereabouts and company, even though there might be no one else on earth to whom she would feel free to direct such questions. It is not even unusual for a husband to take his wife's telephone calls for her, and to deal on her behalf with whatever matter the caller brings up, even though she may be sitting only a few feet away. Similarly, wives have been known to open their husbands' mail and then expect an explanation of its contents. Husbands and wives have been known to arrange with friends for the surveillance of their partners, in order to receive secret intelligence concerning their activities, and have apparently found in such spying no breach of faith or even of civilized manners. It is needless to say that no one would think of treating anyone else in the world in such ways, and the right to do it in this case is strangely thought to derive from the vows of love and fidelity that were once gravely affirmed. If any employer found himself so treated by a subordinate—found his telephone calls or mail being intercepted, for example, or his activities spied out—then the offending employee would be dismissed on the spot. Yet it is strangely supposed that the vows of everlasting love and fidelity upon which a marriage rests do allow abominations of this sort. Parents do not ordinarily feel free to treat even their own teenage children in this fashion. Thus no mother could, without being deeply resented, surreptitiously scrutinize her son's or daughter's incoming mail or insist upon knowing their personal and private feelings and activities.

The marital commitment, even that found in a marriage relationship, is considered by some to permit barbarism and indecency. In fact this is so common that to many married persons it seems almost a simple matter of right, involving no question of conscience whatever, nor even any incompatibility with the demands of their own vows. Faithlessness, in every imaginable expression except the sexual one, seems by some to be allowable under the most solemn promise of fidelity.

What is needed, then, are rules that can serve as guides for persons married to or living with each other when one or the other is thought to be having an affair, and also rules for those involved in the affair. There is a need to cope with love affairs in ways that will at least improve upon the usual reactions of the sort just described and that will reduce the power of these reactions to destroy other precious relationships as well as individual personalities. The relationships and personalities so affected are not only their own, but often those of others, sometimes including children. It is not an easy task, but certainly we can improve upon the present practice of letting those who feel betrayed make up their own rules and then lash about with this immense destructive force.

Rule One: Do not spy or pry.

By spying I mean any devious effort to learn whether someone is having an affair, regardless of who initiates the probe: a husband, a wife, or the partner of a marriage relationship. Its worst form is to watch, or arrange for others to watch, someone's comings and goings; but of course it also includes surreptitious looking at mail, eavesdropping, poking through waste paper, and things of this sort.

Such behavior betrays a total lack of confidence in another person's judgment and determination of his own conduct, thus amounting to a declaration that he or she cannot be trusted. But, in addition to this, it is degrading to the spying partner. To be reduced to fishing through wastebaskets or pockets, putting one's ear to doors or telephone receivers, or, worse yet, engaging an ally to watch and report is inherently ignominious and degrading.

But, one is tempted to reply, he or she "has a right to know." Not quite. One has perhaps a keen desire to know, but a right only to ask. Asking is, with respect to matters of this sort, the only acceptable form of inquiry. A suspected wrong on the part of one person cannot justify a clear and incontestable wrong, such as spying would be, on the part of another.

Moreover, besides being inherently disgraceful, spying is a clear breach of faith, or infidelity, in the strictest sense. It is an injury to the person spied on, of a kind that needs no more to be tolerated within marriage or a marriage relationship than within any other. To spy on a friend would be equivalent to declaring that no friendship exists at all, and a lesser standard can hardly apply within the closest and most intimate kind of friendship. Just as a person forfeits a friendship by turning from friend into spy, so too does a wife or husband, for example, forfeit a marriage in its meaningful sense.

When directed to someone who is cared about, questions concerning matters of this sort might not always yield true answers. To be sure, this is exactly the kind of information that the person asked might be most reluctant to yield. The question of the obligation to be truthful will be considered separately; here it need only be said that the desire for information does not justify the use of *any means whatever* to obtain it. Such a desire must stop short of what is base and faithless in its very nature, which means, to stop on the side of asking. Even here, asking cannot extend to quizzing and prying, to raising accusatory or prosecutorial questions, or to badgering and harassing with suspicions. Behavior of this kind has every bad quality of spying even though it is not covert. In particular, it amounts to a declaration of distrust, and an attempt to take upon oneself the role of governor and judge of another's conduct.

Beyond the ethical objections already offered, there is another, purely practical matter of immense significance: A spying person risks forever losing the respect and with it the love of the person spied upon, and in so doing probably contributes more to the destruction of the relationship than any third person ever could. Consider, for example, a wife who confronts her husband with a tender note ferreted from a wastebasket, or a snapshot lifted from his wallet, or telltales dug out of his pockets. She *wins,* at one level; that is, she proves her point, and the more so if such things constitute proof that he has lied to her. But she also *loses* something less abstract, namely, her husband's respect, and she runs a great risk of losing him as well. She is then likely to lay the blame for this not on herself, where it belongs, but on the outsider who she considers to be behind it. No husband can abide being treated like a child or a fool, even when he may appear to his wife to be acting like one; nor can he long feel affection for anyone who treats him so, or admire someone who debases herself by such spying behavior. The same, of course, follows for any wife.

Consider, for example, the following true case: A wife, rifling through her husband's wallet, finds there a snapshot of a woman known to her and suspected of having an emotional involvement with him; whereupon she blackens the face in the snapshot with ink and replaces it in the wallet. What has she gained by this incredibly puerile action except the momentary expression of her anger and resentment? And what, in comparison, has she lost? A wayward husband or wife can sometimes be brought back to conformity by such humiliations as this, but the problems for the marriage are not then over. On the contrary, that is where they begin, and it is rather seldom that they can ever be resolved at all after the debasement of one partner and the mortification of the other. Such wounds to one's self-respect sometimes never heal, and the damage to a marriage can often be irreparable.

Of course the bare enunciation of this rule against spying leaves unresolved the problems of the one who feels forsaken or, as they say, "cheated" on. If you must refrain even from finding out what is going on, except only by polite inquiry, then what can you do to ease the tormenting jealousy and suspicion? This needs to be dealt with, but not until we have considered a second rule, which is closely associated with the first.

Rule Two: Do not confront or entrap.

The one who feels forsaken and deceived is sometimes tempted to walk right in on the partner, trapping her or him in circumstances with a third person where no out is available. Here the aim is not, of course, to find out what is going on, since this appears to be already known, but to humiliate in the most effective and devastating manner possible. Thus a husband or wife will return home a day earlier than announced, or turn up unexpectedly at some likely place such as a motel to which the partner has been followed. Certainly a more total victory cannot be imagined. There is nothing the "guilty" party can do when "caught" but collapse in total mortification, and to this is added the relish of a devastating humiliation delivered to the third person.

There is no doubt that this is the ultimate horror of unmarried lovers, for the married partner of one of them to actually walk in, and it is for that reason the single most destructive blow that can possibly be delivered. Many people will vicariously feel the terror described in this next episode, a terror made even more acute by its purely accidental nature:

Let me tell you about the most terrifying moment of my life. Susan, my wife, and I had known Debra and her husband for years. On that day I was at home, and in bed with Debra. Susan was out of town at a meeting, and wouldn't be home until dinner—or at least, that is what I thought. But then I thought I heard a car drive into the yard. I almost didn't bother to look, because I wasn't sure I had heard anything, and even if I had, there was no chance of it being Susan. But I got up and looked out, and to my horror there was my wife's car, parked in the drive—which certainly meant that she had seen Debra's car and would be walking in any second! There was no escape. Our ranch house had neither basement nor upstairs. I leaped into some clothes and stepped out of the room, but no Susan. I dashed out the back door, but still no Susan—which meant either that she had gone in the front door, which opened almost onto the bedroom door, or else she was about to. It was an inescapable trap.

I returned and called out, from the kitchen, for Debra to hurry up; then I stepped into the hallway only to see Susan, standing right next to the bedroom, casually removing her coat and hat. I was paralyzed! She stood looking at me in astonishment. I stammered something; she said something about the meeting being canceled, and that she had a headache anyway and was going to lie down—in the bedroom, where in the next minute she would be confronted by a terrified, disheveled, and probably still stark-naked Debra! At that moment the world seemed to end for me.

Susan could hardly have failed to hear me call out for Debra to hurry— besides, she had already seen Debra's car—so the confrontation could only be anticlimactic anyway. I almost begged her, in a burst of confession, not to go in there, but something stopped me. I sat down and watched helplessly as she opened the bedroom door, staring at me in puzzlement, and walked in.

The very next moment Debra emerged from the *bathroom*. I could not imagine how she managed to get in there. She was dressed and calm; she chatted casually, then walked outside and drove off.

Still, I knew we had been caught, even if the ultimate humiliation had somehow been avoided. The car in the drive and my call for Debra to hurry were enough. Trembling and covered with sweat, I pondered what to say. Denials would have only made me a patent liar on top of the rest. I decided to say nothing, hoping that maybe the years would erase the wound and the humiliation.

Strangely, my wife said nothing about this nightmare, and it was not until the next week when I saw Debra again that I was able to piece together the sequence of events during those dreadful seconds. Hearing my exhortation to hurry, she had fled the bedroom, her clothes under her arm, and into the bathroom. So Susan had not heard my shout. Therefore, she must have entered the house a second after Debra had closed the bathroom door behind her. The seemingly inescapable and ultimate horror had been eluded by the smallest particle of time. That moment was certainly the most critical one of my life. Not only humiliation, but years of deep unhappiness had turned on the most exquisite timing imaginable.

I have been tempted to think that guardian angels were managing the scene during those awful seconds, and I have sometimes felt like spending the rest of my life in penance. But since there are no angels, my feelings turned instead to adoration for my wife. Maybe she knew what was happening and arranged to avoid the unthinkable, then forever after keep it to herself and pretend it had not happened. But I guess that is not really possible.

Reading this, one can hardly help wondering whether Susan did not, perhaps, understand the situation and deliberately avoid a confrontation. It would, in any case, be the very best thing to do, though not something that many wives (or husbands) would find very easy.

Certainly the opposite behavior, that is, the deliberate effort to entrap or confront, is a blow that must not ever be delivered, for reasons that are already obvious. For someone to entrap you is not merely to treat you like a child, but rather, as a foe, as someone to be injured in pride and self-respect in a singularly hideous way. Now, to be sure, someone might, in fact, feel exactly that way toward his or her partner. But then certainly the questions to be asked are: Who has been faithless to the promise of love? Who has withdrawn the respect and affection upon which any love must rest? Whose actions have actually destroyed the relationship?

*   *   *

Here, one is tempted to say that sexual infidelity by itself is the ultimate faithlessness, such that no response to it can be inappropriate, and that when it occurs the relationship is already bankrupt. The one who is forsaken might as well salvage his or her remaining pride by gaining the final satisfaction that possessing clear proof of infidelity brings, thereby rubbing the mate's nose in it for the sweet and final relish.

This is beyond a doubt the fundamental and most widespread error in people's thinking on these matters, namely, that infidelity is of necessity sexual, and that an adulterous partner in marriage, for example, proves by his or her very actions that love for the other is dead and that the marriage now exists in appearance and name only. People do think this way, but it is totally the result of cultural conditioning, besides being completely false.

A Moslem man believes that if his wife is raped, by enemy soldiers, for example, then she is irrevocably defiled and no longer fit to live with, so she is simply discarded. We look upon such an attitude as heartless and primitive, as one that could not exist in any intelligent and enlightened mind. But our own attitude toward sexual inconstancy is no less mindless and irrational. Like that of the Moslem man, ours is the product of nothing more than religious and cultural conditioning. Our emotional reaction to it is likely to be intense, but it is no less irrational. Like the Moslem's, it is a dreadfully destructive reaction.

People who are strong, good, even noble, and who are utterly devoted to their own partners nevertheless occasionally become entangled in love affairs with others. No exhortations from pulpits, no reminders of vows or promises, no inner resolutions are going to change this fact. The terse "Thou shalt not" long ago ceased to deserve any but the most simpleminded tribute. To think that even the strictest ethic of marriage can consist of this command alone is to dishonor husbands and wives by supposing that they have little capacity for feeling and thought and are unable to rise to a higher standard of conduct than to be conditioned, like apes, to a largely groundless taboo.

It is also insufficiently appreciated that while a love affair is likely to have an intense impact upon the personalities of the two people immediately involved, it is apt to be temporary in the case of people who are married, and the feelings elicited are almost never as rich and meaningful as either partner already has for the husband or wife who is there in the background. Sometimes, to be sure, a wife or husband leaves to marry someone else, but, by the very nature of things, this happens only in those cases where profound needs were unmet in the original marriage. Shortly, we shall consider this type of situation. But for now consider the case of a perfectly happy marriage wherein one or the other partner becomes entangled in a love affair. This cannot happen, you say. But it does, and fairly often. Nothing on earth is perfect. Every man, for example, has a boundless ego, and even though he can imagine no woman more wonderful than the partner he has, he can easily imagine someone in addition to her, and often finds himself in the company of such women. Similarly, a woman may feel in every way blessed in the partner she has, but this does not mean that she will take no notice of someone who, for example, appreciates elements in her personality or talents to which her partner is somewhat insensitive. To suppose otherwise is to presume a kind of human nature that exists nowhere on earth. What, then, of a happily married wife and mother who becomes infatuated with her English professor? Or the sincerely devoted husband and father whose animal vigor seems to him suddenly and rather overwhelmingly evoked by his secretary? The mere description of such things suggests, in its banality, the proper assessment of them, namely, that love affairs arising from circumstances like these are destined to be temporary and probably brief if left to themselves. Not much can actually be made of someone's admiration of a poetic soul, or of a woman's apparent sense of collapse in the presence of sheer prowess in a man who impresses her. Very little indeed—but love affairs can be made of such things. And because the basis of these relationships is of such limited value, the affairs are likely to be of limited duration.

Putting all of this another way, we can say that a couple who have had a long and happy marriage have innumerable things holding them together, and the product of all these things is a sincere and meaningful devotion to each other. There are memories that stretch over years, many things have been undertaken together, the successes and the failures; there are likely to be children and all the memories and feelings associated with their upbringing, and so on endlessly. Such a marriage can withstand many assaults and buffetings and still remain, not wholly intact, but not really damaged either, so far as the relationship itself is concerned. If things are left to themselves, anyone having such a marriage will never abandon it in favor of a relationship that is likely to be based upon only one or two things of comparatively trivial value. The appreciation of a woman's poetic skill, her loveliness, or her felt need for more esteem than she has may easily lead her to the singular thrill of forbidden and passionate love, but it will not by itself lead her to the destruction of a marriage that is of inestimably greater worth to her. Similarly, the lure of sex, in and of itself, will easily lead almost any man into an affair, even at considerable risk, but he will never let that destroy the good marriage he already has. Not, that is, if things are left to take their course.

And that brings us to our next rule.

Rule Three: Stay out of it.

What, then, is to be done when you are almost sure your partner is having an affair? Nothing, really, except to try to cultivate a certain attitude of serene confidence which will serve to put things back in order more effectively than anything else. It is almost impossible not to feel jealousy and resentment, and sometimes an appalling sense of insecurity, but these should be concealed, or at least expressed to some sympathetic ear other than that of the wandering mate. Beyond that, the most effective instrument, both for the preservation of one's own self-respect and sense of balance and for putting things in their true perspective, is a sense of humor from which you are careful to exclude any bite or edge. A husband of middle age, for example, whose ego seems suddenly carried aloft by the blandishments of a young, shallow, and bosomy nurse—secretary, student, or whomever—can be fairly comical. He views everything with gravity, finds inestimable virtue and nobility where none was apparent before, is borne down by the tragic overtones of these overpowering circumstances, and solemnly plays out the comic role until, sooner or later, he sees these new things for what they are worth, which is very little—provided, however, that things are left to run their course, without wife and friends leaping into the act. A wayward wife, on the other hand, spellbound by the first man who has ever appreciated her as a person—in other words, he nourishes her vanity—is not so comical, because she is not driven by the boundless ego of most men. The watchword for her husband should be patience rather than amusement; for in her case, too, things will run their course.

Imagine, for example, a wife in love with her music teacher, her hairdresser, or whomever, a man who is in every way a lesser person than her husband. Suppose she learns, in her husband's presence, that this lover has left forever. The natural reaction of a husband to this news, so crushing to his wife, is an inward satisfaction followed by declamations to her on how worthless he was anyway and how slight is the loss. But the right response, upon which no improvement could be made, would be sympathy. This could be expressed, for example, by asking: Would you like to be alone? A response of this sort would be neither natural nor easy, which means that it would require a man of significant strength who could rise to the occasion. But it should also be noted that it is the only kind of response that is really in keeping with the lasting love he once promised her.

What most often happens, however, when a husband or a wife finds out about an affair of the other, is everything that should not happen. That is, he (or she) throws himself (herself) into the act, becoming deeply and emotionally involved in it, enlisting the support of friends, and commencing, perhaps with their help, endless remonstrations and accusations. This never has any good result, other than the temporary release of emotion, and in fact produces exactly the result that should be prevented at all cost. The partners in this love affair now feel themselves beleaguered, friendless except for each other, and thus driven to each other's arms. Foolish as this may be, it is nevertheless virtually inevitable the moment anyone makes a great thing of their affair, for the needs that drew them together to begin with are now vastly increased in intensity, and the road to destruction has been made clear.

*   *   *

Of course there is still the real possibility that an affair can destroy a marriage relationship. Wives do leave husbands of long standing, and husbands leave wives, in favor of others who appear on the scene. Marriage relationships that have no legal protection are even more vulnerable to this threat, which can become overwhelming and can drive one to the brink of breakdown when, in addition to the threat to home and affection, there is also a threat to one's security. This is especially threatening to numerous women, who have formed an economic dependence upon their husbands. It is clearly not enough, then, to say that someone thus threatened should just disregard what is going on, as though it were of the least importance.

But here what needs to be said once more is that no good marriage relationship can be threatened by a love affair so long as others keep out of it. A bad relationship can be endangered, and many do come to exactly this end: one partner or the other yields easily to the solicitations of what certainly looks like something better. We have to add, however, that no one is obligated to maintain a dead marriage anyway, and promises spoken long ago cannot still have meaning under these circumstances.

What is a dead marriage? Simply one in which no love exists on one or both sides. Regardless of what else may be said for such a home, how good it may look to the world, that its partners present the appearance of constancy, conspicuously adhering to every conventional standard and upholding the values that are honored everywhere, however appealing they may perhaps appear in a setting which includes beautiful children, that marriage has already failed in case love is not abundant in either partner. And it is, indeed, vulnerable to destruction by the first person who shows the slightest sign of offering a love to one partner that the other has withheld.

Thus, though a wife may be ever so dutiful, faultless, and virtuous in every skill required for the making of a home, if she lacks passion, then in a very real sense she already is without a husband, or he, at least, is without a wife. Similarly, a husband who is preoccupied with himself and his work, who is oblivious to the needs of his wife and insensitive to her vanities, who takes for granted her unique talents—whether they are significant or not—and who goes about his own business more or less as though she did not exist, has already withdrawn as a husband, except in name.

Consider, for example, a husband who works late into the night and then sleeps through most of the morning, but whose wife goes to bed early and rises at dawn; they are rarely awake in bed together. If this is the general picture of their marriage, then it is really a marriage in form only, and there is not much that would be threatened if the wife happened to fall into a love affair—except, of course, her husband's ego and pride. She never promised to protect these, however.

Let us imagine a wife who is absorbed in her children and her home to such an extent that these appear spotless and beautiful to the world; she is a woman who lives her children's triumphs and sorrows as they grow up, glories in the praise and envy that her house evokes from others, and, in addition, pours her remaining energy into clubs, garden, church activities, and similar laudatory things. Suppose that with all this she is cold, neither imaginative nor seductive, entirely accepting of sex but very far from her husband's apparent preoccupation with it. This marriage, too, has already failed, and there is nothing but the visible shell of it left to crumble when some third person offers the basic ingredient that is missing.

What must be remembered by those persons who wish to condemn adultery is that the primary vow of marriage is to love, and that vow is not fulfilled by the kind of endless busyness exemplified in the industrious and ever-generous husband or the dedicated homemaking wife. It is true that one of the partners in marriage may well be awakened to the startling realization that the other partner has been engaged in a full-fledged affair. What has to be stressed, however, is that the first infidelity may not have been committed by the one who is having an affair. The first and ultimate infidelity is to withhold the love that was promised, and which was originally represented as the reason for marriage to begin with. In such cases adultery is not infidelity, but a natural response to it.

16

Rules About Feelings

Love is strong as death;
Jealousy is cruel as the grave.

—Song of Solomon

The first three rules were concerned with the *actions* of those who think, or perhaps even know, that their partners are having an affair. These guidelines are meant to minimize the damage that is likely to follow such a suspicion or discovery. But there are also certain feelings that must be avoided, and for the same reason. They are the feelings of jealousy, guilt, and the impulse to show off to the other person, all of which give rise to three additional rules.

Rule Four: Stop being jealous.

Jealousy is the most wrenching and destructive of human passions. Not only is it painful, but the pain is self-inflicted; and unlike most other emotions, no good ever comes from it, not even the release of tension or the assuaging of pride on the part of the jealous person. On the contrary, this passion is as destructive of oneself as it is of others. Other emotions, even painful ones, are usually redeemed in some way, but not jealousy. Anger, for example, though ugly, is sometimes justified, and may even produce some genuinely worthwhile result, even if it consists of no more than the salvaging of an angry person's pride. Anger is sometimes called "righteous," although jealousy can never be so described. Anxiety, although painful, is seldom self-inflicted, and sometimes has its place in warding off actual evils. Pity, though unpleasant, can sometimes be tender and even ennobling. And resentment, to take still another passion, is sometimes a goad to the correction of evils, such as injustice.

Jealousy, however, is never good for anything at all. It is a pain that is unredeemed, self-imposed, debilitating, ugly, and utterly destructive in its inward and outward effects. Rather than providing a kind of outlet for bad feelings, it has an amazing capacity for feeding on itself, festering away, nourishing depression, and defeating every good and generous impulse that could make itself felt. It does not even protect the pride of its victim, but on the contrary makes him more and more shameful both to himself and in the eyes of everyone else. To be overpowered by jealousy is the ultimate self-defeat.

*   *   *

Of course, it would be ridiculous to suggest that jealousy is an emotion that can just be turned off at will. It would in fact be hard to think of any feeling that is more difficult to control. Even persons with great self-control, for example, can recognize something of themselves in this particular account:

> After two years Gene and I had decided that our affair was over, and it was never going to be like it had been. I knew by then that he was never going to leave his wife; besides, all our time together was spent fighting anyway. When we finally broke it off I was as ready to quit as he was.
>
> But then I heard he had gone back to a silly woman, Jean, he'd been involved with before he knew me, and I began to go completely out of my mind. I found out where she lived, and one night I got in the car and drove past there. Sure enough, there was Gene's car out in front! I couldn't think straight or see straight, and went driving off into the night in no particular direction, going through stop signs and lights and paying no attention to anything, until finally I rammed right into a tree, demolished the car, and gave myself a broken jaw. It was lucky I wasn't killed.
>
> Then a couple of weeks later, my jaw still wired together, my supervisor called to say that no one had showed up for work on the night shift, and could I come in. Wasn't Gene there? No, she said, he hadn't turned up either. So my first thought was that he was with that stupid woman again. I drove over there, and sure enough, there was his car again! I went completely to pieces, but this time I didn't drive off. I went to the door to knock it down and confront him face to face, and I stood there at the door for ten or twenty minutes, thinking I was going to knock it right down. And I would have, if I hadn't realized the satisfaction she would be sure to get having Gene there with her and seeing me make a complete fool of myself. So I went home and stayed up all night. I swore that I wouldn't say a word next time I saw Gene at work. But that didn't last ten minutes. I went right over to his desk that morning and stood over him and demanded to know where he had been that night. Then I told him that I already knew, so he wouldn't have to lie to me, and I made a complete fool of myself; I didn't even know anymore what I was saying. He just leaned back in his chair and was as cool as could be, and polite and sympathetic, the way he had always been.

The above remarks illustrate not only the intensity that jealousy can reach, and its irrationality, but also its necessary cause, namely, some third person. It is this which distinguishes jealousy from another destructive emotion, envy, in which no third person need be involved. And it is significant that in the remarks just quoted, fierce jealousy was aroused over a man who had been more or less willingly abandoned. The role of the third person, in this emotion, is larger than the role of the person to whom one jealously tries to cling.

The appropriate response to a jealousy-provoking situation is to be cavalier, even jocular; but there must be no bitter edge to the jocularity. A telltale article discovered—a piece of jewelry, a note, something of this sort—can be placed neatly and without comment on the husband's or wife's desk, for example, and if that person more or less guiltily brings it up, then the proper response is amusement, not questioning. Or reflect upon the effectiveness of the attitude displayed by the wife described here:

> I was invited to a conference in Hawaii, all expenses paid, lasting several days; and, if I wanted to bring my wife, her expenses there would be paid too, although I would have to buy her airfare. It fell exactly on our twentieth wedding anniversary, so I eagerly accepted. It then turned out, however, that her plane ticket would cost a thousand dollars, and she preferred to go instead to Florida, with our daughter, for a fraction of that cost, where I could join her after my free trip to Hawaii. When I protested that I had no desire to be in Hawaii alone, her perfectly candid reaction was that there would be lots of attractive women in Hawaii, that she was sure I could make someone there very happy— just so long as I didn't come home and tell her about it! I immediately canceled my arrangements to go to Hawaii, even though I had spent weeks composing a paper to present there. Why would I want to be in Hawaii, no matter what company I might find there, if I could be in Florida with a woman like that?

*   *   *

Jealousy always has its source in something almost as ugly as itself, namely, in the attitude of possessiveness towards another person. A man is likely to look upon his wife as *his* in the sense of a personal possession, and with this starting point he feels quite justified in imposing rules and restrictions just as he would upon any other thing to which he claims ownership. Thus the marriage relationship, which is supposed to inspire the most exalted love and friendship, becomes instead debased, reducing a partner to a mere chattel, a *thing,* or worse than this, a thing *owned.*

There is no doubt, however, that this conception of conventional marriage is generally thought to be perfectly natural and acceptable. It is hard therefore to imagine, for example, any clergyman remonstrating with any member of his flock for having exactly this conception of conjugal love, for thinking of his wife as literally *belonging* to him. The same holds for women; that is, wives are similarly possessive of husbands. But strangely, the degree of possessiveness considered allowable for wives is somewhat less than for husbands. Like a man, a woman may restrict her partner's association with other persons, but his violation of these restrictions is considered less serious than it would be had she been thus confined, and similarly, his outrage is deemed more to be feared than hers. Of course this is arbitrary and unfair, but nonetheless true.

Take male possessiveness, for instance. In its worst expressions, a man thinks himself justified in knowing whom his partner might be corresponding with, and even entitled to read such correspondence without asking, or insisting that it be terminated. He feels no restraint in asking whom she has seen and where, what she may have said to this person or that, or what she may have heard. Men have even been known to object to their wives dancing with other men, even men who are virtually unknown to them, and within full view of everyone; or in other words, they have been known to assert their property rights even when not the slightest threat has been posed. There are husbands who believe they are entitled to decide for their wives whether they may work or not, and where and with whom; what careers or even what hobbies they may feel free to pursue; what travel they may undertake, when, and with whom; and whether or not they may make trips by themselves to distant places. In short, there are husbands who consider it acceptable to exercise every control over their wives that they would exercise over an infant child. There are wives who die emotionally and psychologically as a result, and who eventually become hardly more than spiritless appendages to their free and lordly husbands. And, we might note, it is little wonder that such women are vulnerable to the attention of the very first man who befriends them and treats them as persons, and, in fact, they seem ready to fall in love almost at an instant. Thus jealous possessiveness, which springs from weakness and uncertainty, destroys the very thing it was intended to ensure, that is, the secure possession of another person. One can hardly fail to see a hint of justice in this. A man will try to *own* a woman at his peril, for it is almost a prescription for losing her to someone else, in heart and mind if not outwardly— and surely that is as it should be. The infidelity is his, not hers.

The question here is not, of course, how far such rights of possession extend between the sexes, but rather, whether any such right exists at all. It should be quite clear that it does not. No human being can be owned. Even children are not literally the property of their parents, however much some parents may wish to think otherwise. How much less so, then, is an adult an item of property. Furthermore, apart from property rights, this kind of possessiveness is inconsistent with the most basic requirement of ethics: that a person be treated, always and by everyone, as a person and not as an object. And it is likewise inconsistent with the fundamental ethical requirement of any marriage relationship, which is, very simply, that its partners love each other.

Rule Five: Stop feeling guilty.

A sense of shame and guilt is thought by some people to be the appropriate accompaniment to a love affair or, as it should be called in this context, an adulterous relationship. The very word *adultery* has the connotation of sin and guilt. This is the view of those who enjoy analyzing everything in terms of morality rather than common sense. That such feelings of guilt produce nothing but harm, that they are often a screen for the infliction of cruelties, that they produce lasting dislocations in the relationships of husbands and wives, these things do not matter to such people. Adultery, it is thought, is shameful, and no adulterer should be satisfied or complacent for having sunk to it. He should feel guilty. His feelings of guilt should be deep and intense, to match the gravity of his wrongdoing.

The idea is seldom expressed in just those terms, but it is nevertheless a familiar one—so familiar, in fact, that a husband or wife who is "faithless" (another guilt word) is apt to lapse, even wallow, in guilt without even pausing to think about it. It seems to some that the stain of wrongdoing will somehow be wiped away by that reaction; if one feels sorry enough for what has been done, then this will in some way compensate for having done it.

Oddly enough, though, married partners are apt to feel less guilt, or no guilt at all, for things that are really worse than getting involved in a love affair. Thus a man who strikes his wife, or raises his voice to her in anger, may (or may not) feel remorse, may (or may not) later regret it, but he is quite likely to feel no real sense of guilt at all. It is a lapse he can overcome, even possibly rationalize in his own mind. Or one who consistently treats his wife as if she were a mere possession or an ornament, tells her what she may and may not do in areas that are none of his business, and who adds the role of master to that of husband is likely to feel no guilt or remorse about this. He may even think of it as the proper role of a husband. All this can take place in spite of two fairly obvious facts: First, such behavior is very likely to be more injurious to her than any sexual lapse would be, especially if the latter were unknown; and second, that while the goadings and promptings of *eros* are inherent to any man's nature, and therefore no real fault, violence, anger, and a consistent lack of awareness are not, and are, therefore, real faults.

Interestingly enough, women usually feel less shame arising from sexual inconstancy than do men. A woman who regularly and over a long period of time has many lovers is quite likely to feel something rather like shame, namely, a sense of debasement of herself as a woman; for she is likely to see herself more as a thing or an object of desire than as a woman. But apart from this, the guilt reactions of the two sexes are significantly different.

That there should be this difference is instructive, for part of the explanation is not hard to see. A woman does not usually have any overwhelming desire for another lover, assuming she cares for the one she has, unless he treats her with a consistent insensitivity and is inconsiderate. She is moved, then, partly by the goadings of her natural and justified resentment of him, as well as by the solicitations of one who is perceived actually to care about her. One man treats her as a chattel, the other as an angel, and together these two things are quite enough to quench any sense of guilt she may have. A married woman in this position is, in fact, very likely more or less consciously to seek a lover just in order to express resentment for her detested husband. Under these conditions genuine feelings of guilt can hardly emerge.

A man, on the other hand, feels guilt because he is more likely to view his feelings and behavior as expressions of a fault within himself, rather than in the woman he cares for. She may indeed be an angel, and be so perceived by him. This hardly renders him blind to the lures and blandishments of others. It only makes him more ashamed to yield to them—which he does, nevertheless, with fair regularity, unless he can find sufficient distraction somewhere else, most likely in his career.

*   *   *

Not all women dwell in anxiety for the security of their homes, and as the conventions governing marriage relationships change, and a decreasing number of men assume the role of "head of household," such women do become fewer. But most still are, quite understandably, vulnerable to such anxiety. And when a man actually declares to his wife that another person has filled for him the place that she thought was exclusively hers, then the anxiety she feels is likely to intensify so much that she may never really recover from it. Certainly the sobs, tears, and chest beating of her husband are not going to give her any assurance. His behavior indicates that he is thinking only of himself and not of her. He is staging an act, in which he sees himself as his own engrossed audience. If he were really thinking of her, and making the slightest effort to fulfill the commitment of love for her that she expects, he would say not a word of what she wants least of all to hear about, and would, with whatever effort it might take, quietly bring his outside involvement sooner or later to some sort of decorous conclusion. That is usually not an easy thing to do, of course. It is much easier for him to wallow in guilt, to spread misery around himself, perhaps in the process to unsettle all the things that he and his wife do genuinely cherish, to act like a child—and possibly to continue as before in the other involvement. Such a scenario is not at all uncommon in such cases.

There is, of course, another effect of this guilt-wallowing, and that is the emotional abasement of the wife. For just as there are such things as vicious lies (along with the occasional merciful ones), so also are there vicious truths—that is to say, truths that wound and destroy, and which are in no way redeemed by being true. A man who tells an unsuspecting wife such a truth as this stabs her with a weapon against which she has no defense. For a wife who genuinely cares for her husband, it is as crushing a blow as she could receive. Apart from this, it is to any woman a declaration of her own inferiority. Whatever may be said, what she clearly hears is that another woman is more desirable than she is, which wounds not merely her vanity and pride, but her sense of womanliness. And this is sometimes precisely what a husband intends by his confession, however much he may attempt to disguise it. That is, he pretends, perhaps even to himself, that he is moved by his regard for the truth, for honesty between partners, and by the wish to rid himself of the guilt of wrongdoing. But in fact his confession may be an act of sheer malice, aimed at hurting. On the other hand, he may very well be seeking nothing more than to alter his wife's behavior towards him. What he is saying, in other words, is something like: "See what she does for me. Now you see, you could treat me that way too, and then you would have my love, instead of her." Because this message is slightly subtle and quite concealed, it does sometimes work—for a while. That is to say, it is notorious that marriages are sometimes infused with new life and excitement, especially sexual excitement, following the voluntary disclosure by the husband of some love affair of his. But it is also notorious that this marital euphoria is short-lived. Sooner or later this husband is seen not as the glorious recipient of the love and desire of others, but as the same imperfect and dissimulating man that he was before. On top of this is added the contempt and anxiety already described.

It is, on the whole, a very bad show. And not one bit of it was necessary. It was prompted by nothing but the sense of guilt, which was artificial from the start. There is nothing artificial, however, in the feelings of contempt and anxiety that emerge, nor in the husband's inner malice that the sense of guilt so thinly disguises in many cases.

Rule Six: Don't give it away.

There is on the part of some men a strange and perverse need to have their love affairs discovered, even when this means the almost certain ruination of the affair itself and severe damage to their marriages or marriage relationships. Women are less predisposed to do this, and are thus more discreet. Men sometimes, and at least half deliberately, leave tender notes where their wives will find them, or leave telltales, such as pictures, or perhaps an item of jewelry. Rarely do they come right out and tell their wives what has been going on, unless this has been discovered anyway, or unless they are prompted by disordered feelings akin to shame or guilt, as already discussed; but they sometimes seem to come as close as they can, as if courting the excitement of risk. In response to the same inner workings of their minds, many men feel an urge to do something even more strange, namely, to arrange encounters between wives and lovers. In my talks with male students, a constantly recurring description had to do with encounters between two girls with whom they were simultaneously involved. Sometimes these were even agreed to by the girls in question. The man suggests, for example, that they might all have dinner together, or he invites one of them to a party he knows the other will be attending, and tells her so. One might wonder why any woman would go along with such a suggestion, and the acute discomfort of the situation proposed, but there is perhaps a natural desire on her part to meet, and thereby size up, a rival. The man, for his part, is put in the deliciously exciting position of beholding *two* beautiful people competing for his affection and, most delicious of all, possibly falling into overt rivalry or even a veritable fight before his very eyes or, better yet, the eyes of his friends. A man's ego can hardly hope for more.

A woman, on the other hand, does not ordinarily relish the idea of meeting and being expected to be affable with the *wife* of her partner in an affair, for obvious reasons. The wife was there first and has a firmly established prior claim and advantage. But men often rather like the idea. Thus a man who has planned a day of sailing, for example, will invite his partner in a love affair to come along too, with her husband, of course, only the two of them knowing the delicious secret they share. It is a risky business, because lovers sometimes say more by their behavior—by the way they quite unconsciously look at each other, for example—than they do with their tongues, and those messages can be picked up by anyone.

One of the more bizarre expressions of this kind of behavior was described to me this way:

> Tim had had love affairs before, but this time he decided to bring his girlfriend right home with him, even told me he was going to, and got me to promise to be nice to her and make her feel welcome in our house. Well, he did that, he brought her home for dinner, and both of us, his girl and I, were awfully uncomfortable. It didn't seem to faze Tim a bit. He just acted as if it was the most normal thing in the world, and as if he expected the two of us would have lots in common and probably hit it off just marvelously. Joan, his girl, could hardly wait to leave, and I couldn't help wondering how he'd talked her into this in the first place. As for me, I felt absolutely squelched, having this beautiful young girl, half my age, right in front of me. I felt old and fat, and just knew I could never be competition for her.
>
> That affair finally broke up, and Tim's next stunt was even more audacious. He brought his next girlfriend home to *live* with us. And that's how we lived, for a whole year—a threesome. It was the most miserable year of my whole life. Some nights I'd sleep with my husband, and some nights he'd be in the adjoining bedroom with her. I never knew until bedtime which bed he was going to be in. But then he started going further, and arranging for me to find out when the two of them had been making love. For instance, I would come home and find *my* bed, that I had made that morning, stained. Once it was my most beautiful white satin bedspread.
>
> I loved him, and was willing to do anything he wanted to make the marriage work. I actually thought that if I conquered jealousy and just tried to think about things intelligently, then this ménage à trois might actually work. He didn't see any reason why it couldn't, and I wasn't able to come up with any.

That is far from typical, for even though men sometimes enjoy this kind of thing, their partners in the love affair seldom do. A woman is usually quite uncomfortable in the company of both her lover and either spouse. If both her lover and her husband are present, then she would much prefer that one of them, namely her husband, be elsewhere; but if he must be there, she finds no spice of excitement when the other is also present. On such an occasion she is apt to outdo herself in decorum, has no desire to exchange flirtatious glances or innuendos, and will, if there appears to be even the remotest need for it, quietly exhort her lover to treat her husband, the very husband she wishes were not even there, with seemingly excessive deference and politeness.

What is the explanation of all this? It is the male ego, and nothing more mysterious. A love affair is the most powerful fuel for that ego. When a man is loved not only by his wife, a woman whose love can be more or less taken for granted anyway, but also by another woman whose love can by no means be taken for granted, it is almost like breathing the excitement of life twice over. And then somehow to be able to convey to your wife, as if by accident, that you have this enviable blessing, that you are loved not just by her but by another, seems to many men to be nothing short of an authentication of their power and glory. Leaving notes or telltales for a wife to discover, and the joint presence of both women, are like unspoken boasts. Of course, if a man reflects upon it, he does not really want the message to be received, knowing that this will mean the end of everything. Still, the temptation is there. And even if his wife remains blind to the messages, he is nevertheless able to display to *himself* these reminders of manly glory. It is this alone that explains the impulse and temptation many men have to bring lovers and wives together in their own presence. There are probably no normal men who have not, in fact, indulged the fantasy of being made love to by two women at once; but the world being what it is, this usually has to remain a fantasy. Men settle for much less, such as the somewhat silly and incongruous arrangements just described.

But behavior of this kind is not only silly, it is worse than pointless. It is destructive. No woman was ever moved to awe or admiration for her husband upon discovering that he has proved irresistible to someone else, nor does it occur to her to put that interpretation on things. All she sees is a kind of childish display of egoism, not unlike a fowl spreading himself before two or three hens at once. Besides that, she sees a total disregard for her and her feelings. If she already dislikes her husband as a person even if not as an essential part of her home, which may be precious to her, then she may use her discovery of artfully placed notes and telltales for subtle efforts at blackmail. She might, for example, exercise less restraint henceforth in her spending, knowing that any protest by him can be effortlessly silenced. If, on the other hand, she has adored her husband up to now, then the effect of such discoveries is simply the damage, or even the total destruction, of that feeling, along with the demolition of her own pride and sense of worth. To say that she feels betrayed is, usually, to say the very least.

*   *   *

Do women ever behave in a similar fashion? That is, do they leave notes and tell-tales? Certainly not from any similar motive. It is usually no part of a woman's proof of her femininity to be found to have many lovers, as it is, strangely, the proof of a man's masculinity, as he is apt to imagine. A woman's inclination to have but one lover is usually as strong as a man's inclination to have many, for reasons already explored, and this augments the very practical reasons she has for maintaining the strictest secrecy concerning any love affair.

The attitude of women with respect to disclosure was, I thought, typified in one of my interviews. After the person I was interviewing had described her current affair at some length, and the complete absence of love in her marriage, I asked her what she would do if her husband found out. "I would deny everything!" was her instant and astonished response, as though there could ever be the slightest question of what common sense would dictate in those circumstances. This was a woman of the most conventional standards imaginable, who would never consider lying an acceptable practice, nor tolerate it in her children, for example; but in such a case as this, the stupidity of admitting even to a truth that had been discovered seemed too obvious even to discuss.

Yet a wife will sometimes quite deliberately let it be discovered that she has, or has had, an affair—typically for one of two motives. For one thing, she may use this means to express her resentment of her husband, for whatever reason, particularly if she can easily afford to lose him, and would like to. Such a discovery can be as severe a blow to a husband's ego as his similar behavior is a blow to his wife's vanity or, as it should perhaps be called, self-esteem. The other motive would be to even a score. That is, a wife whose husband has carried on an affair has a certain inducement to have one too, however briefly and casually, and to let it be known that she has, just in order to show that she can. Affairs of this sort, however, are not likely to be serious, and cannot even really be called love affairs, as we have been using the term.

In any case, the tendency of a wife to betray her own love affair is usually so minimal as to be almost nonexistent, arising only in special and more or less harmless circumstances. The similar tendency of a man, on the other hand, is strong and constant. The rule that emerges, therefore, really applies mostly to men, and consists simply in this: Do not tell, hint at, or in any way betray the fact of such a love affair; but on the contrary, scrupulously guard its secrecy, at least from your wife, until it has been buried in the past—and work to bring that ending about as gently and decorously as you can.

17

The Fulfillment of Need

Him that I love, I wish to be
Free—
Even from me.

—Anne Morrow Lindbergh

Little is said about the obligations, if any, that are shared by the partners in a love affair. Having already broken, as some would suppose, the basic rule of rigidly monogamous love, persons involved in a love affair seem to be beyond the pale of ethics altogether. Anything goes, it seems—no wrong is culpable, no obligation binding, and nothing owed. And, indeed, lovers sometimes act as if this were so, especially if stresses build up or the love affair starts to deteriorate. There are men, and women, who suppose that they can simply forsake a partner whom they have cared about, at whatever cost to that other person in the form of painful rejection and loneliness, just as though no love had ever existed. Worse than this, lovers always have powerful weapons that can be turned against each other, which no laws or conventions forbid them to use. The fact that they share secret knowledge, and the ease with which it can be exposed, sometimes gives them the power to inflict hideous damage. This danger is so real that a person who has been stung will sometimes, in the case of a new love, gather defensive ammunition against the possibility of being hurt again, ammunition consisting of compromising notes, for example, preferably dated and, of course, signed. Thus the ethics of lovers sometimes appears to have no better foundation than the possibility of blackmail.

Clearly lovers need a set of guidelines. The supposition that the relationship is itself wrong does not constitute a reason for allowing it to be a vehicle for misery, the more so if that supposition is no longer obviously true. Good, sincere, and devoted husbands and wives do in fact sometimes fall in love with persons to whom they are not married. The simple and mindless condemnation of this fact will not make it disappear. Nothing will, and there is really no reason to wish otherwise. Love affairs can be destructive of marriage relationships, and we have already explored ways of reducing their damaging effects. They can also inflict significant damage on the lovers themselves. "It serves them right" can never be a good response to this fact. Misery is one thing, relishing it is quite another; and while recognizing the fact is rational, delighting in it can hardly be a mark of decency.

Of course it is impossible to enforce any rules one might make for lovers. No customs and conventions back them up, and obviously no special laws. Still, they are worth enunciating, and heeding, and their strength is in their reasonableness.

Rule One: Be aware of the needs of the other.

This rule is so banal as to seem hardly worth enunciating, and it is in fact the least important of any, yet in a way it is basic. For however they may be romanticized, love affairs rest upon the fulfillment of the needs of partners, and upon nothing more ethereal. Marriage, too, however much it may be glorified and portrayed as the embodiment of selfless love, rests primarily on the fulfillment of needs. When those needs are met the relationships flourish and their partners are happy. When they remain unfulfilled the partners become querulous and, subsequently, relationships are strained or begin to come apart. If lovers do not fulfill each other's needs, then they cease to be lovers; it is just that simple. In case they are married lovers the marriage itself may grind along, perhaps indefinitely, but it will be for all practical purposes a dead one. And in case they are not married lovers, then very quickly nothing will be left at all except, perhaps, resentment. No one will persist in a relationship that gives him nothing.

The needs themselves upon which these relationships rest are various, though some are so common that they can be regarded as normal, others so uncommon and often so destructive that they can be considered abnormal. Of course, that is no profound insight, but I am further convinced that these needs are entirely the product of childhood, which means that they are the product of the kind and the amount of love one received from one's parents. There is nothing rational to it at all. Love is quite rightly thought of as a kind of "chemistry" between people, a kind of equation having two sides, but such that a reaction, whether mild or violent, becomes possible only when the right things are on both sides. But the elements that stand ready to react are, I am convinced, entirely the product of a sometimes forgotten childhood. In that sense, every love affair really begins in childhood, and results not so much from one's choice of a lover as his "choice" of his parents, for it is they who, unwittingly, lay the groundwork. This consideration by itself is enough to absolve lovers of blame, for if any finger of reproach is to be pointed, it should be pointed towards our parents who nourished our needs and feelings, or failed to do so, rather than at those of us who have responded to them, one way or another, as every human being does.

Very little insight into human nature is needed to find this illustrated in the following account:

> I've only had one love affair, and it's still going on, with the director of our department. I work for the income tax bureau, and there are seven others in that department. Steve, who is the head, is quite a bit older than I am, has been married about twelve years, and has been having an affair with someone or other all that time, currently with me. It has caused a lot of bad feeling in the office, and I never realized that people I considered friends could really be so nasty.
>
> It has never bothered me that Steve is married. He is an important person, and it makes me feel important that he cares about me. I think he does this with everyone; he makes them feel important, and not just because of who he is, but because of the way he talks to them. I know he means it; he doesn't just flatter people. The things he tells me I am good at, I really am good at, but he is the first one who has ever told me so.
>
> I have four sisters and a brother, all older than me, and not one of them has ever had any interest in getting married. And no wonder. All any of us can remember about our father is that he spent all his time at home fighting with our mother. He's dead now, and Mother, after all those years, sometimes seems like a real person in her own right, instead of someone who is just trying to please her husband, and never succeeding. Our father was always very much concerned about his children, but we always felt that what he was really concerned with was how we looked to outsiders. If one of us was hurt in a car accident, I'm sure the first thing he would think of was whether it might be bad publicity, whether it might give the family some sort of bad name. I know I never really loved him. None of us did, and I don't think my mother really did either.

If one's needs are not fulfilled by those who officially love them, then other relationships will be created in which those needs are met. This is not, I think, an oversimplification.

That love, especially between men and women, rests largely upon needs, and that these needs are largely the product of childhood experiences is fairly obvious to anyone who reflects for a moment. It would hardly require noting if it were not for the fact that most people seem to go through their lives acting more or less as if it were not true. Thus a husband goes along totally disregarding even the most elementary needs of his wife; for example, her need to be considered a person in her own right with aspirations of her own that are not merely derived from his. When her inevitable resentment begins to show, then he begins feeling rejected, becoming even more self-centered than ever, and as these cycles reinforce each other, both the husband and the wife become vulnerable to the attentions of some outsider who "understands" them. Of course it works as often the other way. A wife is insensitive to her husband's most basic needs, such as his need to be seen by her as he sees himself—strong, resourceful, and conquering.

Again, the marriage grinds down to the inevitable result, either smoldering resentment that fuels resentment on the other side or, very often, a complete breakdown.

Love affairs are even more fragile than marriage relationships. A love affair has almost nothing holding it together except the mutual fulfillment of individual needs. Considered thus, the relationship is in no sense belittled, except on the supposition that our individual needs are of slight importance. They are, in fact, to each of us, the most important things in the world. The obvious implication of this is that anyone who can truly claim to care for another person—whether that person is husband, wife, lover, friend, or whatever—must cultivate, almost to the point of an art, the awareness and fulfillment of that person's needs.

In the following account, it is very easy to see failure in this respect:

My husband is a chemist. He has never taught, to speak of, but for years has lived on grants. The marriage was a shambles when I met Harold, who was an economics professor going through a divorce. So we were both lonely, and liked each other from the minute we met. The second time I saw him I went home with him. We talked easily, there didn't seem to be any barriers, and at first I was very happy whenever we were together. I felt that he liked me, just for what I was. I had never really felt that my husband had. There had always seemed to be something I was supposed to *change* about myself, and yet I could never be sure just what.

But the thing with Harold lasted only two months, and ended miserably. He was trying to start a journal, and this was something I could help with, since I had done professional editing. But he never wanted to pay me, even though he easily could have, and I needed the money. He would just say he'd pay me off "in bed." I can see why he would say that, because it always was very nice in bed; but I wanted to keep the two things separate. I wanted him to appreciate my professional skills enough to pay for them, the way others did, and also to appreciate me for myself, and not mix the two up. I felt cheapened both ways— in my skills, which I was proud of, and in my person, which I was sensitive about. But he never did pay me for the editing, and even wanted me to take some of my savings and invest them in his journal.

Then the other thing that went wrong was his possessiveness. He traveled a lot, and always insisted that I must not see anyone else when he was away. He always quizzed me about this whenever he came home. I never quizzed him. He didn't even want me to be with my own husband. It is true that my marriage was in bad shape, but I still had hopes of saving it. But Harold wanted me to go live with him, bringing one of my children, Jeannie, but not the other, Steven, whom he couldn't get along with very well. I could never agree to anything like that.

Well, one afternoon I had made a date for cocktails with a man I'd never met, also a professor. A friend had arranged it. It was a disaster. He had no interest in me at all, and that was obvious from the minute we met. It was a complete bust, and I felt terrible. So I went over to see Harold who immediately accused me of having been drinking with another man, which was true of course, as if I had done something terrible. I got more and more angry, finally went to the closet and got all my clothes, and just walked out.

And there I was—my Ph.D. husband was gone, and in just a couple of hours I'd lost two more Ph.D.s. I feel as though I have struck out, and yet I don't see why any of these really had to end that way.

And indeed they did not *have* to end that way. But every relationship of this type will most assuredly end if either partner is blinded to the simple needs of the other by his own ego or vanity.

*   *   *

It is this alone that explains the power of certain relationships that sometimes seem so incongruous, for example, the uncompromising attachment that a young and beautiful woman will form for a man three times her age, or a man singularly lacking in charms, good looks, worldly fortune, or indeed any of the qualities normally thought of as virtues and gifts. The gift such a man has is apparent only to her, and that is tenderness or consideration, which simply means an awareness of her needs and solicitude in fulfilling them. Nor are the connections here really accidental. A man of middle age, for example, is quite aware of his lack of inherent personal charm, his disadvantages when compared to men who are younger. Accordingly, he compensates with the one thing that will triumph over those more visible strengths almost every time, namely, with a genuine concern for the needs of his partner. Every man loves to think of himself as a giant of masculinity, strength, and virility. When the picture he has of himself is not a total distortion, as in the case of a man who is young, athletic, healthy, and without significant aberrations in his personal features, then his need to have that image of himself reinforced by lovers is minimal. He therefore believes that he needs to give very little in order to get what he wants. Giving little, in the way of consideration for one's partner, however, he gets little in return in the way of affection. If there appears on the scene a man with more or less the same need who cannot, however, easily confirm that self-image—someone who is, for example, short or balding or of middle age or with little in the way of personal achievement or fortune—then this is apt to be someone who must give a great deal in order to get anything at all of what he seeks. So he does, and, to the amazement of all, he finds himself adored, the winner over competitors against whom he would be thought to have no chance whatsoever. We see this happen constantly. We see women of exquisite beauty and youth drawn to totally incongruous lovers, to men who seem to have nothing whatever to offer. We simply fail to see that the one thing they do offer is the most basic of all, and in the last analysis the only thing that counts, which is genuine affection or, more precisely, a sensitivity to the needs of another person that can, at least sometimes, take their attention from their blinding preoccupation with themselves.

And it is, of course, the same in the other direction, for people are sometimes astonished by the choices men make, or by the partners in favor of whom they have abandoned their seemingly more estimable wives. The needs of men and women are rather different, as we have noted earlier at some length, but they equally demand fulfillment.

* * *

The tendency thus far has been to speak as though the needs of men are essentially similar, and those of women essentially similar as well, and I believe that this is in most cases true. But not always. What seems unexceptionably true is that our needs are the product of our childhood, even of a childhood that is now more or less forgotten, and this, of course, takes them entirely out of the realm of reason. There is no point whatsoever in telling anyone what he *ought* to want or seek or avoid in his relations with others, and especially in his loves and hates, for what he *will* seek has already been decided for him in a part of his life that is beyond change and even, sometimes, largely beyond memory.

Consider, for instance, the extraordinary case which follows. My report of it, much abbreviated, is the product of several talks, and although I was at first astonished by this beautiful person's narration of her joys and frustrations, I ceased to be so the moment I placed what she told me within the context of her childhood:

> I got married to Ted at nineteen, and it lasted several years, though the last two were pretty meaningless. For the first few years I did everything a wife is supposed to do, and we looked like a happy couple. I went to church, my house was always spotless, Ted and I went out with couples our age, and we did everything about the way they did. It wasn't phony, either; that really was me, it was exactly the way I wanted to be. Nor was there anything wrong with Ted. He was devoted to me, kind and considerate, just what you'd want a husband to be. Everyone liked him. He could walk into a laundromat and know everyone there, and everyone would smile and talk with him. Everyone in town liked him.
>
> I don't know why it didn't work out. Certainly it wasn't his fault. No one could ever want a sweeter, nicer man for a husband. I knew nothing about sex, was a virgin when we got married, and never had an orgasm. I didn't even know what it was. But that wasn't his fault.
>
> That marriage was never really happy for me, though I suppose it should have been. I had no women friends at all, and have never had many girlfriends. Ted and I were popular, and had a good social life, but I always assumed it was just because everyone liked him that we got asked to go places.
>
> Anyway, I began flirting with men, which I had always sort of done, and I began to feel that I wanted to be with men, as many men as I could, as much as possible. I stopped going to church, took off my wedding ring, and started seeking men for company. My husband always worked nights, so that made it very easy. At one time I was having relations with six men. They all knew each other, too, more or less, but I don't think any of them ever knew that any of the others were going to bed with me. The strange thing is that I never enjoyed it much. I think now that it was just my way of thinking that I also had something worthwhile. Mostly I did it because they liked it so much, and I wanted them to like

me. These six men were the only friends I had, and I wanted them to like me. I remember I thought then, that even if every person in the world loved me, it wouldn't be enough.

Then for almost two years I was in love, for the first time in my life, really. He was a salesman named Paul, married and eighteen years older than me. He was marvelous company; he saw me every chance he could, and loved doing things for me. He took me to the summer theater, to dinner, and to plays in Ithaca, and it was always fun. But more important than that, he built me up; he made me feel like a real person, someone possessing good qualities. He never missed a chance to tell me how great I was, and he convinced me that I could do things for myself. I was about thirty then, and this was the first time in my life I'd ever believed in myself. It was entirely because of him that I went out and got a good job working for an accounting firm, which was better than anything I'd ever done before. I was still married to Ted, but he knew about Paul and how much I liked being with him, though he didn't know I was having a regular love affair with him. Actually, I never got much out of sex with Paul either; mostly I just did it for him.

But then something happened that changed my whole life. In the accounting office where I'd gotten my new job there was an accountant I just knew I wanted the first time I saw him. I was still married to Ted, and sleeping with Paul, but there was something about Rob, this new man, that was entirely different from anything I had ever seen. That was in March, and I practically threw myself at him from that first day. He was single too, though that didn't make much difference to me, one way or the other. After awhile I managed to get him to have lunch with me once in awhile, even though his other partners strongly disapproved. But it was September—over six months—before I could interest him in coming home with me, and when he finally did, I practically raped him the very first time.

Eventually I was able to get him to come over every Friday night, and I began to just live for Friday nights. Maybe he would have come more often— Ted was never home evenings, and my marriage was dead anyway—but I think he was seeing another girl then.

No one has ever affected me like Rob did, and still does, five years later, even though I hardly ever see him any more, and I cannot explain it. He never does anything for me, hates to spend money on me, in fact he treats his dog better than me. I don't think he has ever told me he loves me, or praised me for anything, or in fact said anything really nice to me even once in all these years. Actually, he doesn't communicate with anyone. Even when clients would come to talk with him at the office he would hardly say a word—would never ask them any questions, or say anything. He was tired after awhile, and that was probably why. He moved to Rochester, where he got another accounting job, but he didn't last long at that one either, because of his personality. I used to go up every weekend to stay with him, and when I would arrive he would almost always be watching television and reading, both at the same time. This is about all he ever did. Usually he didn't even get up to greet me, but went right on reading, with the television on. He was usually unshaved when I arrived, and his apartment was a mess. He read mostly mysteries. He wasn't really interested in anything, not in his work, or me, or anything.

So why did I like him? It was just sex, and nothing else, but that was some-thing I'd never known. It was like one long orgasm, and I didn't have to work at it at all, which I had always had to before. Rob could kiss me and I would have an orgasm. That is not an exaggeration. It is literally true. All he had to do was touch me and I would do absolutely anything for him. When we had worked in the same office, and were there alone, we sometimes made love right there. I was always the aggressor.

He never did anything else for me, except once, when he took me on a trip. He was completely selfish, and I never liked him as a person. He always just wanted to go to bars, and be around men, and I hated going to bars with him. When we went out we always had to get back in time to let his dog out. It was a nervous, horrid dog that barked his head off at every little sound, and it drove me crazy. But that dog was everything to him. Sometimes when I was there the dog would be eating steak, and we had to have sandwiches. I hated that dog, and finally told Rob that if he ever came to visit me, he would have to leave the dog home.

I could never get along with Rob. We were fighting most of the time, about everything. There was nothing in it at all. Yet that is how he affected me, in bed, or just by touching me, and I don't think anyone else ever will.

When I heard this account, it seemed at first to contradict everything my inquiries had led me to believe about the passionate involvements between men and women. When I put it together with the account of the narrator's childhood, however, her underlying feelings and needs seemed to emerge with transparent clarity.

My own childhood was rather strange. My sister was my mother. That is, my sister—the woman I grew up in the same family with and was taught to think of as my sister—was actually my mother. She had me when she was young, and *her* mother—my grandmother, really—adopted me legally, and taught me to think of her as my mother and to call her that too. So I thought that her mother was my mother too, and that she was my sister. Actually, I knew the truth about all this, though no one knew that I did. Once, I even met the man who had made her pregnant—some boy she'd been going with, who didn't mean anything to her. He was my real father; but I was supposed to think that my sister's (really my mother's) father was my father too. I knew what was true, but never said so. I still refer to my grandparents as my mother and father, call them that, and even think of them that way. They were quite old. My father died several years ago, when he was seventy-nine, and my mother is still alive, but very old.

Mother (really my grandmother) never talked to me much. In fact my last year in high school we didn't communicate at all, hardly even said a word. And my father (actually grandfather) and I were always just strangers. I never had any friends my own age, because I was too ashamed to have them come to my house and see how old my parents were. We were also very poor, and on wel-fare. I was much too tall for my age, and self-conscious. And of course I was by far the youngest in the family. My brother was much older, and my nearest sis-ter was ten years older. So I just didn't have any friends. But I don't remember being unhappy. I just shut everything out, and sort of kept to myself. Sometimes, during the summer, I was sent to Buffalo for two weeks to visit my sister (really my mother), who never did get married, but I hated every minute of that.

My (adoptive) mother, besides being so much older, was also very strict, and a very cold person. When I was in high school she saw me kissing a boy, and acted as if I had done the most awful thing in the world. If a boy ever came to the house she would always stay right with us. I don't mean just stay in the house, but stay in the same room every minute. What made it worse, she hardly ever said anything, to anyone. She just did not communicate. Even now she doesn't have anything to do with my brothers and sisters. She hasn't even been in contact with my brother for years, and my sisters hate to even go see her.

I don't remember that my mother ever kissed me, or said anything good to me at all. Though I can remember her hugging me. In fact I have sometimes thought, when Rob hugged me, that it was exactly the way she used to hug me. It all felt just the same, except that my mother never kissed me, and Rob did.

There have been many theories about why people fall in love, and why they sometimes so inexplicably love the people they do. One is that we try through our loves to resolve certain all but forgotten and unresolved relationships. Certainly the chemistry of love is not rational. I leave speculations of this sort to psychology, noting only that the child each of us once was never dies, but still dwells in us for good or ill, to determine all our loves and hates, and with these all our joy and misery, for the rest of our lives.

*   *   *

It is in the light of the simple consideration of need fulfillment that we can appreciate the immense ineptitude of most of the world's would-be lovers, whether they be men or women—though in fact most of the ineptness and stupidity in this area seems to be on the side of men. Consider, for example, a husband who seems to have a rather good reason to be infatuated with himself. He is, we can suppose, preeminent in his business, hence rich, still young, athletic, surrounded with beautiful things, each of them testimony to his superiority over others. Yet he lacks one thing he wants, which is the fairly constant appreciation of his virtues and worth on the part of others and, above all, on the part of his wife. The effect on him, sooner or later, is that he becomes tirelessly flirtatious—it is a familiar thing. But his constant quest for the love of women is equaled only by his failure to get it. His manner is to invite attention to himself, for he imagines, as most people seem to, that the better he can make himself appear—and with this man that is a very easy thing to do—the more attractive to others he will be. Thus, he never overlooks a chance to call attention to his wealth and his victories over competitors. With more or less subtlety he makes known his connections with important people. His skill at sports, or whatever, is not concealed; and attention is drawn to the breadth of his reading, the extent of his travels, and so on—the type is very familiar. And with all this to buoy up his daring, he virtually accosts female companions with feigned affection; loud, almost bellicose proposals of friendship or intimacy; and suggestions he vainly hopes will serve as bait. And he gets nowhere. The whole approach is doomed to failure. He vainly imagines that he makes himself attractive by being attractive, and in the course of all this omits the one thing that is needed, which is a simple concern for the worth, needs, and sensitivities of the person with whom he is trying to ingratiate himself.

The comedy really unwinds to its proper conclusion when this same man, the envy of all, discovers that his wife has become involved in an affair with some contemptible day laborer, someone who has, we shall suppose, been twice divorced and bears every sign of being a worldly misfit and drifter. This husband's reaction is also totally familiar. He asks in astonished outrage, "What has *he* got that I haven't?"—thereby giving away in one question his whole misconception of what is the actual relationship between the sexes. He thought the path to affection was through the perception others have of his own greatness. Exhibiting little personal greatness, the day laborer thought, and quite correctly, that the path to affection is through the perception of the needs of his partner. However insignificant these may seem, however vain and even sometimes silly, they are nevertheless her needs, just as the affection that is sought is also hers to bestow, or to withhold.

18

Extramarital Fidelity

Those who have had great love affairs are forever glad, and forever sorry, that they have ended.

—La Rochefoucauld

The term *extramarital fidelity* seems at first incongruous, as though trying to combine two ideas that do not fit. Yet that is not so, for all that the expression means is that there is a faith lovers should keep with each other, and this should be obvious by now.

This kind of fidelity gives rise to five additional rules, addressing the issues of truth, discretion, accommodation, trust, and constancy.

Rule Two: Be honest.

Friends and lovers have a special obligation to candor and honesty that few relationships can demand, and one that even comes close to being absolute. The reason is that they have nothing but each other. They have no home, no children, none of the other things that go into making a marriage, or even ordinary business associations, such as partnerships. They have only each other and, by common consensus, are not even supposed to have that. Here, within a love affair, there can almost never be any reason to lie except to gain an advantage over the other, and the moment that happens the possibility of genuine love has already been all but canceled. This is not so in other human associations. In the presence of enemies, for example, one lies in self-defense, and has every right and reason to do so. No one will give true answers to a bandit's questions if he can offer lies instead. Again, lawyers lie and distort to protect their clients, for that is what they are paid to do. A defending attorney who simply presented the whole, unblemished truth to a prosecutor would not be worth his fee, and could in fact be rightly thought to have betrayed his client. And even in the case of husbands and wives, as we have seen, though the presumption of truth, candor, and openness is very high, it is far from absolute. Married people have a great deal more than each other. They have a home, and very likely children, and in any case they presumably want their marriage to last. To the extent that any of these things do not hold—if they have no children, for example—then to that extent the expectation of complete honesty is enhanced. The truth can injure sometimes, just as falsehood can, and when home and children are involved the injury can be immense.

But in the case of lovers no truth can really injure, beyond the injury to feelings. Of course the relationship itself can be destroyed, but lovers who have nothing but each other cease to have even that when serious false representations come to be considered acceptable. Here, truth can destroy nothing that lies would not destroy just as effectively. A love affair will survive a thousand unpleasant truths, but sometimes not even a single deliberate and discovered lie.

*   *   *

The clearest example of wrongdoing in a love affair is for one or the other partner to conceal the fact that he or she is married. A woman is unlikely to do this, for it makes little difference to the feelings of a man to discover that an intended lover is already married. It increases his sense of caution, of course, and is clearly seen as an obstacle, but a man's passions are seldom affected by such a discovery. A woman, on the other hand, is likely to lose interest, instantly and completely, in a man she learns is already married, the more so if he is happily married. And it is quite rare for a woman to have any passionate interest in a man whose wife she knows well and admires. Two men, on the other hand, can continue a close and friendly association that they have cultivated for years even though one of them is, unbeknown to the other, deeply involved with that other's wife. Indeed they can part company at the end of a pleasant day of golfing or sailing, and one of them go straightway to the arms of the other's wife. Corresponding behavior on the part of women is far less common.

There is, then, a temptation on the part of a man to conceal the fact of his marriage. He correctly perceives it as being sometimes an obstacle. In my interviews, it was in fact quite common to find women who had been lied to in just this way. I never found a man who had been thus lied to. And it is even more common for men to pretend that they expect to divorce their wives in the near or distant future—"as soon as the children are a little older," for example. Women, it seems, seldom or never say this unless it is in fact true.

The temptation to mislead someone in matters of this kind must absolutely be suppressed, for to do otherwise is sheer exploitation. A single woman—a divorcée, for example—sometimes has a keen and very understandable wish to remarry, and will go to considerable lengths to enhance that possibility. It is a sheer barbarism, violating every conception of fairness and decency, for any man to combine that wish with his own deceptions in order to gain sexual favors from her. Here his purpose would not be a love affair, but sexual indulgence for its own sake, purchased at no cost to himself and possibly at great cost to his partner.

The case is not different in kind if a man misrepresents his marriage, without actually denying the fact of it. Therefore, if a man genuinely adores his wife and takes great pride and joy in his family, he should not pretend otherwise to any partner in a love affair, and for the same reason. The difference is only a small one of degree.

Lovers have no obligation of constancy to each other, that is, of sexual exclusiveness. Having already broken the rule of monogamy, they know that they can break it again and again. But here, too, total honesty is needed. Sometimes lovers agree to a nonexclusive relationship, in which case there is no real need to conceal other relationships. Usually, however, there is an intense desire on both sides that the affair should be an exclusive one, excepting only the wife or husband who is already there; and if this is understood, then no deviation from it should be concealed.

So it should be with respect to everything. Matters of health, wealth, comings and goings, must be entirely open. Often one is known by his partner in a love affair better than he is known by anyone else in the world. It is something about such a relationship that can be terribly frightening, but at the same time tremendously valuable. Such knowledge should therefore be clear, not something that is contaminated with all sorts of misrepresentations.

Rule Three: Do not exhibit and boast.

A love affair is an ego trip for nearly every man, often a very big one. That is rarely all it is, for if it were, his partner would quickly lose interest; but that is usually part of it, and sometimes a very large part. His temptation is therefore to make it known to the whole world, or to as much of it as he dares. To be in love is a heady thing. But for someone to be in love with you is even more inflationary to the ego. And if that other person has every practical reason not to have such feelings, if in fact the whole thing has the aspect of being something forbidden, as in the case of every love affair, then the impact on a man's ego can be intoxicating. Here, he imagines, is someone who has every incentive and many of the strongest of social pressures not to be involved with him, but who nevertheless, it seems, adores him—for no other reason, it would appear, than his own glory and greatness. That perception is essentially illusory, of course, since her affection rests far more on her needs than any qualities of greatness in him. Still, it is a pleasant, sometimes overpowering illusion, to which even men who are quite able to perceive realities in their true light easily succumb.

Now consider what happens when we add to those feelings the perception, on the part of a man, that he is greatly admired by others for this relationship he has been able to establish, and envied by them too. The first perception is almost entirely false; that is, the cultivation of love affairs is a very poor road indeed to winning the admiration of others, although it is a good way to create in oneself the illusion of doing so. But the second perception, that a man in this situation is an object of envy, is certainly true. It is doubtful whether envy from any other cause is so intense. When Freud lists the artist's blessings as being "honor, power, riches, fame, and the love of women," the last has a special quality that nothing else can possibly match.

Now, finally, consider that men who are consistently successful in winning the love of women are not, typically, those who are possessed of the usual attributes of masculine greatness, as we have seen, but precisely the opposite; that is, the very men who are likely to be seen by other men as not being much at all. Here, then, we have a situation where a man of seemingly limited worth, as judged by the usual standards, is nevertheless the envy of all for having what those others deem, secretly or otherwise, to be the sweetest of blessings—the gratuitous and, it seems to them, the undeserved adoration of a beautiful woman.

Given all these things, the temptation of such a man to make known his love affair, to parade it before the envious eyes of all, can be quite overwhelming.

*   *   *

Women, it should be added, have no similar need, or at least not in any similar degree. Whatever it may do for a man's ego, it does little for a woman's self-esteem, or for what we have been calling vanity, to flaunt an illicit affair. It is quite true that a woman loves the attention of a man, and the more so if he is a man of enviable status and position; but the rewards to her are to her self-esteem, her feeling of being appreciated by him, rather than in the envy she can quicken in others. When, accordingly, she makes known this relationship to her friends, it is more of the nature of a confidence shared, whereas in the case of a man it is a boast.

Of course here, as in all comparisons of the sexes, it is a matter of degree. Vanity is no exclusive possession of women, nor egoism of men, and there is no doubt that many differences are culturally conditioned. Still, those differences are real. The feelings of a man and a woman in a group, known by all to be lovers and to be married to other persons, are decidedly different. She wishes to call rather little attention to their affair, and to act, as much as possible, like other people, while he wants to flaunt it. She is made slightly uncomfortable by any allusion to sexual intimacy, while he is exhilarated. He relishes any display of affection between them, and hopes it will be noticed, while she is embarrassed by it, preferring that it be reserved for another time and place.

*   *   *

There is, in this connection, another kind of boasting to which another set of considerations apply, and that is, boasting between lovers themselves. This is something both men and women have an inclination to do, but as usual, for different reasons; and without doubt, men fall into it more than women.

Thus a man sometimes feels a strong, almost perverse desire to convey to his lover that there are others who find him as fascinating as she does. He will leave a note where she will find it, for example, or receive a telltale telephone call when in her presence, even perhaps arranging for just this to happen. Of course this is nothing more than another ego trip for him. He gives himself the deliciously satisfying reminder of having not one lover, but two. There is the additional bonus that such discovery does sometimes produce visible anguish on the face of his lover, which is to him a further reminder of his importance to her. And on top of all this, there is a widespread, almost universal notion among men, that they make themselves more glorious in the eyes of women by such demonstrations of apparent desirability. Thus quite apart from the stimulus to the ego, a man is very likely to imagine that he is on exactly the right track to impressing a woman, and thereby winning her affection.

But it certainly does not work. On the contrary, this kind of exhibitionism almost certainly backfires. To illustrate:

My son needed music lessons, and I'd heard of this guy named Ray, who played with a group in local inns and places like that and gave guitar lessons on the side. So I arranged to have him give Joey lessons. Then I discovered that he had just been divorced. Well, I'd been divorced six years, but I was still only thirty, and this musician was only a little older than that. An affair I'd been having for years with a married man, almost since my own divorce, wasn't going too well just then, and I looked at this musician and thought, "Hey, he's good-looking, lots of fun, and maybe just what I want."

I learned he had been thinking of going off to Cape Cod for a week, so I managed to get myself invited along. And that whole week was just perfect, absolutely perfect. I'm sure it was the most wonderful week of my whole life. We did everything—we danced, and sailed, and walked the beach, and had shore dinners, and smoked grass, and made love day and night. When I came home I was so exhausted that my mother said I looked more like I needed a vacation than like I had just had one.

But that week was the end of it. I learned that he had other women he treated just the same as me. He didn't even try to hide it, after the week was almost over; in fact he seemed almost proud of it, and acted as if I should be impressed. On our very last night at the Cape he practically went straight from our bed into another bed, then went right from there off to New Jersey to spend a week with still another little friend, leaving me to go home alone!

I felt completely destroyed. I felt as though I were nothing but a piece of merchandise. For the next week I would be on the telephone half the night, night after night, talking to my girlfriend; one night I didn't hang up until four in the morning. She only lived a block away—I could have just gone down there to talk to her. She thought I shouldn't give up on Ray quite yet.

But then the strangest thing of all happened. Ray finally came back from New Jersey, called me up, as if everything was supposed to be just the way it was that week on the Cape, and wanted to know how soon we could get together again! I knew then that I didn't have any interest in ever seeing him again as long as I lived. I stopped Joey's music lessons, and I never did see him again.

With respect to the titillations to the ego that prompt this kind of male exhibitionism, the only proper assessment is childishness. No man, behaving in this manner, is showing the least concern for the feelings and needs of his partner. It is pure, but inept, self-glorification in which no man with any true pride in himself will ever indulge.

With respect to the notion that things of this nature do greatly impress a woman, and convey to her a glory in himself that others see, it can only be said that this is totally false. Something like this is the surest way to kill any woman's interest in a man. A single note or telephone call will do it, with dreadful effectiveness. For women do not seek lovers in order to feast their eyes on their greatness. Nor is any woman ever impressed by any power a man may have to impress others. As his motives spring largely from egoism, hers spring largely from her self-esteem or vanity, and nothing is quite so crushing to this as the discovery that she shares a place in his eyes with others. It is the clearest possible reminder to her that she is, for him, nothing special at all—and with this, everything that led her into this affair is apt to evaporate at once. A man and woman may remain friends after an episode or two of this kind, but any love that she had for him is almost certainly irrecoverably lost. While she may feel no real wrath, like a woman scorned, it is just as certain that she will feel no real love, like a woman cherished.

Women, to their credit, have far less tendency to this kind of boastfulness and display, for their sense of femininity, unlike the male sense of masculinity, never requires anything like this. A woman who boasts of other loves or produces reminders of them is likely to be one whose parents never enabled her to think very well of herself, who were excessively faultfinding, for example, or who compared her unfavorably with siblings, and so on. Her behavior is then a somewhat desperate effort to impress. Sometimes, too, a woman will indulge herself in these ways as a reaction to an upbringing that has been excessively narrow. In every case, however, sexual bravado on the part of a woman is an aberration, something uncharacteristic, whereas in a man it is, alas! the very opposite.

Rule Four: Never deliver ultimatums.

This is a rule that applies to all persons who care for each other, whether spouses, lovers, parents, whomever. Every ultimatum produces a counterreaction and, in the area of personal relationships, they tend to destroy the relationship itself. No one can interpret an either-or option as an expression of caring. A wife who tries to modify her husband's behavior by that kind of forced choice, or a husband who thus tries to control his wife, holds a gun that can explode in the hand and never achieves the desired result except at prohibitive cost. And the same is true for lovers.

This is so obvious to anyone who reflects on it that it hardly needs illustrating, but this brief example may show how, in any case, such ultimatums are apt to be delivered more as a means of trying to prove something to oneself than trying to change someone else:

> I started going with Seth when we were in high school, and we both always assumed that we would both go to med-school and someday get married. But there was always too much game playing and trying to control each other. Even in high school, he got me to give up all my friends who were boys, though they were all just friends. And I always pretended not to know what my father did, and let him think that my father belonged to the mafia. If we spent a night in a motel he always kept the key afterwards, so he could mail it to my mother in case there was any need to—in case I didn't return his sweater to him, for example. Then I would allude to personal things I knew about him or his family, with the hint that I could reveal those. The break came when he came to visit me one weekend. I was busy with lots of papers to write, and he wanted all my attention. He finally left, saying that if I wanted to reestablish the relationship I could come visit him in Boston, but he refused to answer my question whether he wanted me to visit him. It was all just up to me. We never saw each other again.

Quite apart from this final ultimatum, which was obviously bound to fail, it would be difficult to describe a relationship in which things could have been done more badly.

Rule Five: Do not betray.

It is rare for a really intense love affair to end happily. The emotions involved are too strong. The needs that were more or less fulfilled in the relationship are now no longer met, and the effect can be agonizing. The ending seldom comes by mutual consent; one or the other breaks things off, sometimes more or less abruptly, leaving the other lonely and depressed and, very often, sunk in anger and bitterness. For reasons that are not very clear, it seems usually to be the male partner of the affair who withdraws. Perhaps part of the reason is that in our culture men are less likely than women to form an emotional dependence on the opposite sex. If set adrift a man can turn to other things or other persons more easily than a woman. A woman is very likely to terminate an affair if she begins to suspect that she is being "used," that is, not loved for herself and the personal qualities in which she takes pride. This almost certainly happens if she discovers that her partner behaves toward, and tries to ingratiate himself with, some lesser woman in exactly the way he does with her. And again, a woman will sometimes drop an affair in great haste if she finds her security, and perhaps that of her children, imperiled. But when fears and discoveries like this do not arise to disrupt things, then a love affair runs its course, to end sooner or later, usually with less emotional damage to the male partner.

The temptation in these circumstances is for the one who feels abandoned to get even, and of course the instrument of revenge is close at hand. One needs only to betray the secret that both have held. In this we find one of the ugliest spectacles in human relationships. Two persons who, until recently, were lovers —even, as they thought, the most genuine of lovers, without ulterior motives— are suddenly converted to implacable adversaries. This also happens in divorces, but two factors usually reduce the ugliness of these cases. For one thing, there are accepted procedures for terminating a marriage, though none for terminating an affair. And for the other, the partners of a marriage usually do not possess secret knowledge of a scandalous nature that can be used against each other, though of course sometimes they do. On the other hand, lovers always do.

If a man withdraws from an affair, leaving his partner emotionally adrift, then she is likely to have letters he has written that she can mail to his wife, or perhaps his boss. A man, of course, can do the same, in case he is the one aban- doned. Weapons of deadly destructiveness are always available. It is all ugly beyond description, especially when viewed in the context of the feelings that, until shortly before, had flourished.

In fact lovers, or former lovers, rarely betray each other this way, though the possibility always exists. What chiefly restrains them is simple decency, together with a perception of the damage that is going to be done to other people. If love let- ters are planted, for example, then the real victim of that assault is the person who discovers them, not the person who wrote them. The effect on him is severe embar- rassment and resentment, but the effect on the person who finds them—his wife, for example—may be trauma. It was not she at whom the assailant was aiming. The same occurs if the sexes are reversed. On top of this is always the real danger that an established marriage, very likely a home with children, can be destroyed by such an act, and is almost certainly damaged by it. These considerations are usually suf- ficient to restrain any abandoned lover from acting out an impulse of vengeance.

*   *   *

There is, however, one circumstance in which these restraints can by no means be counted on, and that is when a man or woman is abandoned in favor of still some third person, that is, someone other than a partner's wife or husband. No one can really be outraged forever at a man who terminates an affair in favor of his own wife, a woman who has been there from the start and whose claims are in every sense prior. But if a man breaks off an affair only to pursue another, then the danger of explosion is immense. Hell does indeed have no fury like that of a woman scorned. Moreover, it is true that the danger of vengeance is greater in the case of a woman scorned than in the case of a man. If a man is forsaken in favor of another man, then his ego is badly injured; but he can hope for no sal- vation whatever by avenging himself against his former lover. This would only make him look worse as a man, so he is reduced to salvaging what he can of his pride, usually through the appearance of lordly magnanimity and, perhaps, through the reassurance that a fresh love affair promises. But if a woman is forsaken in favor of another woman, then her vanity or self-esteem is violated in a way that sometimes leaves little hope of restoration. She has little inclination to magnanimity in such circumstances, and cannot easily take the initiative in establishing a new relationship that will assuage her pride. The wrathful explosion that follows is likely to be devastating, and should be expected under these circumstances, even from what seemed before to be the best and purest heart in the world. It will likely be regretted, but not before the damage is irrevocably done.

The rule, then, is simple: Do not betray. Lovers, though they may become implacable enemies in time, must never betray each other. It is the ultimate foul shot, one that is way out of proportion to any incentive to do it. The trust that this will never happen, no matter what, has to be absolute, because the secret each holds is so dangerous to outside persons, and because there are so few other forces working to keep it hidden once one of them has lost the need to do so.

Of course it goes without saying that this rule applies to outsiders even more clearly. For anyone, knowing of a love affair in which he is no way involved, to convey that knowledge to the husband or wife of those who are involved in it, is sheer meddling. Even the noblest of motives, such as friendship or the love of truth, can never under any circumstances excuse it.

Rule Six: Do not abandon.

The ending of any love affair, whether gradual or abrupt, is more or less wrenching to one or both partners. It is almost certainly unrealistic to think of such a relationship ending in smiles, its partners to be friends who might henceforth enjoy each other's occasional and casual company. The very minimum expectation, however, is that they can avoid becoming enemies, though this is often not easy. Beyond that, the rule should be not to utterly abandon, whatever pressures there might be to do so. The happiness and fulfillment that were once there are gone, but the same needs persist. They cannot be fulfilled, else the affair would go on, but at least one need that both have does not have to be disregarded, and that is the need for simple friendship and respect, even if maintained at a distance.

One reason for urging this is somewhat aesthetic in character. Things that begin well, and go well, really should end well. Whatever may be the popular and vulgar condemnation and moralizing about it, a love affair is a genuinely heavenly thing to its partners, at least for awhile. No taboos can alter this fact. Something so singular and good should really be spared utter ruination by a sad or sickening ending. Even when it can no longer be possessed, the memory of it never dies, and that memory should be a sweet one. Others might understandably protest a love affair itself, but no one can reasonably object to the memory of it, and that memory may as well be one of those things that makes growing old a bit easier.

19

Divorce

Love never fails.

—St. Paul

Sexual infidelity almost always inflicts a wound that is very slow to heal and may never heal at all. This, as has been suggested, need not always be the case. When the impulse to blame is put aside, and the partner who has been "wronged" sees that the infidelity arose not from some deep character fault in the other, and almost certainly not from any third party, but rather from something that was missing in the marriage, then it ought to be possible to direct attention at that. Forget the "other" woman, or man, the home wrecker, or the seducer. You can do nothing about that person. But perhaps you can do something about yourself, and nourish anew your love for the partner you once vowed to love forever, for better or worse.

But this is not always possible. Some marriages become hopeless, for all kinds of reasons, and very often the discovery of infidelity produces the breaking point. What follows is, almost always, deepening bitterness and unhappiness that lasts for years, or even a lifetime.

Attorneys who handle divorce matters unanimously declare that this is the bitterest and most contentious litigation they ever handle. Lawsuits arising from contested wills, unprincipled business practices, highway injuries, and whatever—these are never destructive of the human spirit the way divorce proceedings typically are. People who were once in love, who have shared years of life together, who have sorrowed and rejoiced together, and who, usually, have children that both adore become implacable enemies, sometimes to the extent that each relishes the thought of inflicting upon the other as much injury as possible.

One thing, however, is quite clear in all bitterly fought divorce proceedings, and that is, that everyone loses, with the exception of the attorneys involved. Large amounts of money usually go into their hands, as each attorney becomes, for the client, both weapon and shield. Divorce proceedings are like all wars. One side may in some sense "win," but at such cost that there is, in fact, no winner, and often the losses on both sides are overwhelming.

It is not hard to see why divorces are so bitter and destructive. A wife with no significant means of support beyond what her husband has provided imagines herself confronted by poverty. A husband imagines his wife "getting everything." Each has the deep dread of "losing" the children. The presence of lawyers on both sides feeds paranoia, for each knows that the lawyer on the other side will use every device he has to gain all he can for his client with little regard to the injury inflicted on the other. Bickering and haggling over details becomes the norm. Partners once moved by mutual affection are now moved by threat and fear. And, in case the dissolution of the marriage has been precipitated by an affair, there is added to these destructive forces deep jealousy and resentment against the third person, the outsider, who is seen as the destroyer.

It has been said that anyone facing divorce needs three things: a good lawyer, a good bank account, and a good psychiatrist. In short, one needs strong defenses, psychological and other, against the onslaught that is impending. Divorce proceedings are seen as a battle, and the cost of defeat in this battle can be very high. If one of the partners has been involved in an affair, then that puts a powerful weapon in the hands of the other. And if one of the partners is perceived as having a "better" lawyer—that is, one who is more resourceful, skilled, and cunning in this kind of battle—then anxiety and paranoia rise further still. It is a kind of battle without mercy for the enemy, in which no prisoners are taken— except, perhaps, the children, who are sometimes scarred forever. The pain to children, in witnessing the contentious breakup of their parents, is comparable to the loss of a parent by death. A child's world, and security, are deeply unsettled by it, and the injury is lasting. Eventually children of divorce learn to cope with it, and recover to the point of living successful lives of their own, but it has been my consistent observation that the damage, even when it in time becomes no longer obvious, is lifelong. Their feelings towards others, often marked by a certain distrust and cynicism, are forever different.

Even when a divorce proceeds through its several stages decorously, without mutual recrimination or hostility, the fact that it is, legally, an adversarial proceeding has negative and sometimes bizarre consequences. Everything, for example, must somehow be *divided*, so that the claims of both parties are, so far as possible, met. Children can, of course, not be divided, so the time that each parent "gets to spend" with them is somehow divided in a way that seems, as nearly as possible, fair to each. One or the other "gets" custody of them. One or the other gets stuck with primary responsibility for support payments for them. With respect to tangible and intangible property, the effort is often made to somehow divide everything in half, without regard to need. The wife may always have thought of the house as somehow "hers," but if it is jointly owned, then the husband is entitled to half. If the wife wants to go on living there, then she will have to give up something in return. If the two cannot agree on how much the house is worth, then they will have to get three appraisals, add them up, and divide by three—something like that. The husband may learn that his cherished library, which he has spent years and much money collecting, and which has been of no interest whatever to the wife, is now suddenly half hers. The husband must sell it and divide the proceeds or, if he is to keep it, he must make some comparable concession to her.

All this eventually degenerates into haggling. Questions never before entertained must be answered, problems never before felt come into focus. How much does the husband owe his wife for the years she worked so he could do graduate work? How much does he owe her, over the years to come, from his income, thus enhanced by his advanced degree? Who gets the car? How shall furniture be divided up? Who gets the heirloom clock? And so on, sometimes to the smallest details. The two, very likely detesting each other more with every passing month, must somehow come to agreement on everything, giving and taking, and for everything yielded by one, there must be some comparable concession by the other. A lawyer once described to me a couple who eventually found themselves haggling, with lawyers present (and keeping track of professional time thus expensively consumed) over the cans of paint in the basement. (It was finally decided, after perhaps a hundred dollars or so of enhanced attorney fees, that the husband would get all the opened cans, and the wife those that had not been opened!)

There should be a better way to dissolve a marriage. And indeed, there is. Something so painful as marital dissolution should not take the form of an adversarial proceeding in the first place, and yet, that is the only form it *can* take once lawyers become involved. It is the responsibility of any attorney to defend the interest of his or her client, without regard for the interests of the other party, who must, therefore, engage his own attorney. Thus the conditions of battle are established and the lines are drawn, and what follows is deepening bitterness, resentment, and often outright hatred between persons who once thought their love for each other would be everlasting.

The better, vastly less destructive way to dissolve a marriage takes some very special doing, and indeed, magnanimity on the part of both partners. It is not easy, but instead of everyone losing, everyone wins. The marriage is, of course, not saved, but everything else is. Paranoia and bitterness are avoided and, instead of enmity, mutual respect is achieved. Children are never put in the position of feeling that they must take sides, for there are no opposing sides. What this approach achieves, in short, is an amicable termination of a marriage that, for whatever reason, did not work. All that is required is mutual agreement upon some rules and steps, and then steadfast adherence to them.

Here, step by step, is how to do it.

Step One: Keep lawyers out of it.

When it becomes apparent to both husband and wife that the marriage must, for whatever reason, be terminated, then the very first thing both must agree upon is that neither will engage an attorney or even informally solicit the advice of any attorney. A lawyer will be needed eventually, simply to complete the proceeding, but at that time only one lawyer will be necessary and, in the meantime, neither husband nor wife should even think of consulting a lawyer. For either to turn to a lawyer is to cross a point of no return. It is a fateful step which renders forever impossible any of the advantages to both that are achievable by the alternative approach outlined here.

For as soon as either party engages a lawyer, then the other feels compelled to do the same, as a matter of self-protection, and the whole procedure is, from that moment on, cast into the form of an adversarial proceeding. No matter how proper, ethical, and even high-minded these attorneys may be, each is bound to fight for the interests of his or her client and, perforce, against the interests of the other. That, and that alone, is the attorney's role. It all takes on the form of a tug-of-war between the two lawyers, one that may last a very long time, the fees of both lawyers constantly mounting, and the bitterness of their clients constantly deepening.

It is not here being suggested that there is something wrong with the way lawyers handle such matters. On the contrary, this is the work they are trained to do. Lawyers are not marriage counselors. They are trained to do battle, to take a side against what they correctly refer to as "the other side," and how well they do this is the measure of their professional skill. The more an attorney can "win" for his client the better he is as a lawyer, no matter what may be the cost to the other side. If the adversarial party is destroyed, then blame should fall not on this attorney, but on the one who was supposed to be defending the interests of the loser.

This first rule, then, must be adhered to with the utmost strictness. There is no danger or risk in this, for neither husband nor wife can pose a legal threat to the other, so long as no lawyer is in any way involved. Thus neither needs to hire a lawyer just to protect his or her interests. The very prospect of divorce is threatening, to be sure. A husband might, for example, profoundly fear that he might lose the children, or a wife might feel the threat of poverty. But, it must be understood at the outset, that the involvement of lawyers will only exacerbate such threats. There are ways of removing the threats, as we shall see, but having a lawyer at your side is, emphatically, not one of them.

Step Two: The assessment of need.

The next step is for each, independently of the other, to draw up a list, not of those things that he or she *wants*, and emphatically, not the things he or she feels *entitled* to, but, quite simply, the basic things that he or she *needs*. The lists should be confined strictly to those. They should be in writing, and with, as may be necessary, an explanation of each.

Thus, for example, each may be entitled to half the house, but this should be set aside. Instead, let it be determined which *needs* the house or, if both think they need it, which needs it more, and why. Merely expressing the need will not, of course, be considered to settle the matter, but it puts things in a proper perspective for a settlement that will eventually come. Next consider finances. If the wife, for example, has no income, and the husband does, then let her figure up not what she thinks she can get, but what she actually will need, and for how long. This too is, of course, tentative, subject to revision, but it is a starting point. Perhaps she will need special training, for example. Estimate for how long and at what cost.

What, next, are their respective needs concerning the children? Here the question must *not* be who gets custody, but rather, how much does each parent wish to be with the children, and what are their special needs with respect to school, and so on. For example, if the husband has a busy schedule weekdays, and the wife does not, then it might work best for the children to be with her through the week and with him on weekends. Whatever arrangement each wishes to see put in place, it must be in the light of considerations like these—the needs of all concerned, against the background of work schedules and so on. One must, above all, avoid any temptation to *withhold* the children from the other. Nor must the fact that one or both might remarry have any effect on this. Each must banish any fear, for example, that the children might come under the influence of, and form an affection for, a stepparent. The need of each parent is to retain the children's affection, and not to deprive someone else of it, even if that other person is viewed as a detested rival.

Those are likely to be the most basic things, the kinds of things that are hardest to settle, and, it must again be stressed, the things that are impossible to settle in any reasonable way by an adversarial approach. Beyond these—house, finances, children—there will be others, far less overwhelming. Who should have the car, for example, or which car? Let the question not be who paid for it, but rather, who needs what. The same for furniture. Here the temptation will be for the wife to "claim" everything she picked out, or everything she owned before they got married, or whatnot, or for the husband to take a similar view, but that absolutely must be avoided. Ask, instead, simply, who needs what. A wife has no need for the husband's tools, or books, and so on, and he does not have the same need as she does for the kitchenware. Nor does it matter how much, for example, the computer is worth, or who paid for it, but rather, who needs it more. And so on to everything else. It is seldom difficult to see, with respect to anything, who has the greater need for it. On the other hand, it is next to impossible for two people to assess the cash value of things, and try to arrive at a settlement in which each gets his or her "share." To approach things in that way is simply to invite bickering.

Step Three: The comparison of needs.

Each having listed, with comment and explanation, and in writing, his or her felt needs, the next step, obviously, is to compare these. *And it is here that the most important step of all is to be taken.* Each must, at this point, ask: *How far can I go, to meet the other's needs?*

This, it must be seen, is quite the opposite from the usual approach to negotiating, in which each side asks: What must I yield, in order to get what I want? For each asks, at this point, *not*: What do I want? What am I entitled to? or even: *What do I need?* but rather: *What can I do to enable the other to get what he or she needs?*

What we have here, in other words, is an approach that is quite the opposite of what is usual, each party working towards the *other's* fulfillments rather than towards one's own. It is a kind of calculated unselfishness. But, as you can see if you think about it, it is a kind of unselfishness in which the basic needs of each person have a good chance of being met, precisely *because the other tries to make it so.* And it is an approach that goes a long way towards banishing anxiety and animosity. Indeed, it fosters a sense of friendship, even in the kind of personal relationship that, more than any other, usually fosters bitterness and often hatred.

Step Four: A separation agreement, first draft.

Having got to this point, one or the other now writes out a tentative agreement embodying, so far as possible, the needs of each and how they might be met. It is important that this agreement *not* be composed by a third person and, emphatically, not by an attorney. It will, in any case, be a preliminary agreement, subject to revision, and subject to modification by subsequent agreements that will be composed as additional matters occur to each person. You might find, for example, that nothing was said in the first draft about the children's schooling, or under what conditions they might move with one or the other parent to another city.

This initial separation agreement should, in any case, follow a certain obvious form. Thus, it should be labeled a separation agreement between the two persons, who are named. Subsequent references to the two persons can be by first name only. It should state at the outset when and where they were married, and list the children, by name and date of birth. After that, each paragraph should be given a number and a title, thus: (1) Support, followed by specific amounts, periods of time, etc.; (2) The house, identified by address, and who shall own it; (3) The children, who is to have custody or (better) how custody is to be shared; and so on, with respect to every other matter which has been touched upon in the informal listing of respective needs. Each provision of this tentative agreement, it must be emphasized, should aim so far as possible at the fulfillment of every need, of whichever party, that has been listed. If, for example, either party has expressed a need for privacy, that is, for complete freedom from scrutiny by the other, then this should be included.

The tentative agreement having been thus composed, it should be signed by both, dated, and notarized. This does not mean that it is final, but only, that it is what has been more or less settled so far.

In the days or weeks that follow, it is very likely that other matters, not touched on in this agreement, will arise, and at this point an additional agreement, normally a very brief one, should be composed, stating that it supplements, but does not replace, the first. It, too, should be signed, dated, and notarized. And if still more matters should come up, things that no one thought to include in the original agreements, then still another can be added, with dates, signatures, and notarization.

These documents, drawn up by one or the other of the two parties and agreed to by both, can form the basis of a *legal separation*. They need only to be *filed* with the court having jurisdiction. They need not be modified or, for that matter, even read by an attorney, whose role at this point is simply to have them duly filed with the court. It is for this reason that notarization is important, for that is the only proof of their dates, which can, in time, become important.

In due time, when the dissolution of the marriage is to be formally completed, these agreements can be incorporated in one way or another in the divorce decree itself, and *at that point they will have the force of law*. An attorney will be needed for drawing these papers and filing them, but only one attorney, rather than one for each "side." Who it is to be should be agreed to by both, and it should be made clear to that attorney that he, or she, is not to represent either party, but only to ensure that the things both have agreed to will be incorporated in a decree. The fee for this will, of course, be minimal and, what is still by far the most important consideration of all, husband and wife will be able to go their separate ways not only without haggling and bickering (since each gave foremost consideration to the needs of the other), but without enmity and even, to some extent, with lasting respect and friendship.

*   *   *

Is this sort of thing possible? Can two people, whose marriage is breaking up, and who thus have overwhelming reasons to resent, distrust, and dislike each other, set their own most basic interests aside and give first consideration to the needs and interests of the other?

Yes, it can be done, for, in fact, it has been done. There are people who have gone their separate ways, through separation and divorce, in precisely this manner, and with exactly the result described. But to appreciate the significance of this, two things have to be emphasized.

The first is that working out a separation and divorce in this manner amounts, in a very real sense, to turning things upside down. No one jockeys for position, no one tries to negotiate an acceptable deal for himself, no one tries to strengthen his or her own position or to hold back, no one grudgingly yields in return for something grudgingly given. Indeed, no one tries to win—and the result is that both win. If your primary aim is to see that, as far as possible, I get what I want, and my primary aim is to see that, as far as possible, you get what you want, then clearly we shall both come out ahead, and with the least cost.

The second point is concerned with the problem of vulnerability.

Few things nourish the sense of vulnerability like the breakup of a marriage. You feel at the mercy of all kinds of forces that can threaten some of your deepest interests. In the course of a marriage, various documents will have been signed, investments made, property shared, and, more than likely, children will have been born. Now these arrangements and relationships are all threatened. It is no wonder that your first impulse is to seek the support of a lawyer to protect them. But that, it cannot be overemphasized, is the fatal step, beyond which nothing of the kind here envisioned is even remotely possible.

So, you are apt to think, what if you approach things in the magnanimous manner here described, putting someone else's needs ahead of your own— indeed, giving priority to the needs of the very person who embodies everything you feel threatened by—and then that person takes advantage? Having helped him meet his needs, how do you know he will do the same for you? Might he not, on the contrary, having so effortlessly won all that, try to win even more, and at your expense?

In response to this kind of fear, it should be noted that the approach described is one for arriving at a *tentative* agreement and arrangement or, more likely, a succession of these. *Nothing has been filed with any court yet, everything is subject to reconsideration,* so no one is really threatened. But the beauty of it is that, as each party sees those things that are more precious to himself or herself protected, through the consistent effort on the part of each to help the other, then things move forward. What is here described is a method of moving along, making progress, and even preserving friendship. There is little inclination on either side to try taking advantage when all the advantages are more securely and completely won by this other approach. Then finally, when everything has finally taken shape, and each finds what was important reassuringly embodied in a written agreement that the two of them have put together themselves, it can be turned over to an attorney who, for a modest fee, files it with the court. The attorney's role is, up to this point, limited to that. Attorneys were not needed for "both sides" because, in a very real sense, there never were two sides to begin with. The "versus," meaning "against," which appears at the top of every document of a formal litigation, is simply out of place here.

That this manner of dissolving a marriage is possible is shown by the following account.

My marriage lasted thirteen years, and until almost the very end, I had no doubt that it was the most successful, romantic, and fulfilling marriage in the world. We had two beautiful, bright, well-adjusted children, and we lived for each other. I still have a thick folder filled with love letters, many of them written after we were married. Whenever my work took me away from home overnight, I would find sweet little notes in my pockets, some of them tender, some whimsical. I still have a box full of these.

Toward the end, I sensed that things were changing, but for several months I refused to face it. I kept thinking that things would, in time, get back to what they had been. It did not seem possible that love could be so total and then change. But people do change, especially when they marry young. It seemed to me that my wife was, quite simply, losing interest in me, and I was sometimes at my wit's end. When, one day, she actually spoke of leaving for awhile, to get her thoughts and feelings together, I actually urged her to do that. She had no money and no job, and I felt sure she would see the foolishness of what she was talking about. But to my astonishment, she actually went out to look at apartments.

The marriage began to come apart very fast after that. We were outwardly amicable, but, for the first time ever, sarcasm and annoyance sometimes entered her conversations with me. She seemed to find my very existence objectionable. Soon she began to sleep in another room, something that both of us, a year or so earlier, would have considered unthinkable. Then, one day, she said outright that she felt no love for me anymore, and wanted out. I was plunged into a depression that, at times, was almost suicidal. For weeks I moved around like a zombie, only half aware of what I was doing and what was going on. I tried to compensate for this overwhelming loss by increased involvement with our children, but that never really took my mind off the awfulness of what was happening.

At first I tried to use subtle pressure tactics to get her to reconsider, reminding her of how difficult things could be for her, but this, of course, did nothing to revive things. Sometimes I would not come home at night, imagining that she would be alarmed. Sometimes I sat around all day in silence. I even sought the casual company of other women, who meant absolutely nothing to me, thinking this might stir jealousy in her. But none of these stupid tactics worked.

The marriage really was over, and I had to face it. The unthinkable had become real, and nothing would ever bring things back.

Then, one day, I hit upon what turned out to be the most wonderful idea I had ever had in my life. I suggested to my wife that she sit down and write out exactly what she wanted in life, exactly what her needs were, without any consideration of whether or not they were possibilities, and to do this with as much thought and explanation as she could. She did this. Her basic need was to be independent. For this she needed an income until she could somehow become self-supporting. She estimated how long this would be. She needed a place to live. And she listed all the lesser needs—a car, furniture, things like this. None of these were things she was, in any sense, entitled to.

She having done that, I did the same. I wanted to stay in our house and to have all the furnishings left there. I wanted to ensure that our children's future, and their education, were secure, that they would not move away, that I could be with them whenever I wanted, and so on.

Then we both did quite an astonishing thing. We each studied what the other had written out, and resolved, each of us, to go as far as we could towards meeting the other's needs. *We would, we agreed, put our own needs second, and the other's first*—the exact opposite, I think, of what usually happens in cases like this.

My morale immediately improved, and something resembling the love and unselfishness that had given such life to our marriage replaced the fears and resentments. We began drawing up tentative agreements, made many revisions as new things occurred to us, and several fresh drafts. I pledged my life's savings to buy her a new house, thus meeting one of her most basic needs. No court of law would have required this. She relinquished all claim to my rather large annuity benefits, thus ensuring the children's education, which was important to me. She had no obligation to do this. She was glad to leave all the furniture in the house, other than the things for which I had no need, even though most of this had come from her family. I, in turn, agreed to pay for the furniture for her house. We agreed that we would both pay the children's costs, as we were able, that they would not be removed from their present school district, that neither of us would make any custodial claim against the wishes of the other, and so on, to the smaller details.

No lawyer was consulted in any of this. We, together, looked for a new house for her, and finally found just what she needed, somewhat in the spirit of newlyweds buying their first house; yet how different this all was! Before long each of us found ourselves doing somewhat *more* for the other than was actually called for under our agreement. We were now both animated by a spirit of genuine friendship, and managed never to slip into attitudes of rivalry and competition, or worse, animosity or warfare. Our approach remained, not what we could get, or felt entitled to, but what each of us could give to the other.

Once things were pretty much settled, we took our agreement to a lawyer to be incorporated into a divorce decree. This was our first, and only, involvement with any lawyer. The decree was routinely rendered, and what we had agreed to thus had, for the first time, the force of law. But the important thing is that neither of us was compelled to give up anything, yet both of us got everything that we wanted, within the realm of what was possible, precisely because what each of us sought was not what we thought we could get, but what we could give.

Now, years later, we are still friends, though we seldom see each other. Neither of us has ever spoken a word against the other, to anyone. We consult from time to time, over lunch or tea, about matters having to do with the children. No problem has ever arisen, for either of us, which was not immediately resolved, usually with a brief phone call. The children go back and forth according to arrangements we make as we go along, according to what suits both of us, and the children, best. They have not been scarred by the divorce, because they have never witnessed animosity between us. On the contrary, they see us as friends, though not, to be sure, very close friends. Both of us have made new lives for ourselves. It is, in the very nature of things, sad for any marriage that was once filled with love and happiness to come to an end, but, if it must end, then I cannot imagine it ending better than this. I think we'll always be proud of how we did it.

Is that unbelievable? It should not be, because it actually happened. Even a good and fulfilling marriage can, in time, come apart, because people, and especially young people, sometimes change. And just as marriage is sometimes, albeit perhaps rarely, the fountainhead of life's deepest joys, its dissolution is usually the source of the deepest bitterness and resentment. But it need not be so. The same love that animates a beautiful marriage can be the spirit of its dissolution.

Epilogue

The Taboo

What is done out of love always takes place beyond good and evil.

—Friedrich Nietzsche

I have tried in these pages to encourage more tolerance of love affairs. That there has been an immense change in attitudes concerning the relations of the sexes over the past several years is obvious to everyone, but there are still very strong feelings about triangular relationships, especially when one or more of those involved in them are formally or legally married. There is a deep-seated feeling that we are, or at least ought to be, monogamous, that for each man there should ideally be one woman and vice versa, and that once such a man and woman have to any degree committed themselves to each other, whether by formal marriage or otherwise, then outside loves should be excluded from their lives. To be sure, people have come to accept the cohabitation of the sexes in what I have called marriage relationships, even in the cases of those that are assumed to be temporary; but a large number still emphatically reject the simultaneous emotional and sexual involvement with more than one person.

No doubt there are advantages, both to individuals and to society, of strictly monogamous relationships between the sexes. But I have tried also to show that there are sometimes great values in love affairs, that the joys of such a relationship can be unique and unmatched in their intensity, and that for those involved in them they can sometimes be more meaningful even than the fulfillments of monogamous marriage. Above all, as I have tried to show, they are not in any significant sense "immoral."

Because of attitudes that are still widespread, my inquiries were not always made easy. Inducing conservative newspapers to accept my ads, for example, was sometimes difficult. One simply returned it with the comment "unacceptable," no reason being given. Another finally accepted it, after much consternation, many telephone calls, and consultations within its staff, but only on the condition that responses would be sent to them and then forwarded to me.

All of which illustrates a strange ambivalence that people still feel about sex. It is not so much that many ideas on this subject are fixed in their minds, otherwise there would be intense objection to a great deal of popular entertainment. It is, rather, that many are confused in their feelings, and what confuses them they tend to fear and withdraw from, or deal with irrationally.

Of course, I have discovered the same fear and ambivalence in some of the people I have talked with. Some consider even the discussion of such a subject, however serious and well motivated, to be a kind of impropriety. Several expressed the fervent hope that my book would be a total failure, not read by anyone. And more than once, describing my project to strangers of chance encounter, I appeared to be regarded as someone whose very utterance was an indiscretion. Thus one woman, of evident standing and education, whom chance had seated next to me on an airplane, became intensely interested in my description of what I was writing about, but also visibly agitated, referring to men as being, in her words, "sometimes weak." Strict monogamous marriage was, in her mind, so fixed a principle that even the suggestion of its violability had to be repelled with polite abuse. Nor was it hard to see why this was so in her case. She was married to a leading physician and professor of medicine, and her several children were all in the very best universities. In short, her stake in that marriage was very great, and she could not abide even a purely hypothetical threat to what seemed to her one of its foundations. When our plane had landed my traveling companion of the moment withdrew until I was at a safe distance before falling into the waiting arms of her husband—illustrating once more, I thought, the fear under which so many married persons live, and under which they are actually encouraged to live. It is sometimes a fear, not merely of violating some more or less understandable custom, but of violating even the most capricious, unreasonable, and jealous wishes of their husbands or wives. Perhaps such solicitude for even the irrational feelings of spouses tends to hold marriages together, perhaps it does not; but it is quite certain that it is destructive of our most generous feelings.

Before my book was finished its existence became known, by the most unlikely of accidents, to a reporter for the largest daily newspaper in Rochester, New York. A few days later the headline appeared: "Affair Not Inherently Immoral," followed by "Ethics Professor Tells How to Have One." The accompanying story produced a torrent of letters and telephone calls to the newspaper, to me, and to the reporter. Many of them expressed outrage, in spite of the fact that the story made very clear that I strongly defend the institution of marriage. The volume and intensity of this response became the subject of still another story by the same reporter, which appeared in several newspapers across the country.

Another consequence of this somewhat premature publicity was numerous invitations to be interviewed on radio and television, some of which I accepted. For two of the radio interviews listeners were invited to call in to air their opinions and solicit my responses. Many of these, too, were negative and impassioned, but not all. On the contrary, I found, and have since learned in other ways, that there is a vast amount of agreement and support for my ideas among thoughtful people.

Much of the outrage directed against me has come from evangelical clergymen and their followers—none of whom, it should be noted, had actually seen a single line of my book. Violation of the seventh commandment appears to their minds to be the paradigm of immorality. Indeed, most persons, when they think of immorality, think first of sexual immorality, the clearest example of which they believe to be adultery. This is so clear to them that to inquire into the *reasons* for its immorality is something they choose not to consider unless the question is put to them point-blank. The other group whose members were likely to condemn my ideas, even before I had been given a chance to express them, were the wives of stable and successful men, such as physicians. Their reactions sometimes went beyond mere disagreement and spilled over into anger. I never received this kind of angry response from husbands, except when religion seemed threatened.

Disagreement with someone's opinions can usually be explained on intellectual grounds, but intense negative feeling cannot. Persons of evangelical orientation do not, for example, become overwrought if someone fails to keep the Sabbath, or indulges in covetousness, even though these, too, are violations of holy commandments. It is the idea of *sexual* freedom that stirs their ire, or the person who suggests, as I do, that such freedom is not necessarily wrong. There are many possible explanations for this, but part of it must be the feelings of guilt that are associated with sex, especially in the hearts of the pious. Another part, I believe, is the feeling of deprivation in persons who have led faultlessly monogamous lives. I believe they quite naturally resent that deprivation, the more so upon hearing that it might have been pointless and unnecessary. To suggest this is to open up the possibility that their moral goodness, which has been the chief reward for their constancy, may be illusory. It is like hearing, too late, that a rich and fulfilling life has been eschewed, and all for the sake of some abstract ideal that someone has dared to suggest was chimerical to begin with.

The resentment on the part of conventional wives of successful men has, of course, a different source, and one that is not hard to fathom. Such persons are likely to have submerged their lives in their homes and children. The suggestion that any obstacle to sexual infidelity, such as the moral obstacle, might reasonably be removed is a profound threat to them. Even though the general sense of wickedness might not be terribly strong in such women, their sense of security is strong indeed, and they easily recognize even the most abstract threat to this.

Oddly enough, whenever those persons whose condemnation of love affairs is most intense are asked, point-blank, what they think is *wrong* with these affairs, they are apt to talk about how damaging they are, especially to homes and to children. One would suppose, then, that they would rejoice upon learning that someone has been giving thought to the problems of how to make them less damaging, and has undertaken to write a book having just that purpose, and that they would wish him well. Yet the very opposite occurs. It is as if someone were to point with alarm to the famines caused in parts of the world by soil erosion, and then vilify someone who undertakes to make those changes of climate less damaging—advocating instead the condemnation of the weather!

Love affairs are like wars: Everyone finds them exciting, yet everyone knows they carry with them the risk of untold destruction. But just as wars are not going to be stopped by piously intoning "Thou shalt not kill," neither are people going to stop falling in love and acting on those deep and beautiful feelings just because someone says "Thou shalt not commit adultery." Wars and the kinds of "moral equivalents" that people find in prizefights and football can be made less destructive, and so can love affairs, together with such substitutes for these that people find in fantasy and literature. We really need no barren, spiritless, and negative prohibitions, here or anyplace else.